AF342630

INCOMPLETE FICTIONS

INCOMPLETE FICTIONS

The Formation of English Renaissance Dialogue

K. J. WILSON

The Catholic University of America Press
Washington, D.C.

Library of Congress Cataloging in Publication Data

Wilson, K. J. (Kenneth J.), 1944–
Incomplete fictions.

Bibliography: p.
Includes index.
1. Dialogues, English—History and criticism.
2. English prose literature—Early modern, 1500–1700—History and criticism. 3. Dialogue. 4. Elyot, Thomas, Sir, 1490?–1546—Criticism and interpretation. 5. Ascham, Roger, 1515–1568—Criticism and interpretation. 6. More, Thomas, Sir, Saint, 1478–1535—Criticism and interpretation. I. Title.
PR756.D52W54 1985 832′.2′09 84-21455
ISBN 0-8132-0598-0

To the Memory of

RICHARD S. SYLVESTER

1926–1978

and my parents

KENNETH J. WILSON

1922–1974

and

BETTY WALLACE BLEAKMORE WILSON

1922–1977

CONTENTS

PREFACE

Dialogue has always presented a problem to literary theory. Since Aristotle, the ambiguity of its position between narrative and drama has made it difficult to define as a genre. This problem is compounded by the fact that, like other forms, dialogue bears the imprint of historical change. That impression could hardly be more intricate than in the era of humanism, when personal ambitions and social reform combined in complex patterns. Moreover, if the sheer number of humanist dialogues testifies to their popularity, it also dictates selective analysis; and this results inevitably in the omission of examples favored by individual specialists.[1] The 1520s and 1530s stand out as a high point in the development of English prose dialogue, but there has never been a satisfactory study of this phase in the long tradition of the art. Such is the intellectual richness and artistic force of dialogue in the early Tudor period, however, that it is worthwhile to confront these difficulties.

We must begin with classical dialogue. Indeed, nearly half of this short book is devoted to an analysis of classical materials since it was from these that the humanists fashioned a new form. This book attempts, first of all, to locate dialogue in relation to narrative and drama by examining Platonic dialogue in light of Aristotle's theory of fiction. Secondly, we turn to

1. A series of Harvard dissertations has mapped the extent of nondramatic prose dialogue before 1750. Roger Lee Deakins identifies 56 dialogues written between 1500 and 1558 in "The Tudor Dialogue as a Literary Form" (1964); John T. Day, Jr., finds 206 between 1558 and 1603 in "Elizabethan Prose Dialogues" (1977). In "The Non-Dramatic Dialogue in English Prose" (1918), p. 442, B. V. Crawford plots a graph of the production of dialogues from 1550 to 1750.

Cicero's rhetorical modifications of the Platonic form. In this way we can determine the intellectual and aesthetic resources of classical literary dialogue before attempting, in the third chapter, to delineate its new formations in the Renaissance and their historical significance in the humanist program of studies. The second half of the book consists of three case studies—of Thomas Elyot, Roger Ascham, and Thomas More—by which I hope to indicate the spectrum and intensity of response to the resources of dialogue in this period. From a better understanding of the nature of the form, as well as the circumstances of the authors' lives, more complete, and perhaps unexpected, meanings may emerge in the readings of individual works.

Early Tudor dialogue signals with particular clarity "the entry of humanism into vernacular literatures by no means severed from Aristotelian aesthetic norms," as Dermot Fenlon has in part characterized the New Learning of the Renaissance.[2] In some ways Aristotle's model for argument proved highly amenable to a distinctive new preoccupation with the self:

> Always, in dealing with any proposition, be on the look-out for a line of argument both pro and con: and on discovering it at once set about looking for the solution to it: for in this way you will soon find that you have trained yourself at the same time in both asking questions and answering them. If we cannot find any one else to argue with, we should argue with ourselves.[3]

It is in the humanists' dialogues that we observe a transmutation of this principle in an increasing consciousness of the mental processes which question-and-answer entails. In their dialogues we find them exploring new reaches of dialectical thought. Thus we are concerned with the inward experience of an art which encompasses not only ideas but the responses they generate.

The modern theoretical literature on dialogue is a pretty dis-

2. "The New Learning, the New Religion and the Law," *The Historical Journal,* 17 (1974), 195.

3. *Topica,* trans. W. A. Pickard-Cambridge, *The Works of Aristotle,* ed. W. D. Ross (Oxford, 1928), vol. 1, 163b.

appointing affair. Often overlooking the implications of rhetorical strategies for our understanding of the dialogist himself or his themes, it easily ignores the larger patterns of invention and imagination through which a powerful mind achieves expression.[4] There has been illuminating work, however, on the dialogue in antiquity by French classicists, chief among whom is Michel Ruch, whose study of the art of dialogue is original and provocative, though unfortunately it does not take up the post-Ciceronian evolution of the form.[5] The whole question of the continuity of dialogue in the first millennium and the Middle Ages still awaits a comprehensive historical analysis.[6] As my own treatment of that question here is cursory and incomplete, I have tried to provide at least some bibliographical guidance in the notes to Chapter 3.

This book then is not a history of dialogue. It inquires to what

4. Rudolf Hirzel's ponderous survey, *Der Dialog, ein literarhistorischer Versuch,* 2 vols. (Leipzig, 1895), is devoted primarily to classical dialogue in contrast with Elizabeth Merrill's sketch of the modern period, *The Dialogue in English Literature* (New Haven, 1911). Walter J. Ong's *Ramus, Method, and the Decay of Dialogue* (Cambridge, Mass., 1958) offers a number of theoretical directions, and Lisa Jardine's *Bacon: Discovery and the Art of Discourse* (Cambridge, England, 1974) begins with a useful chapter on "Dialectic and Method in the Sixteenth Century." *Le Dialogue philosophique dans la littérature française du seizième siècle* (The Hague and Paris, 1976), by Mustapha Kemal Bénouis, engages the theoretical problem but is cluttered with too many names and historical digressions; it provides a basic chronology of sixteenth-century dialogues and a bibliography. Another chronology may be found in Gottfried Niemann's *Die Dialogliteratur der Reformationszeit . . .* (Leipzig, 1905). David Marsh's *Quattrocento Dialogue: Classical Tradition and Humanist Innovation* (Cambridge, Mass., and London, 1980) traces the influence of Cicero's dialogues upon the rhetorical theories and productions of Bruni, Poggio Bracciolini, Valla, Alberti, and Pontano.

5. *Le Préambule dans les oeuvres philosophiques de Cicéron: essai sur la genèse et l'art du dialogue* (Paris and Strasbourg, 1958). One should also consult *Le dialogue platonicienne de la maturité* by Jean Laborderie (Paris, 1978). Kent F. Moors provides an overview of the philosophical function of dialogue in his essay "Plato's Use of Dialogue," *Classical World,* 72 (1978), 77–93. Additional studies of Roman dialogue are found in Chapter 2, Notes.

6. See K. J. Wilson, "The Continuity of Post-Classical Dialogue," *Cithara,* 21 (1981), 23–44.

extent early Tudor dialogue may be conceived as a projection of the classical model into the era of the Renaissance. Yet even a *forma rediviva* can scarcely escape the influence of contemporary events, and so this account strives to approach its selected dialogues as products of their time.

The first three chapters address the theoretical problems mentioned at the outset, i.e., the obstacles to aesthetic criticism of dialogue, the qualities of characterization, the impact of Roman oratory, and the role of dialogue in the humanist educational reform. I have tried to examine two key problems which have hitherto been neglected or ignored, though both require much more investigation: the theoretical basis for a criticism of dialogue and the gradual formation of dialogue during the Renaissance. It is against this backdrop, I believe, that the private and social roles of particular dialogues will best be discerned. Elyot's introspective Platonic dialogue *Of the Knowledge Which Maketh a Wise Man* and Ascham's confident Ciceronian manual on shooting with the long bow, *Toxophilus,* illustrate the enormous range of the humanist pedagogues, while More's *Dialogue Concerning Heresies* and his *Dialogue of Comfort* explore the most intimate contours of Aristotle's model of intellectual debate. These examples reflect a personal rather than representative choice; their subjects are certainly not the only concerns of Tudor humanists. Nevertheless, they are remarkable as ambitious, highly evolved dialogues which possess a complexity of form adequate to their subjects. It may also be advantageous to reconsider their perennial subjects—the exercise of wise judgment in civic action, the possibility of attaining true eloquence, and the force of will and belief against the worldly powers—in relation to the dialogue form.

Reading, as the writers of dialogue knew, is no solitary enterprise. In writing these pages I have had in mind a reader like those fellow students whom it has been my good fortune to know in the Tudor seminar in several universities. From our colloquies I have learned that one tends to belabor those points that took one longest to comprehend, and often to neglect those that came easier. I doubt that these pages are free from that "seminar effect" (as few of those seminarians would fail to point out), but I have tried to avoid it no less than errors of fact. I hope my reader will read as those friendly combatants conversed. "Conversation," Erasmus noted hopefully, "is the medicine for a burdened spirit."[7]

7. *Adagia* 2099, in *Opera omnia*, ed. J. Clericus, 10 vols. (Leiden, 1703–06; repr. Hildesheim, 1961–62), II, 744D–745C: "Animo aegrotanti medicus est oratio."

ACKNOWLEDGMENTS

This book grew out of a paper on the form of dialogue in Professor Richard Sylvester's Tudor seminar at Yale. I was astonished that formal criticism of imaginative literature provided such clumsy tools for handling the scholarly productions of the age of humanism. In following years my interest came to center on the motives behind the humanists' forays into fiction. My own experience teaching the literature of the imagination helped me to see that dialogue holds a flickering status in that dimension. As Professor Sylvester knew, it was necessary to investigate dialogue as *an art of ideas.*

Since his death, a number of other scholars have read the manuscript and offered helpful criticism. These include Lewis White Beck, William T. Bluhm, G. R. Elton, D. B. Fenlon, George M. Logan, Richard Marius, and Louis L. Martz. Their learning has guided me past many pitfalls; for their candor and courtesy I offer heartfelt thanks. The faults which remain must of course be counted my own.

Grateful acknowledgment is also due the Folger Shakespeare Library and the American Council of Learned Societies for generous fellowships which permitted research in Washington, D.C., and Cambridge, England. As an associate of Clare Hall, Cambridge, during a year's leave from teaching, I enjoyed the privilege of frequent conversation with Professor G. R. Elton; no student could hope for a more generous, more uncompromising master. For their assistance I would like to thank the staff members of the Bodleian Library, the British Library, the Folger Library, the Library of Congress, the University Library, Cambridge, and Yale University Library.

Chapter 5 is a modified version of an article entitled "Ascham's *Toxophilus* and the Rules of Art," which appeared in the Spring 1976 number of *Renaissance Quarterly.* I am grateful to the editors for permission to reemploy it. The manuscript was expertly typed and retyped by Helen Craven and Claire Sundeen. The initial capitals used at chapter openings are taken from a copy of the 1557 edition of Thomas More's English *Workes* in the University Library, Cambridge.

It is a pleasure to remember those who shared in my labor with many forms of encouragement: my teacher Margaret Tuck, who opened my eyes to literature, John R. Mong, Alan and Peggy Fisher, Rowland L. Collins, Ian and Sarah Fyfe, Thomas Spence Smith, Paul Pickrel, Richard H. Schlessinger, Phyllis Andrews, Speed Hill, Marjorie Currie Woods, Stanley Novak, Clarence Miller, Peter Lang, and Warren Hunting Smith. Finally, I would like to thank my friend Ronald Federico, whose cheerful, flawless patience is a continual example. *Pax cum eis.*

1

The Aesthetic Position of Dialogue

I

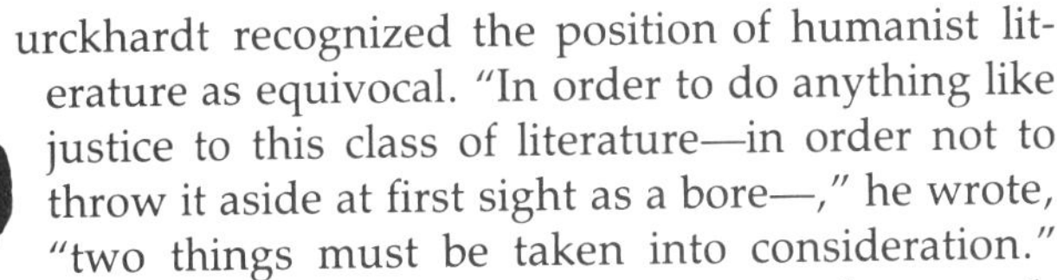

Burckhardt recognized the position of humanist literature as equivocal. "In order to do anything like justice to this class of literature—in order not to throw it aside at first sight as a bore—," he wrote, "two things must be taken into consideration." The first was the active public role of the humanists; the second, the nature of their literary achievement. "The century which escaped from the influence of the Middle Ages felt the need of something to mediate between itself and antiquity in many questions of morals and philosophy; and this need was met by the writer of treatises and dialogues. . . . The language, too, in this form of writing, whether Italian or Latin, moved more freely and flexibly than in historical narrative, in letters, or in oratory, and this became in itself, the source of a special pleasure."[1] Burckhardt may be said to have characterized the humanists as *mediators* between their own age and antiquity, and this role was

1. Jacob Burckhardt, *Die Cultur der Renaissance in Italien* (Basel, 1860): *The Civilization of the Renaissance,* trans. S. G. C. Middlemore, ed. Ludwig Goldscheider (Oxford, 1944), p. 144.

expressed primarily in literary activity. The art they practiced was a pedagogic duty.

This view of the role of the humanists is probably derived from the more clearly perceived and articulated system of mediation by the Church. Mediated religion, the interpretation of Christ to society by the priesthood, is the unalloyed expression of the educational and interpretative role which the humanists played on the secular stage. The mediating function of Renaissance humanism was an intellectual ideal: to create a dialectic between present and past. In the dialogue humanists discovered a literary form uniquely receptive to this function. Dialogue could re-create an almost limitless variety of mental processes, and in so doing it could place the reader in an intimate, sophisticated relation to his intellectual ancestors.

Though hundreds of examples are known, the form of the dialogue has long been imperfectly understood. On the one hand, theorists neglected the aesthetic principles of a "didactic" form, while on the other, critics failed to perceive that dialogues themselves were expressions of the humanists' historical role as mediators. As a consequence, for the early Tudor period in particular, our picture of humanist literature has remained distorted. Dialogues in a sense comprise a significant part of the imaginative literature of humanism. By investigating the combined historical and subjective contexts in which dialogues were produced—by tracing the processes of their creation—we can hope to improve our picture of one of the preeminent arts in the *studia humanitatis.* If we are fortunate, this venture may give access to certain pathways of the humanist mind.

The work of recent historians of the Renaissance encourages a renewed effort to analyze the humanists' public role into components consisting of differing individual attitudes. As Charles Trinkaus has argued, ". . . more significant by far than the established institutions—political power-centers, ecclesiastical temporalities, professions, economic organizations (all drastically and sometimes catastrophically important)—were the *elements of consciousness*: ideas, purposes, feelings, behavior, beliefs, hopes and fears. . . ."[2] It is these elements, along with "the characters and differences of urban and rural communities; individualism and community-identifications; conceptions of and believed relations with supernatural beings and forces; technologies, habits, and skills, . . . sometimes regional, frequently totally individual, . . . [which] in fact comprise the sum-total of the culture itself." Indeed, it is "only through conceptions, purposes, moods, feelings of the living humans who enact and suffer them" that institutions can be understood.

Humanist literature in the early Tudor period could not develop unmarked by the revolution, or transition, of that age. In its dialogues the changes in consciousness are abundantly written. To understand these works, however, the analytic study of form alone will not suffice; the elements of consciousness, as Trinkaus urges, "must be grasped not taxonomically but *dynamically* because they are evanescent and only exist in relation to and interaction with experience."[3] We must endeavor to move between historical and formal perspectives, acknowledging the impossibility of a balance. It is virtually a principle of the life of dialogue that it develops *in between* "conceptions, purposes, moods, feelings"—in between traditions or institutions and

2. "Humanism, Religion, Society: Concepts and Motivations of some Recent Studies," *Renaissance Quarterly*, 29 (1976), 687; my emphasis. Trinkaus's essay follows from Paul Oskar Kristeller's "Studies on Renaissance Humanism during the Last Twenty Years," *Renaissance Quarterly*, 9 (1962), 7–30. In *The Renaissance in Historical Thought: Five Centuries of Interpretation* (Cambridge, Mass., 1948), Wallace K. Ferguson summarizes the views of such literary historians as Legouis, Sidney Lee, and L. Einstein, providing too a perceptive understanding of Seebohm's contribution (*The Oxford Reformers*, 1867) and a bibliography of "studies of the origins and development of the concepts Middle Ages and Renaissance." See also Hans Baron, *The Crisis of the Early Italian Renaissance*, 2 vols. (Princeton, 1955), and Ferguson's assessment, "The Interpretation of Italian Humanism: The Contribution of Hans Baron," *Renaissance Studies* (London, Ontario, 1963) pp. 111–21. A stimulating reappraisal of the definition of Renaissance humanism, with close attention to the recent contributions of Kristeller and William J. Bouwsma, is George M. Logan's "Substance and Form in Renaissance Humanism," *The Journal of Medieval and Renaissance Studies*, 7 (1977), 1–34.

3. "Humanism, Religion, Society . . . ," p. 687; my emphasis.

their times. Dialogues, like the humanists, may be approached as mediators, their art as a medial art.

II

A surprising obstacle which the student of dialogue must confront is the lack of definitions or theoretical discussions of the form in ancient or modern times. This phenomenon is traceable to Aristotle and the enormous influence his teaching has exerted over the analysis of literary fiction. It was Aristotle who constricted the definition of fiction, passing over and thus effectively excluding dialogues from consideration. This occurs in an obscure parenthesis in the first chapter of the *Poetics:*

> We have no term to denote the class that includes the farces of Sophron and Xenarchus, and Socratic dialogues;[4]

Aristotle is arguing that there is a nameless class of poetry for certain works in prose. The late fifth-century mimes of Sophron of Syracuse and his son Xenarchus were realistic sketches from everyday life, while the conversational philosophy of Socrates had given rise to a new literary form. It was not Plato but Alexamenos of Teos (whose works are lost) who first wrote in this form; Xenophon also wrote some conversation pieces with Socrates the chief speaker.[5]

> nor should we have one even if the imitating were done in iambic trimeters or elegiacs or any other metre. People append the term 'poetry' to the metre, distinguishing for example between 'elegiac poets' and 'epic poets.' They class them, not as *poets in virtue of the act of imitating,* but according to the metre used. . . . But Homer and Empedocles have nothing in common except their metre; and therefore, while it is correct to call the former a poet, the latter should be called a scientist rather than a poet.

Aristotle points out the error of thinking that the criterion of poetry is meter; its true criterion is *mimesis,* or the imitation of

4. Aristotle, *On the Art of Fiction,* trans. L. J. Potts, 2d impression (Cambridge, England, 1962), Ch. 1, p. 18. All citations of the *Poetics* refer to this edition.

5. Aristotle, *Poetics,* commentary by D. W. Lucas (Oxford, 1968), p. 60.

human actions. "If the mimes and Socratic dialogues were put, for example, into iambics, they would have a common name, but it would be in virtue of their metre, not their content, and so irrelevant *qua mimesis*."[6] Aristotle deplores the error that "imitative works which happen not to be in verse (e.g. Sophron, Plato?) are not recognized as 'poetry,' and . . . non-imitative works which happen to be in verse (e.g. Empedocles) *are* recognized as poetry."[7] The essential element, if a work is to be classified as poetic or fictional in the Aristotelian scheme, is imitation.

Socratic dialogues are impeded from fitting smoothly into Aristotle's mimetic conception by their philosophical substance. To him they seem insufficiently dramatic, excessively didactic. What precisely is imitated in the philosophical dialogues of Plato would become a key question for humanist critics. Clearly Aristotle is reluctant to include didactic works in the class of poetry. As Else maintains (pp. 49f.), Aristotle saw literature as essentially *stories,* and he sought in this early passage in the *Poetics* to distinguish fiction (which includes *stories about men*) from another class which is made up of exposition, or *argument about principles* or things. The influence of this view can still be felt in the disappointment which modern readers of dialogue express toward limitations of characterization, dramatic setting, and plot, even as they continue to adhere to these as criteria for evaluation.

In Else's accurate phrase, for Aristotle "the poetic element is, in short, not the specifically philosophical element" (p. 44). It is primarily for this reason that there has been so little theoretical discussion of the art of dialogue. Discussion has been further inhibited by the fact that after Aristotle includes dialogue in the category of poetry, by virtue of imitation, he then says nothing more about its nature. He imprisons dialogue categorically in the silence of a nameless art.

In passing over the Socratic dialogues Aristotle indicates that

6. Ibid.

7. Gerald F. Else, *Aristotle's Poetics: The Argument* (Cambridge, Mass., 1957), pp. 49f.

he does not regard the form as genuinely or fully fictional. It is as if the Aristotelian concept of *mimesis* becomes more restrictive toward dialogue in proportion to its philosophical substance. At the opening of the *Poetics* we learn that Aristotle could not see Empedocles as a poet. "I am afraid," Else concludes, "it is just here that we can mark the limitations of Aristotle's philosophy and aesthetic capacity. For him a cosmic *drama* could not exist, any more than it could for Plato. The order of the cosmos is eternal, beyond the reach of change. Poetry is of men and men's actions; there is no room for an imitation of the gods . . . in Aristotle's scheme of things" (p. 51). The same limitation, his dramatic bias, prevents Aristotle from seeing the place of Plato's dialogues in his scheme in the *Poetics*. Hence, we may perceive the profound disjunction between his and the alternative Platonic concept of imitation. For "Aristotle nowhere recognizes the *Timaeus*, in which Plato's concept of imitation finds its ripest embodiment (the world as an image of the divine reality, and the 'dialogue' itself a 'likely story' [29D], a secondary reflection of that image in words), as a cosmic drama *or even an imitation.*"[8] For Aristotle imitation, and hence what he would see as poetic in Plato, is imitation of men and their actions; for Plato it is of an altogether different order.

III

In his analysis of the art of fiction Aristotle distinguished three "manners" of poetic imitation: (1) "one can speak invariably in one's own person"; or (2) "one can use actors to imitate the whole thing as though they were living it themselves"; or (3) "one can imitate partly by narration and partly by dramatic dialogue (as Homer does). . . ."[9] These manners came to be known as narrative, dramatic, and mixed. In the *Republic* Plato raises the question of whether to allow imitative poetry in the ideal state. In his discussion of poetic discourse, imitation seems

8. Else, p. 44; my emphasis.

9. *On the Art of Fiction,* trans. Potts, Ch. 3, p. 19. Aristotle lists these in the order 3, 1, 2, which I have rearranged to facilitate the following comparison.

to play a narrower role than it does in Aristotle's; for Plato can conceive of poetic narrative without imitation. According to his scheme, all the fabulists or poets speak by narration; this he analyzes into three types. These are simple narration, or indirect discourse; mimetic narration, in which the poet speaks as if he were someone else; and the mixed type which employs both, as in epic. He distinguishes: (1) "pure narrative, in which the poet speaks in his own person without imitation, as in the dithyramb; (2) narrative by means of imitation, in which the poet speaks in the person of his characters, as in comedy and tragedy; and (3) mixed narrative, in which the poet speaks now in his own person and now by means of imitation."[10]

If, as McKeon has shown, Plato's definition of imitation could contract very narrowly, it could also expand to include all philosophy. It could move in another direction from poetry to cover "all verbal accounts"; in some sense it could be argued that "all discourse is imitation."[11] By contrast, it is evident that Aristotle's innovation was to restrict imitation (in language) to the degree that it became the criterion for poetry. He opted for the single sense of imitation as fiction. The *Poetics* teaches that imitation is "peculiar to the processes of art."[12] It is of particular things and of the actions of men and is "not found in the processes of nature or of knowledge."[13]

For Plato, however, imitation does contribute to these processes, even though the poet does not play the dominant role.

In the *Republic* [the poet] found himself in competition with the dialectician, sadly handicapped by his lack of knowledge: in the *Laws* he is in

10. *Republic* 392D–394C; I quote the paraphrase by Richard McKeon in an important essay to which my discussion is greatly indebted: "Literary Criticism and the Concept of Imitation in Antiquity," in *Critics and Criticism, Ancient and Modern*, ed. R. S. Crane (Chicago, 1952), p. 151. Renaissance critics were well aware of the parallel between this passage in the *Republic* and the theory of the manners of imitation in the *Poetics;* see Bernard Weinberg, *A History of Literary Criticism in the Italian Renaissance*, 2 vols. (Chicago, 1961), p. 61.

11. McKeon, ibid., p. 153, who notes certain defects in Plato's presentation.

12. McKeon's phrase, p. 161.

13. Ibid.

competition with the lawgiver, for the whole state is an imitation of the best and noblest life, which is the very truth of poetry. It is not its imitative character but its lack of truth and knowledge which brings poetry to its low estate. Homer and all the poetic tribe are imitators of images of virtue and of other things, but they do not lay hold on truth.[14]

The whole of the *Poetics,* as McKeon reminds us, focuses on a discussion of plot as an imitation of the actions of men. It is no wonder that the Socratic dialogues, which are largely plotless, are treated ambiguously by Aristotle. Plato focuses on the eternal objects of imitation: ideas, even appearances (themselves imitations), and ultimately the imitation of an idea in the creative mind.

Over against the poetics of imitation stands the poetics of ideas. Plato's dialogues attest to his central concern with the exposition and verification of principles. In the *Phaedrus* he explicitly raises the question of which poetic style is proper to Socratic dialogue. Of the three kinds of poetic style, Plato's term for the first is narration, or *diegesis.*[15] The point of this term is that it denotes description (including description of moral character and action), as distinct from imitation. Socrates says in the *Phaedrus* (246A), when he has finished speaking of the immortality of the soul and now comes to speak of its nature—a very difficult task—, that to tell what it is really like would be possible only for a god and would be a long "tale" (*diegesis*); so instead he will speak not as a god but as a man and more briefly, using a figure of speech, telling what the soul resembles. He then immediately gives the simile comparing the soul to the charioteer with two horses, i.e., an *image.* Thus Plato in this dialogue rejects straight narrative, *diegesis,* and chooses not *mimesis,* but a rhetorical figure, a simile. He sees this method as an expansion of *diegesis* and as perfectly compatible with dialogue. Moreover, whereas the Aristotelian scheme locates Socratic dialogue inside the bounds of *mimesis,* Plato finds a purely narrative basis for dialogue unsatisfactory.

14. Ibid., p. 159.
15. *Republic* 392D; also Aristotle, *Rhetoric* 1416b29.

In the *Republic* Plato advocates the adoption of a poetic style in which imitation serves the narrative discourse. But how much imitation does he sanction? Socrates says (396E) that the "man of the right sort" will adopt a diction that uses appropriately both imitation and simple narration—"but there will be a small portion of imitation in a long discourse. . . ." In Plato's view that narrative discourse will allow only "a small portion" we note some attempt to quantify imitation and hence to locate such discourse *between diegesis and mimesis.* The "debased speaker," on the other hand, Plato deplores as one who imitates indiscriminately; the discourse of this man will contain "little of pure narration." One is tempted to see Plato as ironically implying that the best form of speech for the good man is a slightly or quasi-imitative form, such as dialogue.[16]

Plato's poetics therefore raises the possibility of partial imitation, and this idea in turn leads us to reconsider Aristotle's *Poetics* as implying *degrees of fictionality.* It follows that dialogue may be given a place in the Aristotelian scheme as a partial imitation, and hence a medial art: an incomplete fiction.

IV

The peculiar challenge of dialogue to aesthetic criticism springs from its nature as a didactic art. In the delicate metabolism of its synthetic nature its philosophical usefulness continually threatens its existence as a work of art. "We are in the presence of a work of art," writes George Kubler, "only when it has no preponderant instrumental use, and when its technical and rational foundations are not pre-eminent. When the technical organization or the rational order of a thing overwhelms our

16. A *poesis* of quasi-imitation has not to my knowledge been postulated before, though the French concept of *mi-partition* lurks among many discussions of Aristotle's aesthetics. In his commentary on the *Poetics,* Else, for example, says of Aristotle's remark on the Socratic dialogues: "In recognizing the style of Plato's dialogues as *half-poetic,* Aristotle was not necessarily saying anything about their status as *poesis* [Gk.], that is, as imitation; the remark would even be consistent with denying Plato the title of poet" (p. 43). But by "*half-poetic*" Else does not mean, as I do, quasi-fictional, but simply halfway between prose and verse.

attention, it is an object of use."[17] This order certainly attracts yet in the Socratic dialogues does not overwhelm our attention. However, a division of attention is only one aspect of our complex response. Dialogue insistently raises the difficult problem of how ideas are transmitted in art.

Although he could not analyze its art, Aristotle did not venture to deny the status of dialogue as fiction.[18] Thus the *Poetics* gave dialogue a uniquely sheltered position as a form just inside but unrecognized within the borders of the Aristotelian scheme. It was for this reason that there was so little cognizance of dialogue as a form by subsequent literary theorists.

Although dialogue became a leading humanist form, its success rested upon no clear theoretical definition or aesthetic valuation. As a form, it could scarcely be claimed to belong to the art of fiction at all. Renaissance dialogists, while adopting and elaborating classical models, usually kept silence on method.[19] Yet there are enough observations, intermittent and obscure, in

17. *The Shape of Time: Remarks on the History of Things* (London and New Haven, 1962), p. 16.

18. Wesley Trimpi has commented on this problem historically, observing "the recurring effort to make literature either back into philosophical discourse by a didactic concern for factual or doctrinal truth alone, or back into rhetorical discourse by an exclusive concern with the manipulation of language for its sensuous and emotional effects upon the audience; that is, to reduce it either to its content or to its expression. The corrective function of literary criticism has always attempted to resist each of these specializations." "The Ancient Hypothesis of Fiction: An Essay on the Origins of Literary Theory," *Traditio*, 27 (1971), 8. He adds in a note: "This is even partially reflected in the subsequent history of the two principal definitions of poetry, metrical composition and imitation *(mimesis)*. The first states its relation to the prose composition of oratory and the second, in being concerned with the object and representation of certain types of knowledge, to philosophy."

19. This was also true in the early postclassical period. Lloyd William Daly, in the introduction to his edition of the *Altercatio Hadriani Augusti et Epicteti philosophi* (Urbana, 1939), p. 15, observes: "For few forms of literature is there such a dearth of information. It is but few facts about the form that we can extract from the prefaces to these [question-and-answer] dialogues, even when they are provided with such introductions at all, and other literary references are almost totally lacking."

the prologues, prefatory epistles, and commentaries to indicate a continuing desire in that age of eloquence to encompass dialogue in the universal analysis of literary forms. During the proliferation of poetic theory in the Cinquecento, out of a need to classify and justify poetry as part of moral philosophy, rules to cover the new genres of poetic art were established.[20] Yet because of its marginal status at the edge of the realm of art, dialogue was largely exempt from the attempts at regularization by the theorists.

An exception to this state of affairs was an episode in humanist literary criticism which only demonstrates the unassailability of the Aristotelian verdict. Sigonius[21] and, under his influence, Tasso[22] reiterated Aristotle's scheme as the basis for their rare studies of dialogue in 1561 and 1586. Writing on the imitative aspect of dialogue, they boldly appropriated to this single form Aristotle's three categories for the whole art of fiction. They adopted his manners of imitation intact, attempting thereby to derive from the *Poetics* a true "art of dialogue." Concerning the narrative manner of dialogue, Sigonius specifies that the narration must allow the speech of other people to stand out.[23] Of the dramatic manner, he writes that in dialogue the material is set

20. Weinberg, *A History of Literary Criticism in the Italian Renaissance*, pp. 797–813. We shall return to this "need" in the next chapter. As Weinberg notes (p. 349), "the text of the *Poetics* became available only at the very end of the fifteenth century and became generally known only toward the middle of the sixteenth."

21. Carolus Sigonius (Carlo Sigonio or Sigone), ca. 1524–1584, Italian humanist, historian of Greek and Roman antiquities and the Kingdom of Italy. See articles in the *Biographie Universelle*, the *Encyclopedia Britannica* (11th ed.), John Edwin Sandys, *A History of Classical Scholarship*, 3 vols. (Cambridge, England, 1908–21), III, 143–45, and Weinberg, pp. 455–57, 482–85.

22. Torquato Tasso, 1544–1595; his *Rinaldo* and discourses on the art of poetry appeared about the time of Sigonius's *De dialogo liber* (Venice, 1561). I use the Bodleian Library copy of Signonius's *Opera omnia*, 6 vols., ed. P. Argelati (Milan, 1732–37). The *De dialogo* is found in VI, 431–88; cited hereafter as "Sigonius."

23. Sigonius, 450C: ". . .alter, cum narratur ita, ut aliorum etiam assimulata extet oratio. . . ." Cf. Tasso, *Discorso dell' arte del dialogo* (Venice, 1586): "L'una può montare in palco. . . . Ma un'altra ce n'è che non può montare in palco,

forth "as if acted on the stage, not narrated."[24] The same manner produces tragedy and comedy. As examples of the dramatic manner, Sigonius cites the *Phaedrus* and *Gorgias,* dialogues which follow the procedure of plays, with the speakers' names set at the head of their speeches, and which have no introduction or explanation. Tasso similarly assigns this manner to Plato (as well as to Lucian). The narrative dialogue, says Sigonius, is typified in Cicero's *De Oratore,* and Tasso concurs.

Aristotle conceives of the third, or mixed, manner of imitation not as an oscillation between story and speeches but rather as a unified, continuous form. He gives Homer as his example. Later in the *Poetics,* when he gets around to discussing epic in detail, the stress of his argument falls on the unity of this mixed form: "Clearly, its fables should be put together dramatically, as in tragedies; concerning a single whole and complete action with a beginning, middle, and end, in order that it may give its own individual pleasure like a single whole picture" (Ch. 24, p. 51). Its unity derives from the fact that the epic imitates one object. Thus the *Poetics* argued the territorial integrity of narrative, dramatic, and mixed as forms of fictional art.

Logical problems were to arise, however, with the adoption of such a system to classify the forms of dialogue. These are obvious in the treatment of the third manner.[25] Sigonius's and Tas-

perciò che, conservando l'autore la sua persona, come istorico narra quel che disse il tale e 'l cotale" (333f.). The *Discorso* can be found in *Torquato Tasso: Prose,* ed. Ettore Mazzali, *La Letteratura italiana* . . . (Milan and Naples, 1959), vol. 22; cited hereafter as "Tasso."

24. Sigonius, 450C: ". . .unus est, cum ita res exponitur, quasi agatur in scena, non narretur. . . ."

25. Sigonius, 450C, says simply: ". . . tertium ex utrisque confusum est." Tasso, p. 334: "E c'è ancora la terza maniera: ed è di quelli che son mescolati della prima e della seconda maniera, conservando l'autore la sua prima persona e narrando come istorico; e poi introducendo a favellar *dramatikos* [Gk.], come s'usa di far nelle tragedie e nelle comedie; e può, e non, montare in palco: ciò è non può montarvi, in quanto l'autore conserva la sua persona, è come l'istorico; e può montarvi, in quanto s'introducono le persone rappresentativamente a favellare. . . ." Having distinguished this manner, Tasso adds rather lamely that Cicero made some dialogues like this, and then drops the subject.

so's dilemma is instructive. Following the analogy with Aristotle, the mixed form of dialogue should have embodied various combinations of the narrative and dramatic manners and should therefore have produced a counterpart to epic. But in fact dialogue itself seems to be a formal alternative to epic, for all dialogues are in a sense mixed. Aristotle may have chosen epic simply as the most salient example. It is not certain he would have seen dialogue as a type of either the dramatic or the narrative manner. At any rate, Aristotle's omission of dialogue as a form of the mixed manner allowed Sigonius and Tasso to argue for three forms when they might better have argued for three manners of a single form. The concept of one mixed manner, with elements combined in various proportions, found no place in their scheme.

In reviewing the methodology of the literary theorists in the cinquecento, Weinberg (p. 51) illustrates the common practice of borrowing Aristotle's method in the *Poetics* for the analyses of genres (e.g., romance) which Aristotle did not analyze. Weinberg shows some of the errors and unintelligent misunderstandings of Aristotle which commonly resulted when critics incorrectly applied the *Poetics* to genres, and how they got embroiled in futile discussions of the meaning of "imitation." Sigonius's theory goes down under this new wave. As Weinberg remarks (p. 485), "what starts as an attempt to apply Aristotelian distinctions to a new genre [dialogue] thus becomes little more than an expression of the current theory of decorum in literature. Clearly, Sigonio still writes at a time when the implications of Aristotle's method are not clear, when it is easy to pass from one critical context to another, when there is no notion at all of methodological rigor."

Tasso's contribution to the theory of dialogue is more significant, though it is unfortunately only a sketch. Writing of Plato and Cicero in his brief *Discorso dell' arte del dialogo,* Tasso characterizes dialogue as the imitation of reasoning, *imitazione di ragionamento.*[26] He retraces some of the arguments found in

26. Tasso, p. 335 et passim.

Sigonius, and undoubtedly he knew the earlier work. But Tasso's theory for an *art* of dialogue makes more searching use of the *Poetics* than his predecessor's. Tasso is especially original in clarifying the relation between dialogue and dramatic imitation. Tragedy and comedy imitate the actions of men, and to the degree that dialogues portray these actions they may be characterized as one or the other. Tasso goes so far as to call the *Crito* and the *Phaedo* tragic, the *Symposium* comic; but these, he adds, are not true tragedy or comedy. Rather, in dialogues the action is partially (or as if) joined to reasoning, *ne' dialoghi l'azione è quasi giunta de' ragionamenti.* By "reasoning" Tasso means something more than disputation (*le quistioni*) or even dialectic; he is aware that reasoning exercises men's fullest human capacities. The "perfection" of a writer of dialogues, such as Plato, he says, derives from his position *midway* between the poet and the dialectician.[27]

Perhaps the most prescient of Tasso's allusions to Aristotle is made almost in passing (p. 337): "quale è la favola nel poema, tale è nel dialogo la quistione," as the fable is to the poem, so the disputation is to the dialogue. This simple ratio is an invaluable key to the interpretation of the dialogue form, for it brings the very core of the *Poetics* to bear upon the dialogue. Speaking of the essential components of tragedy, Aristotle says that the chief of these is the fable, i.e., "the whole structure of the incidents";

> for tragedy is an imitation not of men but of doings . . . ; it is their characters that give men their quality, but their doings that make them happy or the opposite. . . . Thus it is the incidents (that is to say the Fable) that are the end for which tragedy exists; and the end is more important than anything else. (Ch. 6, pp. 24f.)

It is clear from Tasso's analogy that he considers Aristotle's argument equally true for dialogue. The end for which dialogue exists is the imitation of reasoning. Tasso thus qualifies dialogue as an *art* by fully reckoning reasoning among the doings of men. The end of dialogue, like the end of other forms of imitation, is the creation of an image of human life.

27. Tasso, p. 345, "mezzo fra 'l poeta e 'l dialettico."

In Plato's dialogues the dramatic elements and the philosophical dialectic are related in a reciprocity whose completeness Aristotle refused to acknowledge. The critical problem before Tasso was to depict that reciprocity as mimetic, and thus the problem has been cast in our own era. In a magisterial study on the genesis and art of classical dialogue, Michel Ruch asserts:

l'action extérieure 'mime' presque toujours l'action intérieure, souligne les grandes divisions du raisonnement, marque l'économie de l'ouvrage et les phases du dialogue. L'art dramatique facilite la compréhension de la discussion philosophique.[28]

That the dramatic element thus enhances an unfolding argument is an observation of fundamental importance, but it falls short of defining the reciprocal nature of *mimesis* in dialogue. Tasso's concept extended the range of the mimetic principle by the assertion that the exterior action is as it were *joined* ("quasi giunta") to the action of reason. This term argues a deeper unity in dialogue that even Ruch supposes: the whole narrative, not simply the dramatized dialectic, is an imitation of reasoning. Tasso's discourse may be seen as a heroic attempt to seize dialogue for the Aristotelian camp. A Poet was seeking to mediate between dialectic and drama by means of the *Poetics.* Yet even so clever a proposition had its limitation, and that was the rather curious way in which his aesthetic analysis of dialogue held aloof from the resources of the Socratic Method.

V

The tendency in modern literature, especially drama, e.g., in the plays of Samuel Beckett, to have only two characters—protagonist and deuteragonist—may indicate a dual purpose on the part of the creator. Beckett speaks in *From an Abandoned Work* of "a mind like the one I always had, always on the alert against itself. . . ." Like the drama of our time, certain ancient and Renaissance dialogues offer representations of the striving of a divided mind toward resolution. In them, as in modern drama,

28. *Le Préambule dans les oeuvres philosophiques de Cicéron: essai sur la genèse et l'art du dialogue* (Paris and Strasbourg, 1958), p. 378.

it is sometimes impossible to distinguish between an author's psychic conflict and the process by which he discovers where intellectual arguments really lead. As Tom Stoppard has remarked,

'I don't write plays with heroes who express my point of view. I write argument plays. I tend to write for two people rather than for One Voice. Rosencrantz and Guildenstern were two sides of one temperament. When I start writing I find it difficult, except on simple questions, to know where I stand. . . .'[29]

In Plato's representations too, the intellectual struggle of the dialectic acquires the power of personal affect from other sources than dramatic conflict.

It has been argued that Plato's dialogues were "dialectical mimes," composed for (written and recited to) a listening audience. For much of his career Plato was a teacher of dialectic, and his dialogues provide instruction in that skill by representing such disputations dramatically.[30] Their intellectual intention is clear. Dialogic speech in Plato can be characterized by a phrase in his seventh epistle (344B): "benevolent disputations by the use of question and answer without jealousy. . . ." For Plato dialectic has its own power, and this can be understood by a comparison with the power of drama. Aristotle speaks of the revelation in drama which produces a purgation or purification of the soul, catharsis. For Plato the goal of dialectic similarly is revelation, which Aristotle described as "a change from ignorance to knowledge."[31] "At last," Plato asserts, speaking of the process of dialectic,

a flash of understanding . . . blazes up, and the mind, as it exerts all its powers to the limit of human capacity, is flooded with light.[32]

29. Interview in the *New York Times,* 29 July 1979, Section 2, p. 22.

30. Gilbert Ryle, *Plato's Progress* (Cambridge, England, 1966), Chs. I and II.

31. Aristotle's definition of dramatic revelation, *Poetics,* Ch. 11, p. 31; further elaboration is found in Chs. 14 and 16.

32. *Epis.* 7,344B. Unless otherwise noted, all quotations from Plato are taken from *The Collected Dialogues of Plato including the Letters,* ed. Edith Hamilton and Huntington Cairns (Princeton, 1961).

Plato is here describing insight, the revelation of knowledge, but in a way that suggests a mental version of catharsis as well. The intensity of the flash claims for the moment of insight a primacy in Plato's view analogous to that which disclosure claims for the crisis of feeling in Aristotle's theory of complex tragedy.

The analogy between dialectic and drama points up two important differences between Plato and Aristotle. Aristotle argues that revelation comes sometimes from an external agent, which awakens in the protagonist the sense of something familiar and hence causes a recognition, while Plato implies that revelation always comes from within. The second difference, implicit in the first, is that while Aristotle probably means that catharsis is experienced by the audience rather than the protagonist, Plato may be said to attribute both revelation and catharsis to the mind of the reasoner. These attitudes of Plato's underlie the fundamentally interiorized quality of his dialectical dialogues. In the seventh letter he asserts that in the dialectical act of understanding, the mind experiences a positive release of its full powers. In the experience of drama the analogous moment would be called cathartic. The questions and answers of dialectic seek to create an intellectually purifying form of drama. The *events* or what happens in dialectic might thus be characterized as a mental version of the dramatic element; dialectic relates men to one another as minds.

One may distinguish two worlds to which Plato's thought refers: the world of *discourse* and the world of *contemplation.*[33] The first has to do with logical method, the second with aesthetic experience. Extending the line of Tasso's argument that reasoning and dramatic action are "bound together," one might regard the whole world of dialogue as composed of thought. Then it might be posited that the degree of fictionality of a dialogue could be ascertained by determining whether, at a given moment, the dialogue addresses the world of discourse or

33. John Alexander Stewart, *Plato's Doctrine of Ideas* (Oxford, 1909; repr. New York, 1964), Part II: "The Doctrine of Ideas as Expressing Aesthetic Experience."

the world of contemplation. Usually in Plato the aesthetic, contemplative experience is stimulated by an image, and so images might provide one gauge. But what if we grant that dialogues belong primarily to the world of discourse? It then becomes possible to see aesthetic experience in a dialogue as contributing directly to its discursive experience.[34] Might we not see the creation of "discursive experience," rather than *mimesis,* as the basis of the art of dialogue?

The Socratic dialogues do not grant us admission to their rational order by means of the recognized Aristotelian techniques. Their characters live a mental life but they do not live; they exchange their ideas but do not become involved in plots which we long to see untied; their language often keeps to the lower slopes, hooded in obscurity. The discursive experience which they sometimes create reminds us of drama, but that is a deceptive resemblance; Sigonius and Tasso were both betrayed by it.

Socratic dialogues and those in their tradition are about "mental events in the characters' minds." Paul Hernadi has examined this phenomenon in the novel:[35]

> While mental events (whether rational, emotive, volitive, or sensory) are not strictly verbal, no articulate account can be given of them, not even to the mind in which they occur, save by means of words. Thus, whenever a person is fully conscious of his mental operations, something related to, yet different from, verbal communication can be assumed as present in his mind. . . .

Thus mental events, being neither verbal nor nonverbal, are *quasi-verbal,* and Hernadi submits that those events constitute "a third distinct realm of *mimesis.*"

When a few Renaissance critics struggled to articulate the rela-

34. Ibid., p. 172: "We now see how natural it is that aesthetic experience should 'contaminate' the discursive experience of a man of [Plato's] temperament and calibre, without at all vitiating his conception of the method of Discourse—without causing him for a moment to forget that, in Discourse, the *eidos* [Gk.] is not an individual thing apart, but a point of view generally applicable."

35. The novel is the only prose form which has received critical attention comparable to that devoted to poetry and drama. *Beyond Genre* (Ithaca, 1972), pp. 197f.

tion of drama to dialectic in dialogue or, more broadly, of action to reasoning, their strength lay in Aristotle's analysis of action. Critics of the novel have concentrated with increasing precision on the ability of that form of prose to represent a variety of mental states, including quasi-verbal ones. After the psychological and aesthetic elaborations of novel criticism, the suggestion that dialectic or reasoning has a variety of states, including quasi-verbal ones, should not seem excessive.[36] We know that reasoning is accompanied by many mental events, and not all of these are rational. Alcibiades disturbs the banquet toward a new harmony; Bembo's auditors are taken unawares by the dawn. An unfolding argument is attended by doubts, fears, objections—in short, the elements of consciousness—each prompted by its own particular cause. Logic is usually the least obstacle! Following its own needs, the "other" *mimesis* of dialogue has recourse to Aristotelian *mimesis* from time to time.

To represent dialogue as a lesser art tapping a greater would be very cumbersome and far from my purpose. The fact of the matter is that dialogue centers on ideas and the responses or mental events they create. Its references to the sensory world, that is, to the world of Aristotelian imitation, are all in the interest of intelligibility and are therefore essential. Its status as an art has a rough correspondence to that "intermediate reality" which Plato suggests in his discussion of the soul. This intermediate reality is only the hint of a certain intelligible liaison between the Idea and the sensory world.[37] This link Plato understands as the soul. It is this sense that I intend in calling dialogue a medial art.

36. Malcolm Bradbury has discussed the problem of defining a poetics of fiction, ranging widely over the definiton of the novel. He regards the novelist as "mediating verbally a devised succession of events." "Towards a Poetics of Fiction: 1) An Approach through Structure," *Novel*, 1 (1967), 45–52, 50. One must mention two influential studies in this field, Wayne C. Booth, *The Rhetoric of Fiction* (Chicago, 1961), and Robert Scholes and Robert Kellogg, *The Nature of Narrative* (New York, 1966); but I must confess I have not found these pertinent to the unique problem of narrative dialogue.

37. See M. Guéroult, "La Méditation de l'âme dans le 'Phédon,' " *Revue de Métaphysique et de Morale*, 33 (1926), 469–91.

It is an art, moreover, which mirrors the Renaissance humanists' role as mediators between the ideas of antiquity and their own sensory world.

The term *incomplete fictions* may be used to sum up the position of dialogue inside the Aristotelian scheme. Because it is but intermittently mimetic (and sometimes the theatrical trappings grind noisily) dialogue intermittently resembles drama.[38] Centered on ideas and their actions, however, dialogue would only be diminished by the achievement of complete fictionality such as Aristotle conceives. With reference to Aristotle it is evident that dialogues comprise no genre. Rather we ought to speak of their aim, which is primarily didactic. The essential purpose of the rational order of dialogue and of every fleeting affiliation it makes with the art of fiction is pedagogical.

What implications follow from this conclusion? No one can fail to recognize this purpose in the vast bulk of dialogues, which seem to bear a wearying load of facts and uninspired arguments like slaves of Morpheus. We need not look there for any formal excellence beyond utility. Obviously didacticism, as we thus normally conceive of it, threatens to decay the form of dialogue into a barren formalism. In Kenneth Burke's capsule: "Atrophy of form follows hypertrophy of information."[39] But a few dialogues merit our sustained attention. As we have seen, didacticism may be equated with the creation of mental events. This Platonic conception of an extended world of thought allows us to shift the basis of our analysis from Aristotle's aesthetics without discarding his criteria of fiction when they are useful. To acknowledge as primary the pedagogical purpose of dialogue

38. The fashion of putting Plato's dialogues on the stage never enjoyed a diffusion outside boys' schools, where the pious wishes of classics masters could be harmlessly indulged. Besides such performances in humanist schools during the Renaissance, some of Plato's lighter dialogues, according to Plutarch, were sometimes performed by boys as entertainments at the symposia of the Romans in his time. See Thomas Twining, trans., *Aristotle's Treatise on Poetry* (London, 1815), p. 135n.

39. *Counterstatement* (Berkeley, 1953), p. 144.

allows us to examine some of the masterpieces of dialogue as intellectual creations which stimulate intellectual creativity.[40]

40. A. L. Kroeber holds that "intellectual creativity and aesthetic creativity behave alike historically, presumably because they operate in equivalent ways: they both produce intrinsic values." See his *Style and Civilization* (Ithaca, 1957), p. 151.

2

Platonic vis-à-vis Ciceronian Dialogue

I

Although the humanists customarily linked Plato and Cicero as masters of literary form, Platonic dialogue differs markedly from Ciceronian. To imitate the Greek form committed the writer to a different ethos and set of conventions than those of the writer recasting Cicero. Other classical authors live again in Renaissance dialogue. The Greek dialogists Plutarch and Lucian inspire the salty diction in such Renaissance table talk as Erasmus's *Colloquia* and the satirical banter in More's *Utopia.* But Plutarch's *Moralia* were then known in far fewer editions than Plato, and it is significant that Erasmus and More translated into Latin only a few of the more high-minded of Lucian's dialogues. The scope of their influence remained distinctly secondary. It was Plato and Cicero who provided models for serious philosophical argument. Because English humanists formed new dialogues upon these sources, often intermingled, it behoves us to follow their practice of returning *ad fontes* before taking up their innovations. The humanists were chiefly interested in three elements in Platonic and Ciceronian dialogue: the *characters,* the *subjects,* and the development of an *oratorical style.*

That dialogue imitates reasoning, as Tasso maintained, has important consequences for characterization. In Plato the characters may be regarded as aspects of a central intelligence.[1] His dialogues represent "articulated thoughts"—objectified and personalized in the characters.[2] Yet, as we have seen, it is the reasoning rather than the character of men which is the object of imitation in dialogue—a fact which imposes definite restraints upon characterization in Plato. The spirit of free inquiry that pervades the dialogues is in fact the essential trait of Plato's characters. His attention to individual traits, as for example in the *Phaedrus,* follows from a desire for dramatic verisimilitude, i.e., for a credible sequence of responses. But ultimately, as Pierre Grimal has argued,

> La personne de Phèdre, de Ménon, de Criton, et des autres n'entre plus en jeu; il n'y a plus en présence que des êtres raisonnables, et, comme tels, interchangeables. La fin même du dialogue est, en somme, de surmonter le caractère individuel des interlocuteurs et de les amener à découvrir ce qui, en eux, est universel.[3]

The communal discovery of truth is necessarily sought through successive stages. Phaedrus is not portrayed as simply an "être raisonnable" in the beginning. If his individual traits and those of other interlocutors are finally insignificant, it is still true that in the initial stages the characters are clearly defined in order to accredit the imitation of reasoning.

1. In the *Theaetetus* (189E–190A) Socrates defines the thinking process as "a discourse that the mind carries on with itself about any subject it is considering. . . . [W]hen the mind is thinking, it is simply talking to itself, asking questions and answering them, and saying yes or no." Plato recurs to this definition in the *Sophist* (263E).

2. Irwin Edman, ed., *Works of Plato,* Modern Library (New York, 1928), p. xxvii. "The closet drama of an inner argument among the conflicting voices of one intelligence becomes the objective drama of audible discussion of the diverse characters in a Platonic dialogue."

3. "Caractères généraux du dialogue romain: de Lucilius à Cicéron," in *L'Information littéraire,* 7 (1955), 194; cited hereafter as "Grimal."

Ethopoeia, or the delineation of character, attains the level of an art of portrait-making in Plato.[4] In the *Lysis* Socrates enters into dialogue with four characters; in each conversation his speech is adapted to the individual, thereby refining the portraits of the interlocutors. With the philosopher Ctesippus, Socrates holds a polite debate appropriate between equals; with Hippothales his conversation is jesting with a lovesick boy; to Lysis he takes obvious pleasure in giving gentle, chastening instruction; with Menexenus, Socrates follows a line of strict reasoning in making a formal attack. In this way Socrates' speeches help to characterize the other figures. Moreover, just as the conversation is bilateral, so too the art of portraiture in dialogue involves at least two points of view. The responses of each speaker reinforce the perception of his character implied in Socrates' tone.

The central portrait in the *Lysis* is Socrates himself.[5] As the protagonist, he directs the conversation and in so doing reveals through his language his own extraordinary flexibility of thought and sensitivity to the thoughts—expressed or obscure—of his interlocutors. The character of Socrates is of course recurrent, and each of the Socratic dialogues contributes some detail concerning his person or his temperament.[6] As Ruch observes, the consistency of this portrayal testifies to Plato's vener-

4. Michel Ruch, *Le Préambule dans les oeuvres philosophiques de Cicéron: essai sur la genèse et l'art du dialogue* (Paris and Strasbourg, 1958), p. 33; cited hereafter as "Ruch." "Personne n'avait fait de portraits aussi complets, et en caractérisant d'aussi près chaque personnage, par son langage, sa façon de s'exprimer et ses mille particularités. Hérodote, Thucydide, Aristophane, Euripide, n'avaient pas développé le même art du portrait."

5. Cf. Julius Stenzel, *Plato's Method of Dialectic,* trans. D. J. Allan (Oxford, 1940), p. 2: "the principal subject of [Plato's] poetic imitation is Socrates. . . . The question of literary style is thus seen to be bound up with that of Socrates' personality. . . ."

6. Especially in the early dialogues, what the ancients called the *Sokratikoi logoi* (the sketches of Socrates) are, in H. J. Rose's judgment, "probably, allowing for a little natural idealization, . . . very like what he really did and said" (*A Handbook of Greek Literature,* 3d rev. ed. [1956; repr. New York, 1960], p. 263).

ation, which encompassed not only the substance of Socrates' teaching but even his turns of phrase. His sobriety, his daily routine, his mannerisms find expression in the dialogues. Above all, Plato adopted his method of teaching—the Socratic dialogue—from the desire to retrace not only the words of Socrates but also his image and, by extension, that of his interlocutors.[7]

Yet the characterization of Socrates differs radically from that of the other figures in Plato. Besides being a primary subject of imitation, his character is always, from the outset of every dialogue, fully formed.[8] Socrates may not be said to undergo any "character development." His personal aspects, though gradually revealed, are seen as parts of an integrated whole. In the figures of his interlocutors, on the other hand, progress toward enlightenment may be seen to work upon their character. Here then are two points, to which we will return in later chapters. First, in Plato we observe a tendency toward character development in the interlocutors; in Cicero and certain Tudor writers this tendency becomes a prominent feature of dialogue. Second, the unique relation between Socrates and his interlocutors is a distinctive characteristic of Platonic dialogue. Socrates is the constant, they the variables. Let us look more closely at the second point.

One of the principles we have inherited directly from Plato, intermediately through the humanists, is that human moral character is not given at birth but is perfected through self-knowledge. Socrates' success in persuading Phaedrus of the truth of his arguments depends in large measure on his perception of Phaedrus's personal character. Indeed, as Socrates says, an orator must "know what types of soul there are"; in order to persuade an individual he must apply certain arguments in a

7. Ruch, p. 34.

8. In *Der Dialog* (1895; repr. Hildesheim, 1963), Rudolf Hirzel observes: ". . . die sokratischen Dialoge [erinnern] an die Evangelien, nach welchen der Gottessohn bereits bei seinem ersten Hervortreten im Tempel sich im vollen Besitze der höchsten Weisheit zeigt" (I, 178 n. 1).

certain fashion suited specifically to him.[9] In following the stages of Socrates' argument—in resisting, demanding qualifications, and finally assenting—Phaedrus reaches a new level of enlightenment and vows to act accordingly. We regard him as a changed man. So too the character of Lysis may be seen to expand by virtue of his reasoning with Socrates.

In the *Symposium* Socrates gives an unusual glimpse into his own personal development by recounting his dialogue with Diotima. The truth he learned on that occasion changed his whole life. The episode is an archetype of personal growth; it also typifies the relation between Socrates and the other characters. Throughout the dialogues Socrates assumes the role of Diotima, the interlocutors developing in response to his guidance. It is this relation which the reader silently rehearses, and in this way dialogue may become the vehicle of change. The method of Platonic dialogue is "educational" in the root meaning of the word, for Socrates is engaged in "drawing out" the characters of men. In this sense the dialogues of More, Ascham, and Elyot follow the Platonic method. Such is the form characterization takes in Plato. Like that in drama, it must be deduced from the speeches; in addition there are such narrative supplements as prologues and indications of scene.

This view of the form accords with Grimal's assertion that the goal of Platonic dialogue is ultimately to surmount the individual character of the interlocutors and to lead them to discover the universal in themselves. I have proposed that Socrates, though he himself does not develop, is the agent of development in others. We can see that Plato's attention to the individual character of the interlocutors is limited virtually to elaborating their relation to Socrates. Thus it holds true that dialogue imitates not the character of men but the process of their reasoning. Grimal regards Socrates' role as essentially abstract: "to call everything into question. . . ." This is the meaning of Socratic irony, which is not modern irony but rather the dis-

9. *Phaedrus,* 271D–E. See also the *Laws,* 651.

semination of "systematic doubt."[10] Every statement by the interlocutors is subject to this irony; it is inevitable that they are chiefly characterized by their relation to the Socrates principle.

From the abstract function of characterization in Plato we turn to Cicero, whose characters have more concreteness and autonomy. They share the burden of the dialogue more equally. Cicero's dialogues are commonly said to be aristocratic. There is doubtless a recurrent emphasis on personal glory, on such things as the titles, offices, and lineage of the characters. Cicero's characters belong to the category of family portraits. Such a method of character delineation deeply affects the form of his dialogues. Further, the Roman sense of the concrete helps to explain the tendency towards historicity in the characterization in Ciceronian dialogue.[11] Cicero's characters are chosen precisely because they are real individuals. As important as the opposition of doctrines is the opposition of men, with their particular humors, temperaments, and prejudices.[12] It is characteristic of Roman "realism" to grasp individual traits carefully, in order to shed light on what renders each man unique rather than to express his participation in universal humanity.[13]

The extent of Cicero's divergence from Plato in this respect is illustrated by the contrast between the *Symposium*—with its set doctrinal speeches by Pausanias, Eryximachus, Aristophanes, Agathon, and Socrates, whose speech subsumes them all—and Cicero's *De Oratore,* with its digressive conversations, which are given their shape by the individual temperaments of Crassus, Antonius, Catulus, Caesar, and the others. In Cicero, not only the opinions but the personalities of the characters are played

10. See Søren Kierkegaard, *The Concept of Irony, with Constant Reference to Socrates,* trans. Lee M. Capel (London, 1966).

11. Grimal, p. 195.

12. Thus Grimal characterizes the dialogues of Lucilius, which directly influenced those of Cicero.

13. Grimal, p. 196.

off against each other. Thus the autonomy of each character reinforces the integral validity of each point of view.[14]

This principle is preserved even in the characterization of minor figures, those who are not present to debate but to observe and learn from the debate. Sigonius says in 1561 that such characters should not be lacking in learning or humanity, but neither should they be superior to the persons taking the principal parts in the dialogue. "Neque decorum ullo modo, aut consonum, eum audire, cui sit docendum, praecipere verò, cui discendum" (*De dialogo liber,* 458C).

Cicero's dialogues partake of a profound duality, which Grimal has admirably described (p. 196): Roman dialogue, instituted upon some general problem, of a spiritual nature, takes place between definite characters, whose personality, rather than becoming an extension of the debate, tends to impose its own limits on it and, as it were, to keep it down to earth. The attachment of a general problem to a definite personality is epitomized in the double titles of such dialogues as *Cato Maior De Senectute* or *Laelius De Amicitia.* In grounding the philosophical problem in character Cicero has thus contrived for one to be understood in terms of the other.

The increased importance of personal character is one of Cicero's major contributions to the dialogue form. This fact was not lost on the Renaissance humanists. Cicero develops any given philosophical theme in accordance with a dramatic fiction involving the encounter of several characters. But there is not the tendency towards synthesis or dogma which is found in Plato. For the concreteness and autonomy of Cicero's characters bespeak his conception of dialogue as the representation of equally viable views.

The necessity thus arises that each view be expressed by a

14. Francesco Tateo, in *Tradizione e realità nell' umanesimo italiano* (Bari, 1967), p. 239, singles out the initial encounter between Antonius and Crassus in Book I of the *De Oratore* as typical of the balance of roles in Ciceronian dialogue and goes on to point out that the debate between Crassus and Scaevola has neither victor nor vanquished.

qualified *porte-parole.* Ruch observes: "Ce qui précède toujours l'élaboration d'un ouvrage dialogué, c'est le choix des personnages susceptibles d'illustrer les thèses philosophiques. Autrement dit, le dialogue n'est pas possible que si l'exposé logique peut s'allier à une fiction dramatique."[15] Cato the Elder, the consul happy in his old age; Gaius Laelius, whose noble friendship with Scipio Africanus the Younger was famous; Crassus, the most illustrious Roman orator before Cicero—such are the protagonists, and such their qualifications, that Cicero chooses. Moreover, Cicero surrounds them with distinguished peers and juniors also known to his audience; in this way he establishes the *auctoritas* of his dialogues. It was more satisfying to the Roman reader, Grimal has held (p. 196), to know that the precepts emanated from a personage he knew well, whom he respected and considered a good patrician. A result of buttressing the arguments with personal authority in this way is to set them, like the characters themselves, on a par with each other. One of the most successful Tudor examples is Thomas Starkey's *Dialogue between Reginald Pole and Thomas Lupset.* In Ciceronian dialogue the dramatic development and the philosophical development move together not toward a crisis or conclusion but toward equilibrium.

Finally by way of contrast with Plato we should note the appearance among the *dramatis personae* of Cicero himself. In a genetic account of the dialogue form, the argument might be made that Plato pretends to be his characters and in so doing incorporates dramatic elements into his imitative art. As Gerald Else has maintained: "For both Plato and Aristotle the dramatic mode is imitation *par excellence.* For Plato it is so because imitation means to him a personal experience and a direct relationship."[16] This principle is, one might say, the soul of Plato's dra-

15. Ruch, p. 307. Cf. Sigonius, 454E: "Quod si eos, qui hac luce fruantur, induxerimus, tum, ut dixi, videndum erit diligenter, ne ad earum eos artium disputationem vocemus, quarum constet ignaros illos esse. . . ."

16. Gerald F. Else, *Aristotle's Poetics: The Argument* (Cambridge, Mass., 1957), p. 97.

matic fiction. But it is quite another thing for the author to be present in his work in his own person. Perhaps Cicero's practice of appearing as a character in his dialogues follows the procedure in the lost dialogues of Aristotle.[17] Where the author assumes the role of protagonist, as Cicero does for example in the Tusculan dialogues,[18] the function of character is expanded in a variety of ways, and these should be enumerated, as they will be useful later in our examination of Thomas More's dialogues.

(1) Sigonius argues (456B and 457A) that, whereas some characters function to confirm, some to teach, some to refute, and some only to listen, the protagonist of a dialogue almost always expresses the opinions of the author. This is true enough in *De Amicitia* or *De Senecute;* the difficulty arises in *De Oratore* that it is not always clear who the protagonist is (Crassus?) or whether Cicero assumes his role without reservation. (2) Considering the autonomy of the other characters, we see that Cicero's role as protagonist imposes a certain limitation on him as a writer. This limitation Sigonius sees (457D) as the problem of preserving the "dignity" of the characters. Opponents, he says, should not be forced to defend false positions or to retire from the discussion shamefully beaten; their arguments should be probable, their positions agreeable to them. In other words, the writer as protagonist establishes his own authority at the risk of undermining that of his interlocutors. (3) Cicero's self-inclusion in the mimetic representation of reasoning complicates

17. Ruch (p. 40) argues that "la grand innovation d'Aristote fut évidemment de se mettre lui-même en scène, soit en identifiant son rôle avec celui d'un interlocuteur, soit en assumant le rôle du protagoniste." He goes on (p. 45) to single out the "trait commun à tous les dialogues imités d'Aristote: l'auteur est en même temps protagoniste." Cf. Hirzel, *Der Dialog,* I, 321 n. 1.

18. That Cicero has been speaking in his own person is made clear at the close of Book V, though it is evident throughout. In the Renaissance, the medieval siglum "M" for Magister was taken for Marcus; an interesting discussion of the *Tusculans'* sigla is found in Jean Andrieu, *Le dialogue antique: structure et présentation* (Paris, 1954), pp. 297f. In *De Senectute,* 3, Cicero states that his own views on old age are voiced by Cato. Sigonius (457C) would include in this category *De Finibus, De Divinatione, De Legibus,* and *De Claris Oratoribus.*

the dramatic fiction; e.g., the presence of the author insures a built-in commentary, often ironic. The author's assumption of a role in his dialogue increases the psychological depth of both the drama and the dialectic, just as it would if the Socratic dialogues were written by Socrates.[19]

II

"A dialogue," says Diogenes Laertius in his *Life of Plato* (3, 48), "is a discourse consisting of question and answer on some philosophical or political subject, with due regard to the characters of the persons introduced and the choice of diction." Having regarded in the first chapter the function of question and answer and, above, the characters of the persons introduced, we turn next briefly to the subjects of Platonic and Ciceronian dialogues and finally to their choice of diction.

The philosophical and political subjects in Laertius's definition of dialogue, in the judgment of Sigonius (445D), comprise two kinds, "quae cognitionis sunt, & quae actionis." Here Sigonius's understanding cuts deep; he uses Laertius's observation to throw into relief the two essential concerns in all of Plato's dialogues: knowledge and ethics. It is interesting to note the analogy between this classification according to content and Renaissance classifications according to form (narrative and dramatic). Neither method provides headings under which to rank the dialogues, though Laertius is ingenious in devising inclusive subdivisions (3, 49–51). Rather, just as Plato's dialogues blend narrative and dramatic elements, so their concern is both epistemological and ethical. Hence the subject like the form of his dialogues should be seen as synthetic; Plato studies the nature of the moral life.

Such is the general subject from which the individual dia-

19. The exiled Cicero, in composing the *Tusculan Disputations*, does in fact represent himself as a kind of Socrates. His adoption of the Socratic manner inspired Tasso (*Discorso*, p. 340) to exclaim: "Such is the power of the love of philosophy in an old Roman senator, father of his country, who disputed after the Greek custom, perhaps in this way to deceive himself and console himself in bondage!"

logues branch. This is the point of Laertius's subdivisions: physics, he says, is *represented by* the *Timaeus;* logic, by the *Statesman, Cratylus, Parmenides,* and *Sophist;* ethics, by the *Apology, Crito, Phaedo, Phaedrus,* and *Symposium;* and so on. More important, the discussion within individual dialogues elucidates the general subject by the particular. Cicero is concerned with many of the same subjects—with logic, rhetoric, and law, with love, inspiration, and death. He shares the central subject of the nature of the moral life. It was for an age beyond the Renaissance to debate Cicero's relative deficiencies as a metaphysician; as moralists, to men such as Sigonius, Tasso, and the English humanists, Plato and Cicero were rivals.[20] To them their works differed in form, not in subject. Though ultimately a less original philosopher, Cicero consistently professes the Aristotelian aesthetic doctrine, derived to a considerable extent from Plato, that imitative art in its highest form is an expression of the universal element in human nature.[21]

From what has just been said it may seem that the extraordinary thing about the dialogues of Plato and Cicero—considering the magnitude of their general subject matter, i.e., the universal element in human nature or the nature of the moral life—is their particularity of focus. Each dialogue is devoted to a specific problem. We need not refer to the doctrine of the Forms to see that for both Plato and Cicero the ideal is revealed in the particular. Such is the explicit task in the *De Oratore:* "we have to picture to ourselves in our discourse an orator from whom every blemish has been taken away, and one who moreover is rich in every merit" (1, 118). The picture is composed of minute particulars, from the quality of voice to the quality of soul; the Orator is universal because his virtues are humanly attainable.

Humanist conversation pieces, in contrast to medieval *quaes-*

20. "Fra tutt' i dialogi greci, lodevolissimi son que' di Platone. . . . Ma Cicerone e primo fra' Latini, il quale volle forse assomigliarsi a Platone . . ." (Tasso, p. 341). See also Thomas Elyot, *The Boke Named the Gouernour,* ed. H. H. S. Croft (London, 1883), I, 93f.

21. See S. H. Butcher, *Aristotle's Theory of Poetry and Fine Art,* 4th ed. (1911; repr. London, 1932), p. 150.

tiones or other scholastic dialogues, consistently stress the connection between the particulars of their subject and wider meanings. Often, as in *Toxophilus* or *Utopia* or *A Dialogue of Comfort,* the result is allegory.

We have already seen that the philosophical dialogue is a method of instruction. The Socrates of the Platonic dialogues is above all a pedagogue, who lived and died for his teaching. Nor is the pedagogical motive absent from Cicero. Roman dialogue belongs definitively to *praeceptiva philosophia* or the *genus praecipiendi,*[22] that is, to the didactic genre. Yet what mattered to the Roman reader, and no less to the humanists, was that the realities of life should not disappear behind the subtleties of dialectic.[23] It is precisely with this problem that the dialogue method is calculated to cope. Moreover, as Ruch has said, the merit and originality of Cicero consist in the preservation of the didactic motive in artistic forms more complex and more refined than those which descended from the Greeks.[24]

As a rule, Plato teaches the pure abstract, Cicero the many-sided, nature of his subject. As methods, the former is perhaps better suited to the *discovery* of truth, while the latter is concerned with the disposition or *presentation* of knowledge.[25] The two branches of dialectic, which Bacon sought to distinguish in the later sixteenth century, may thus be traced to a more general distinction between two forms of classical dialogue.

III

One element of style definitively separates Cicero's dialogues from Plato's. For Cicero the art of oratory has its roots in the give-and-take of philosophical dialectic. He requires of the

22. Seneca, *Epis.*, 95, 1; Cicero, *De Partitione Oratoria,* 67; see Ruch, p. 71.

23. See Ruch, p. 70.

24. Ruch, p. 71.

25. Lisa Jardine contrasts discovery with presentation in Bacon's dialectical method in *Francis Bacon: Discourse and the Art of Discovery* (Cambridge, England, 1974). On the earlier history of discovery and disposition, see Richard McKeon, "Rhetoric in the Middle Ages," *Speculum,* 17 (1942), 1–32.

orator an Aristotelian integrity, which demands full articulation of any opposition. Cicero writes to Brutus, in the prologue to Book II (§9) of the *Tusculans,* that he has always preferred

> the rule of the Peripatetics and the Academy of discussing both sides of every question, not only for the reason that in no other way did I think it possible for the probable truth to be discovered in each particular problem, but also because I found it gave the best practice in oratory.

In the *De Oratore* he has Crassus assert:

> If anyone ever comes forward who can, in the Aristotelian manner, put forward both sides on every subject, and can with knowledge of Aristotle's precepts develop two contrary speeches on every question, . . . he is the true, the perfect, and the only orator.[26]

As these passages make clear, oratorical technique involves dialectic and, by extension, the procedure of dialogue. The vital principle of Ciceronian dialogue functions as a counterpart to the dramatized dialectic of the Platonic form; this complex principle is the art of oratory.

The thesis at the core of the *De Oratore* is that the ideal orator is, before anything else, the ideal philosopher. The great Roman art, Cicero is arguing, embraces the great Greek science. Crassus wrily remarks (1, 47), "What impressed me most deeply about Plato [in the *Gorgias*] was, that it was when making fun of orators that he himself seemed to me to be the consummate orator." The joke goes around a second time in *The Courtier* of Castiglione, who uses the *De Oratore* as a model for his dialogue.[27] The dialogue *Brutus,* a literary history of oratory, reveals the Greek influence in another way. "It is my purpose," says Cicero (§137), "to put together [*colligere*] those who have made it their business in civic life to be regarded as orators. What their progress was and how difficult in every art is final attainment of the best [*optimi perfectio*], may be judged from what I have to say." Here we recognize the two dominant traits of Cicero's

26. Oxford edition, 3, 80. Cf. 1, 158.
27. *Il libro del cortegiano* (Venice, 1582), I, xxxvii.

method. The first comes from Aristotle: to put together (*colligere*) the works of all the great orators. The second is Platonic: to seek, in this art, the *optimi perfectio.*[28] Aristotelian in method, Platonic in matter, Ciceronian dialogue hesitates between rhetoric and philosophy.

If such was the ground from which Cicero's dialogues sprang,[29] this branch of the new *ars oratoria* developed further in the light of its own time. Cicero's claims for oratory are high. The eloquence of the orator, says Crassus,

> is one of the supreme virtues . . . which, after compassing a knowledge of facts, gives verbal expression to the thoughts and purposes of the mind in such a manner as to have the power of driving the hearers forward in any direction in which it has applied its weight; and the stronger this faculty is, the more necessary it is for it to be combined with integrity and supreme wisdom. . . . (*De Oratore,* 3, 55)

Crassus sets himself and his subject apart from "these exponents of the science of rhetoric, who are exceedingly foolish persons":

> they only write about the classification of cases and the elementary rules and methods of stating facts: whereas eloquence is so potent a force that it embraces the origin and operation and developments of all things, all the virtues and duties, all the natural principles governing the morals and minds and life of mankind, and also determines their customs and laws and rights, and controls the government of the state, and expresses everything that concerns whatever topic in a graceful and flowing style. (3, 76)

Scaevola's objection early in Book I (§§35–44) that Crassus overrates the political influence of orators and exaggerates the range

28. Alain Michel, *Rhétorique et philosophie chez Cicéron* . . . (Paris, 1960), pp. 430f. Chapters 2 and 3 of Michel's work treat the complex influence of Greek rhetoric; on this subject see also the commentary in A. S. Wilkins's definitive edition of the *De Oratore* (Oxford, 1892).

29. See Grimal, p. 196. Hirzel (*Der Dialog,* I, 343ff.) traces the gradual penetration of the dialogic element into the body of the rhetorical speech among the early Greeks until, as he says, "der Dialog rhetorischer und die Rede dialogischer wurde."

of their powers follows the Greek view, which Crassus counters with the argument that even if limited to politics oratory calls for wide knowledge; on the other hand, philosophers borrow style from oratory, although style is not as essential for them as a command of matter is essential for the orator.[30] For the orator, then, Cicero claims that entire province of philosophy which deals with human life and conduct (1, 68). Oratory is no longer a skill belonging to professional philosophers but an inclusive art belonging to statesmen.

Crassus's remark on spoken delivery as imitation (3, 214) reveals in a kernel the preeminent position in human activity which Cicero believes the orator to occupy: we have but to compare "the actors, who only mimic reality," with "the orators, who are the players that act real life. . . ." *Ac sine dubio in omni re vincit imitationem veritas.*

The role of oratory in Cicero's dialogues is more thoroughgoing than anyone reading them for the first time might imagine. Oratory like dialogue itself is a way of speaking. Among the maxims which Cicero lays down for the orator, in the *De Oratore* and the short catechism of rhetoric called *De Partitione Oratoria,* we discover many that accurately apply to the characters of a dialogue as well.[31] In the first place, an impressive variety of natural gifts is expected. "In an orator we must demand the subtlety of the logician, the thoughts of the philosopher, a diction almost poetic, a lawyer's memory, a tragedian's voice, and the bearing almost of the consummate actor" (1, 128). His training parallels that of the poet with regard to the cultivation of an appropriate diction; the traditional precepts are to speak, "in the first place, pure and correct Latin, secondly

30. Harris Rackham, trans., *De Oratore,* Loeb edition, p. xvi.

31. It hardly seems necessary to argue that Cicero is addressing the writer as well as the public speaker throughout the discussion of oratory; see, e.g., *De Oratore,* 1, 150–51; 3, 125. As is frequently true in Cicero, the discussion of a particular case gives focus to observations of wider applicability; the orator faces many of the same problems as the prose writer or the poet. I am arguing here for the relevance of these observations to dialogue.

with simple lucidity, thirdly with elegance, lastly in a manner befitting the dignity of our topics and with a certain grace" (1, 144). As for subject matter, the orator should "be able to speak on any subject whatever that is laid before him in general terms" (2, 66). He should be able to discuss both sides of every question. Such are the orator's personal resources with regard to matter and style. The *De Partitione Oratoria* treats the *vis oratoris* more briefly and systematically under the topics *collocatio,* the arrangement of the arguments in a manner suited to the nature of the speech; *elocutio,* the varieties of style; *actio,* the graces of delivery; and *memoria.*[32] It is noteworthy that these resources are enunciated by the two foremost orators of their day, Crassus and Cicero—each in the role of protagonist in a dialogue.

The success of an oration depends above all on *inventio,* the cardinal duty of the orator to attain "a style fitted to convince" (*De Oratore,* 1, 138). The optimal procedure will be (1) to secure the goodwill of the audience, (2) to define the dispute, (3) to establish one's own allegations, (4) to disprove those of the other side, and (5) to expand and reinforce all that was in one's favor while weakening the opposition (*De Oratore,* 1, 143). The *De Oratore* exactly reproduces this structure laid down in the *De Partitione Oratoria* and based on the system of rhetoric of the Second Academy: *exordium, narratio, confirmatio, reprehensio,* and *peroratio.* The point here is not the virtue of this plan (that question Cicero undertakes in both dialogues) but simply that the plan had become the stock-in-trade of the orator. It is no surprise then to us, nor was it to Renaissance commentators, to discover this structure in many of the major speeches in Cicero's dialogues. One could trace the structure in Cato's speech in the *De Senectute* and in several of the long speeches in the *De Oratore.* And in the *Tusculan Disputations,* after the preliminary dialogues, one finds a recurrent structure very like the *oratio* prescribed above.

Cicero the dialogist was above all an orator, whose techniques

32. See Loeb edition (1942), trans. H. Rackham, pp. 307f.

shaped all his narrative writings. Beyond its presence in individual speeches, the system of Academic oratory proved so strong an influence that it came to dominate the fundamental structure of Ciceronian dialogue. And conversely, dialogue often assisted Cicero in unfolding an oration. This is the case in *De Senectute* and *De Amicitia,* where the preliminary dialogue corresponds to the *exordium* and the *narratio.* Thus Cato's and Laelius's continuous speeches virtually dispense with introductory remarks and proceed almost immediately to the *confirmatio.* The same holds true in the *Tusculans.* The *De Oratore* is a more complicated case. Here we have more of a real conversation; only by an effort of abstraction (and some overstatement) can we argue an oratorical plan in the narrative. Cicero begins by telling his brother Quintus that he is going to recount "an old story" (1, 4) which is suited to his purpose. The ever-present narrative "*inquit*" and a running commentary keep the teller and the idea of the dialogue as a tale before our mind's eye. Further, the interlocution is one combined effort; *confirmatio* and *reprehensio,* the allegations and disproofs, function in tandem as the two sides of a single dialectic. This is indeed the substance of the narrator's "story," the true subject of his oration.

IV

Ciceronian oratorical dialogue hangs on the basic narrative skeleton common to most species of persuasive argument. But the influence of oratory courses through the entire body of the Ciceronian dialogue, not only defining its structure but informing its diction and tone. With this last element in Laertius's definition of dialogue, a proper choice of diction, we may conclude this chapter.

In *De Oratore* Cicero writes to his brother Quintus: "In oratory the very cardinal sin is to depart from the language of everyday life, and the usage approved by the sense of the community" (1, 12). Throughout his dialogues Cicero eschews this sin. In the *Tusculans* he even pauses to point out, "we are at present suiting our language to ordinary usage" (*loquimur nunc more communi,*

4, 66). For Cicero, observing the language of everyday life corresponds to the rule of good usage. Indeed, the equation between good and ordinary usage lies at the heart of the oratorical style. It constitutes Cicero's cardinal virtue and amounts to nothing less than a philosophical outlook. Some may speak of faultless friendship with perfect wisdom, says Laelius in *De Amicitia* (§38);

> but I am speaking of the friends before our eyes, of those whom we see, or of men of whom we have record, and who are known to everyday life.

And again in the same dialogue (§21) he exhorts:

> let us interpret the word *virtue* by the familiar usage of our everyday life and speech, and not in the pompous phrase apply to it the precise standards which certain philosophers use.

In the Tudor dialogues we have to examine, this choice of diction, by which an orator seeks assent, is consistently applied: the familiar usage of everyday life and speech.

The ideal diction is both natural and correct. It is true that in his correspondence Cicero takes many liberties in the use of Greek words, neologisms, and colloquialisms. But in his dialogues he strictly forces himself to employ only words belonging to the ancient fund of the Latin language and yet still in current usage and comprehensible to everyone.[33] He purposely adopts a certain grammatical laxity for the style of the *Tusculans.*[34] Laurand (pp. 257–60) cites a selection of conversations from the dialogues which illustrates their variety of diction, ranging from everyday conversation to exchanges that have "more vivacity than naturalness." Throughout the dialogues the diction strikes a balance between correctness and naturalness in the interest of

33. Louis Laurand, *Etudes sur le style des discours de Cicéron,* 4th ed. (Amsterdam, 1965), p. 99; cited hereafter as "Laurand." Ascham and Elyot were repeatedly attacked for their English neologisms.

34. So J. E. King, translator of the Loeb edition, has argued, noting (p. 410) the absence of an apodosis to the last "if" clause in 4, 72, and the incomplete sentence at the beginning of §77.

a conversational tone. The chief purpose of this balance and the consequent tone, as Cicero often says in discussing *inventio,* is to persuade. For to persuade, one must be easily understood, one's thought must be constantly followed. Laurand reminds us that Aristotle had urged in the *De Sophisticis Elenchis* that the dialectician must never speak as a savant but that, to persuade his auditors, he must tell them nothing of which they believe themselves ignorant. For this reason the orator—and the oratorical dialogist—must speak the "language of everyday life." This is why Cicero's historical examples are as well known as possible. Thus from oratory the dialogist learns to seek always to convey the impression that he thinks like everyone else. But since all propositions are not acceptable to everyone, the dialogist must also speak in his dialectic the language of his adversaries.[35] This principle the best dialogists of the Tudor period do not fail to grasp: More caricatures Lutheran jargon in the *Dialogue Concerning Heresies* and Luther himself in *The Confutation,* in the *Ciceronianus* Erasmus mimics the purple Latin of the pseudo-Ciceronians, and Elyot impersonates foolish hedonism in his dialogue of *Knowledge* and flattery in *Pasquil the Plain.*

The open liberality of Cicero's diction contributes to the characteristic leisurely pace of his dialogues. There is time in their deintensified atmosphere not only for digression but also for literary allusion, even extended quotation.[36] The tempo, like the occasions of the dialogues, is "otiose with dignity." *Verum otii fructus est,* says Crassus, contrasting his own manner with the Greeks', *non contentio animi, sed relaxio.*[37] We will examine in detail this sense of the dilation of time in dialogues by Elyot, Ascham, and More. The uncontentious pace and pattern of Cicero's dialogues derive in no small degree from his ideal of the use of oratory. His own practice proves more telling than the portrait of the perfect orator. As Anthony Trollope observed, in

35. See Laurand, pp. 350f.; Michel, pp. 170f.

36. E.g., in the *De Senectute* and Book I of the *Tusculans.*

37. *De Oratore,* 2, 22. A pastoral sketch follows this remark, ending in praise of "nihil agere," the classic Italian *dolce far' niente.*

all of Cicero's works on oratory "he charms us rather by his example than instructs us by his precepts."[38]

Otiose in style, Cicero's dialogues exhibit nonetheless a full range of emotion. A single example may suffice to remind us of the affective purpose of his language. In the *Tusculans* (1, 94) he asks:

> What lifetime in fact is long, or what is there at all long for a human being? . . . All such things are spoken of as long or short according to the proportion in which they are in each case allotted. By the river Hypanis, which flows into the Pontus from a part of Europe, Aristotle says that a kind of small animal is born, which lives for a single day. One of these creatures then that died in the eighth hour has died at an advanced age: that which died at sunset is decrepit, and all the more if it happen on Midsummer Day. Contrast our longest lifetime with eternity: we shall be found almost in the same category of short-lived beings as those tiny creatures.

Translation scarcely detracts from the full pathetic note struck here with characteristic dignity. Thomas More would strike the same note in his *Dialogue of Comfort.*[39]

On the other side of pathos is wit. Sigonius, in the last section of his discourse, shows unbounded enthusiasm for Cicero's humor. But Trollope confesses he finds the master's jokes feeble, though carried off with a lightness of touch. Laurand, after enumerating a host of pleasantries—puns, proverbs, historical and mythological allusions, droll tales, and ironies—proceeds to discuss the difficulty of understanding Cicero's humor in view of the differences in language and culture.[40] Still, occasional flashes are accessible to the illatinate. The solemn *Tusculan Disputations* convey a certain wit in the handling of the dialogue

38. *The Life of Cicero* (1880; repr. London, 1882), II, 312. Trollope admires, for instance, the way in which Crassus and Antonius "differ in the sweetest language, and each, though he holds his own, does it with a deference that is more convincing than any assertion" (II, 314).

39. *A Dialogue of Comfort against Tribulation,* ed. Louis L. Martz and Frank Manley, The Yale Edition of the Complete Works of St. Thomas More, vol. 12 (New Haven and London, 1976), 157/12–158/14.

40. Laurand, pp. 234–55.

form. The logical acrobatics of the opening encounter between A and M are nothing less than a tour de force, not unlike the game of "Statement" in *Rosencrantz and Guildenstern Are Dead;* the hyperdialogic is funny. Throughout Book I, whenever A's response is solicited, he speaks with an air that betrays Cicero's awareness of the playful potential of the form. Thus to M's assertion that "this" (the preceding statement of some 230 lines) "is proof of eternity—unless you have anything to advance," A makes laconic reply (1, 55): "I have found it easy to let no argument to the contrary so much as enter my head; I therefore support the view you have given."

It is characteristic of the Ciceronian dialogue and of many dialogues in its tradition that solemn jesting is regarded as universally appropriate, even to such grave subjects as those of the *Tusculans.* Cicero sets forth his view of the place of jest, humor, and wit in the second book of the *De Oratore* where he pays highest tribute to Socrates, who "far surpassed all others for accomplished wit in this strain of irony" (2, 270). He continues with a concise expression of the duality of form and function that characterizes all true Ciceronian wit:

> This is a choice variety of humour and blended with austerity, and suited to public speaking as well as to the conversation of gentlemen. [Genus est perelegans et cum gravitate salsum, cumque oratoriis dictionibus tum urbanis sermonibus accommodatum.]

Elegant and grave in form, wit is equally suited to oratory and dialogue, which may concern themselves with virtually any subject. "There is no occasion in life"—not even the ascent to the scaffold on Tower Hill—"on which accomplished wit may not fittingly be displayed" (2, 271).

In writing dialogue Cicero drew mainly on the power of persuasion—the *concitatio animi*—which he acquired as an orator. The development of the Ciceronian dialogue form out of the Platonic can ultimately be attributed to the triumph of rhetoric.[41]

41. Tateo (*Tradizione e realità,* p. 236) recognizes this fact: Ciceronian dialogue, he concludes, is "più tipico del 'persuadere' retorico, che del 'dimonstrare' filosofico. L'incontro delle opinioni, attraverso la chiarificazione dei termini, lo

Despite his admiration for Plato, Cicero seems to have lost faith in the absolute irresistibility of dialectical argument. He relies not on the flash of insight, which Plato wrote about in the seventh epistle, but rather on human emotional response to the spoken word. It is this impulse which the orator addresses finally, as Antonius says, rather than the hearer's judgment or deliberation (2, 178).

> For men decide far more problems by hate, or love, . . . or fear, or illusion, or some inward emotion, than by reality, or authority, or any legal standard. . . .

This radical displacement of "reality" (Cicero's word is *veritas*) by "inward emotion" (*permotio mentis*) as the primary element of persuasion not only defines Cicero's humanism; it justifies the role of oratory, with its full emotional range, in the explorations undertaken in his dialogues.

In the third book of the *De Oratore* Crassus pursues the relation of style to philosophy. He makes the crucial point (3, 56) that oratory is not simply a method of "expressing thought" (*pronuntiandi rationem*), whose power Antonius indicated in 2, 178, but a method of thinking itself (*cogitandi*). This faculty of speaking is one of the supreme virtues, "designated by the ancient Greeks wisdom." Having adopted the dialogue form, Cicero continued to reinforce his arguments oratorically. The problem was to sway, and oratory made available to dialogue an affective power equal if not superior to that produced dialectically. It was this power that Renaissance Ciceronians were after. In remaking dialogue, Cicero relied in the same measure on his natural bent as on his training. "To my thinking," says Crassus (1, 146),

---

sviluppo delle divergenze, intese piuttosto come correzioni marginali, aggiunte particolari, smussamento di troppo rigide posizioni, costituiscono l'intimo movimento logico del dialogo ciceroniano. . . . Era pur sempre il metodo socratico della discussione, ma arricchito, o ammorbidito, dal gusto dell' agone oratorio e della conversazione."

the virtue of all rules is, not that orators by following them have won a reputation for eloquence, but that certain persons have noted and collected the doings of men who were naturally eloquent: thus eloquence is not the offspring of the art, but the art of eloquence. . . .

Cicero's imitators would study the art of the oratorical dialogue, but their success or failure would still depend on individual genius.

3

The Formation of Renaissance Dialogue

I

The medieval perspective of recent Renaissance studies has brought into sharp relief the two classes of scholarly literature in the Renaissance—scholastic and humanist. The latter was written in either Latin or the vernacular, while the former employed chiefly the technical Latin of professional philosophers writing in the tradition of medieval university disputation. Each class produced an impressive number of dialogues. Yet for us the precise relation between the two classes of Renaissance dialogue remains as problematic as that between the two general strains of Renaissance thought. A useful contrast is to be found in ancient practice.

Plato's dialogues have been divided into two types, the *philosophical discussions* of his later dialogues and the *elenctic dialogues,* which comprise the dozen works up through Book I of the *Republic.* The second type can be described as rule-governed concatenations of questions, answerable by Yes or No, which are intended to drive the answerer into an *elenchus,* or self-contradiction; these eristic contests are what should be meant by "the Socratic Method."[1]

If we look in the *De Sophisticis Elenchis*,[2] we find that Aristotle perceives two classes of argument in dialogue form. The first he calls, rather loosely, *didactic:* arguments which reason from principles appropriate to each subject and not from opinions held by the answerer. Such arguments are demonstrations, not contests. It is not difficult to tie this class to the philosophical discussions of Plato. Aristotle's second class of argument in dialogue, which corresponds to the elenctic dialogues of Plato, has three parts. (1) *Dialectical arguments* reason from generally accepted premises to the contradiction of a given thesis. They ask a Yes or No answer. But there are also (2) *examination-arguments,* which reason from premises which are accepted by the answerer and which anyone who pretends to possess knowledge of the subject is bound to know. In the *Topics* Aristotle says that these are conducted in a spirit of inquiry, not competition. Examination-argument is a branch of dialectic, and it asks a Yes or No answer. Another name for (2) is *peirastic,* a term to which we will return. Finally, the third part is contentious arguments or (3) *sophistical elenchi:* arguments which reason or appear to reason to a conclusion from premises that appear to be generally accepted but are not so; these are arguments which "beguile by misreasoning from the same principles dialectic uses."

Even if it were possible, as Ryle evidently thinks it is, to distinguish nondialectical dialogues in Plato, the subsequent history of the dialogue form illustrates its continual selective appropriation of dialectic in various degrees. By the Renaissance stage, the two classes into which Ryle would divide Plato's works are no longer distinct. Those Renaissance dialogues which are most "rich in subject matter and solid in concepts"—to use Kristeller's phrase for Aristotelian natural philosophy—all bear the imprint of dialectic.

1. Gilbert Ryle, *Plato's Progress* (Cambridge, England, 1966), p. 119.

2. *De Sophisticis Elenchis,* trans. W. A. Pickard-Cambridge, *The Works of Aristotle,* ed. W. D. Ross, vol. 1 (Oxford, 1928).

Plato and Aristotle are in rare agreement in distinguishing between two forms of question-and-answer, two potentialities of dialectic, or argument in dialogue form. These seem to me to provide the central contrast between the two classes of Renaissance dialogue. The first form is *eristic,* the kind of question-and-answer used in controversy; and this contrasts with the second form, *peirastic,* another name for the examination-arguments of Aristotle, which means experimental, tentative, and above all speculative. Plato and Aristotle constantly make the contrast between the "match-winning" and the "truth-hunting" spirits in which the question-and-answer exercise may be conducted.[3] I would submit that this is the contrast between eristic and peirastic dialectic. Moreover, when we pick up a Renaissance dialogue, we soon know in which of these two spirits it is being conducted.

Eristic may have a pejorative overtone for modern readers (while *peirastic* is a comparatively unknown word). But for the Greeks the former could denote the true Socratic Method, in contrast with the more fluid didactic argument of peirastic. In his eristic dialogues Plato furnished *training* in controversy, just as a body of Renaissance dialogues must count as training manuals or *arts* of disputation. The non-eristic dialogues of Plato were devoted to tentative inquiry, and this peirastic class constitutes the most enduring literary achievement of the Renaissance dialogue form. Eristic includes those dialogues before Book I of the *Republic* which drive toward an elenchus, and the vice of eristic is the illegitimate elenchus—sophistical dialogue; whereas peirastic engages in more speculative philosophical discussion like the post-*Republic* dialogues.

Plato and Aristotle's contrast between eristic and peirastic may provide the necessary contrast between the scholastic and humanist dialogues of the Renaissance. It supports, moreover, our twofold division of Renaissance dialogue by exposing deeper roots to the rivalry of two modes of consciousness. Scholastic dialogues instruct the student in the techniques of con-

3. Ryle, *Plato's Progress,* p. 128.

troversy. They are elenctic, not above sophistic; they give training in the destructive methods of disputation, how to win. The best humanist dialogues, *per contra,* inquire more experimentally after truth, using dialectic for didactic argument and speculation in the peirastic spirit. The concurrence of the two Greek masters on the double potentiality of dialectic affirms that the scholastics and the humanists share a great common ground and, further, that between them and the ancients dialogue made a bridge.

II

Medieval dialogue imbibed life from the prevailing system of learning. Students learned Latin by colloquies, read classical and patristic dialogues, and wrote and recited their own scholarly dialogues. Instruction, examination, and advancement within the university all proceeded by disputation.[4] The mirror the university held up to the world was a method of structured, logical dialogue; this was the instrument which candidates for various degrees were required to manipulate with increasing facility. Such disparate popular forms as elucidaries, catechisms, and poetic dialogues may be organized under the principle of disputation. In the later Middle Ages the repertoire of uses of disputation extended further. It provided exercise not only in the precise logic of scholastic philosophy but also in reasoned argument on a variety of other subjects. As a lecture technique and in moots, it was used in legal training in the inns of court and in practice before the bar. Training in academic disputation paved the way to public disputation in adult life: civil and ecclesiastical trials, parliamentary and other public debates, and the teaching of young scholars.[5]

4. The centrality of disputation in medieval academic life is discussed in my article "The Continuity of Post-Classical Dialogue," *Cithara,* 21 (1981), 23–44. Texts of the medieval ordinances of Oxford University requiring disputation, as well as other documents pertaining to ceremonies and examinations, are found in Henry Anstey, ed., *Munimenta Academica Oxoniensis,* vol. 50 in 2 pts., *Rerum Britannicarum Medii Aevi Scriptores* (London, 1868). See also Andrew Clark, ed., *Register of the University of Oxford,* vol. 2 (1571–1672), pt. 1 (Oxford, 1887).

5. The following works include useful accounts of medieval disputation: Palemon Glorieux, *La Faculté des arts et ses maîtres aux XIIIe siècle* (Paris, 1971), and

To say nothing of the expressive uses of this didactic form! If our own literary mode is the psychological novel whose traditions and tensions reflect the problems of the modern age, then in the range and flexibility of disputation medieval men found a mode amenable to theirs. The ceremonial disputations of the university examination known as inception contained a certain expansive, celebratory potential.[6] In other circumstances, such as the disputation in which Aquinas was "virtually arraigned" by the theological faculty of Paris,[7] it could become harshly constrictive, a weapon of attack. Disputation could be a wide or a narrow mode, as public as Paul's Cross or as private as a cell.

In time the work of scholastic philosophy began to wane; the expense of spirit yielded fewer and fewer new ideas, though this decline was disguised by increasing elaboration. This was what disgusted the humanists. These scholars turned away from Aristotle—but not from disputation.[8] They continued to rely on it for the exposition of ideas and as a way of approaching truth. All during the revival of eloquence and the reformation of

---

his "L'enseignement au moyen âge: Technique et méthodes en usage à la Faculté de Théologie de Paris, au XIIIe siècle," *Archives d'histoire doctrinale et littéraire du Moyen Age,* 35 (1968, publ. 1969), 65–186; Martin Grabmann, *Die Geschichte der scholastischen Methode,* 2 vols. (1909–11; repr. Graz, 1957); and Hastings Rashdall, *The Universities of Europe in the Middle Ages* (1895), ed. F. M. Powicke and A. B. Emden (Oxford, 1936), vol. I. The last is clarified by Gordon Leff, *Paris and Oxford Universities in the Thirteenth and Fourteenth Centuries . . .* (New York, 1968), and A. B. Cobban, *The Medieval Universities: Their Development and Organization* (London, 1975), while Grabmann and Glorieux are supplemented by James A. Weisheipl's important report, "Curriculum of the Faculty of Arts at Oxford in the Early Fourteenth Century," *Mediaeval Studies,* 26 (1964), 143–85.

6. The earliest and most important source is Magdalen College MS 38. For a translation of comical passages from an inception, see Strickland Gibson, "The Order of Disputations," *Bodleian Quarterly Record,* 6 (1929–31), 107f. See also Rashdall, *The Universities of Europe in the Middle Ages,* I, 454ff.

7. See Leff, *Paris and Oxford Universities,* pp. 172 and 228.

8. The often misunderstood term *scholastic method* refers to a medieval development—a questions-objections procedure outlined by Gratian in the *Decretum* (ca. 1140) and by Peter Lombard in the *Sentences* (ca. 1160) but most fully represented by the *Summa Theologica,* which reflects actual pedagogical practice and the form of public debates—rather than any practice in the Lyceum.

the school curriculum, the old form of academic disputation was preserved at the university level. The humanist Leonardo Bruni (1369–1444) urged young men not to neglect

> the custom and practice of disputing, than which I can think of nothing . . . more useful to your studies. For what. . . , by the immortal gods, . . . is of more avail in learning and discussing subtle matters than disputation. . . ? What . . . more refreshes and restores the mind, tired and exhausted and almost loathing these studies from long sittings and close reading, than discussions carried on in assembly. . . ?[9]

In a host of new dialogues, dialectic, far from being rejected, was reassimilated to grammar and rhetoric. The trivium remained a closed system.

Spawned in the tradition of academic teaching and examination, the new dialogues sought an ever-increasing degree of fictionality. Literary dialogues diverged from university disputations in favor of a wider, enthusiastic reading public. In contrast, "the official records of the university . . . tell of nothing but the dreary routine of expiring scholasticism," or at least of formal scholastic disputation.[10] While the history of disputation illustrates the primacy of resistance as a method of learning, it also shows that this essential intellectual conflict—the kind that leads to knowledge and changes that really matter in one's life—cannot be confined within any single formal academic structure. Literary art may preserve in ideal form what in the practice of the real world becomes an arid formalism.

The rise of dialogue in the half century beginning in 1475 can only be understood in the context of a complex network of influences. University disputation had brought in a rich harvest in the autumn of the Middle Ages; now all the fields were being sown anew. Perhaps the fascination of dialogue, as a subject of study for a modern student of the Renaissance, lies in the va-

9. *Leonardi Aretini ad Petrum Paulum Istrum Dialogus,* excerpted in *University Records and Life in the Middle Ages,* ed. and trans. Lynn Thorndike (New York, 1944), Document 102, p. 267.

10. Rashdall, *The Universities of Europe in the Middle Ages,* III, 167.

riety of views it allows into the ways the tradition of old learning was caught up in new aspirations. Some of the influences, such as new social and political forces, are themselves highly complex; but they affect certain dialogues quite specifically, others hardly or not at all. Any pattern of influences must of course be selective. Some of these should be noted before we attempt to follow the new direction of dialogue in this period.

The publication of larger numbers of all kinds of dialogue was made possible by the invention of movable type. After printing, the method of instruction was no longer predominantly oral. Students could now have their own printed books, textually more accurate and uniform than manuscript books, and these could be more complex than those which formerly were dictated. Some of the longer new dialogues must have been *intended* to be read silently, not aloud, and independent silent reading of dialogues must increasingly have supplemented the vocal work of the classroom. Whether printed dialogues played a part in the historical transformation (no one knows when) from an aural to a visual culture, I leave to the reader to decide. At least printing allowed the new dialogues greater ambitions than teaching Latin grammar!

As latinity based on the classics became more desirable, so too did dialogues, which displayed and hence taught eloquence. New interest in rhetoric and oratory encouraged the publication of classical and neoclassical dialogues anatomizing these subjects, and this was coupled with a deepening admiration for a confluence of Greco-Roman virtues which dialogues often treated. The interest in imitation on the part of humanist writers of this period extended to qualities which dialogue imitated. Thus the appeal of the image of man the reasoner, which was implied in classical dialogues, led to the production of new, often topical versions of this image in sixteenth-century dialogues. The best supplied rich aesthetic experience which scholastic disputations were felt to lack. Many dialogues appeared as a result of widespread changes in educational theory; reformer schoolmasters and theorists wrote dialogues providing models for humane classroom conduct.[11] The number of published dialogues also rose in response to the program of educating more people (nonclerics, whether aristocratic or middle-class), a need which sprang from profound changes in social and economic conditions. Naturally a widening audience meant a widening repertoire of subjects treated in dialogue, and the favorable reception of early original dialogues, as well as translations of classical ones, encouraged further exploitation of the form.

While it is undoubtedly true that the influence of established institutions, economic organizations, and differences between communities can be felt in the formation of Renaissance dialogue, it is possible to conceive of dialogue itself as an institution undergoing the influence of the ideas, purposes, feelings, beliefs, hopes, and fears of a culture in transition. To conceive of dialogue dynamically, not merely taxonomically, we must distinguish changes of consciousness in it. For example: Burckhardt argued that the Renaissance was the result not only of a revival of antiquity but also of an independently existing Italian "national spirit," and he taught us to see this spirit in Renaissance works of art. It is equally possible to see expressions of English nationalism in sixteenth-century English dialogues, reflections of peculiarly English social, religious, and other preoccupations in their literary art. Indeed, in England as in Italy the thoughts and feelings that made up the contemporary "national spirit" confronted the thoughts and feelings expressed in the body of classical literature as it became known to a widening audience through the humanists. The result was the humanists' most lasting achievement: even as they promoted the internationalism of Latin, they created a vernacular—that is, a national—literature. Vernacular dialogue epitomizes the re-formation of the past in the image and likeness of the present.

11. A Bömer, in *Die lateinischen Schülergespräche der Humanisten . . .* (Berlin, 1897), treats Mosellanus, Erasmus, Schotten, Hegendorf, Heyden, Cordier, Vives, and others. See §III below.

III

Both the *humanist* class of neoclassical, peirastic, vernacular dialogue, to which the early Tudor form belongs, and the *scholastic* dialogue continued to develop outside the universities. Renaissance scholastic dialogues, devoted to grammar and logic, included both elementary colloquies used to instruct schoolboys in Latin and dialogues for adolescents, which were training manuals or *arts* of disputation. In addition, the patristic tradition of scholastic dialogues is apparent when in the Renaissance they frequently give form to religious polemic.[12] University disputation reached beyond university walls in the sense that it furnished a model of eristic upon which humanists were not invariably loath to draw. It served, that is, as a matrix to humanist dialogue, supporting that which ultimately had to be severed from it. But on the whole, humanist dialogues show a more rhetorical bias, a self-consciousness of style, in addressing various philosophical subjects. The extent and assumptions of both classes of Renaissance dialogue need to be indicated before we turn to the contributions of Elyot, Ascham, and More. The examples in this brief survey will give a preview of topics in the subsequent chapters.

12. For example, the Swiss reformer Niklaus Manuel's dialogue *Krankheit der Messe* and the Catholic Thomas Murner's *Von dem Grossen Lutherischen Narren.* For a chronology, see Gottfried Niemann, *Die Dialogliteratur der Reformationszeit nach ihrer Entstehung und Entwicklung* (Leipzig, 1905). The topic of the continuity of postclassical dialogue—which includes (1) Christian debates, (2) early questions and answers, and (3) the medieval colloquy—awaits a full-scale historical study. The various forms and their transmission are surveyed in my "Continuity of Post-Classical Dialogue," *Cithara,* 21 (1981), 23–44. On 1 and 2, see William Lloyd Daly's important introduction to the *Altercatio Hadriani Augusti et Epicteti philosophi* (Urbana, 1939); Robert J. Menner's introduction to *The Poetical Dialogues of Solomon and Saturn* (1941; repr. New York, 1973); and Gustave Bardy, "La littérature patristique des *Quaestiones et Responsiones* sur l'Ecriture sainte," *Revue Biblique,* 41 (1932), 210–36, 341–69, 515–37; 42 (1933), 14–30, 211–29, 328–52. On 3, see G. N. Garmonsway's introduction to *Ælfric's Colloquy* (London, 1939) and his essay, "The Development of the Colloquy," in *The Anglo-Saxons,* ed. Peter Clemoes (London, 1959), pp. 248–61; and W. M. Lindsay's introduction to *Early Scholastic Colloquies,* ed. W. H. Stevenson (Oxford, 1929).

Though the dialogue form in which the scholastics liked to intertwine grammar and logic did not cease in the Renaissance, its substance changed fundamentally. I spoke earlier of the institutional persistence of scholasticism in university teaching and examinations by disputation. This is apparent on a wider scale when we look at Latin language instruction at the turn of the sixteenth century. In this sphere of knowledge humanism more successfully challenged the theory than the method of grammar. The scholastic theory of *modi significandi* (along with the expression itself) disappeared entirely as Thomas of Erfurt, Peter of Spain, and Alexander of Villedieu were replaced by Erasmus, Vives, and Valla.[13] Thurot explains the failure of scholastic doctrines of grammar as the result of the violation of the Aristotelian precept that each discipline should be governed by its own principles, e.g., metaphysics should not be applied to grammar. It was this fixation on the theoretical, doctrinal aspect of the Latin language (the modes of signifying) that the humanists disliked so intensely in scholasticism. They did not argue the *whys* of usage but simply pointed to classical precedents and the usage of learned men.[14] Rather than merely return to the simple rules of Donatus and Priscian they preferred to demonstrate them in colloquies.

The transformation of scholastic logic which occurred in Renaissance dialogue is more difficult to define. If Erasmus and Vives were hostile to medieval logic chopping, they recognized the place of dialectic in intellectual training; and thus they favored the *continued* use of dialogue for beginning Latin and at more advanced levels. The direct continuation of scholastic logic in dialogue form, however, is to be found in the religious polemics of the Reformation, such as John Fisher's *Assertionis Lutheranae confutatio* and the eighth book of More's *Confutation.* I have

13. Charles Thurot, *Notices et extraits de divers manuscrits latins pour servir à l'histoire des doctrines grammaticales au moyen âge* (Paris, 1868), p. 499. On modist grammar, see Robert Henry Robins, *Ancient and Medieval Grammatical Theory in Europe* (London, 1951); Jan Pinborg, *Die Entwicklung der Sprachtheorie im Mittelalter* (Münster and Copenhagen, 1967); and G. L. Bursill-Hall, *Speculative Grammars of the Middle Ages* (The Hague, 1971).

14. Thurot, ibid.

chosen More's *Dialogue Concerning Heresies,* a full-blown and at the same time transitional example of Renaissance scholastic dialogue, for analysis in Chapter 6. At this point I should like to focus on the dialogues for schools.

The purpose of mustering elementary Latin dialogues into the scholastic class is to counter the assumption that all new school-dialogues were soldiers in the humanist educational reform. In fact they adhered to an established pedagogical tradition. Hence it is difficult to say, for example, whether the new emphasis on *spoken* classical Latin—with the resulting development in two specialized forms, the colloquy and the *vulgaria*—was encouraged solely by Renaissance humanism or by an evolving Renaissance scholasticism.

Some interesting evidence can be brought to bear on the problem. Surprisingly enough, in Italy the number of new school-colloquies seems to have been relatively small. Sigonius uses examples only from antiquity, disdainfully ignoring the colloquies of Erasmus and his contemporaries. It was in Spain, Switzerland, France, and especially Germany, having a language so unlike Latin, that dialogues for schoolboys proliferated. A far cry from the primers such as appeared in England from the pens of Thomas More's teacher John Holt (*Lac Puerorum,* 1497) or Thomas Wolsey in his early vocation as schoolmaster (*Rudimenta grammatices,* 1529), these were works of erudition, of philosophy, a confused repertoire on astrology, medicine, etymology—the sort of thing, declares Massebieau, that would have been wasted on a schoolboy.[15] The charge has been leveled regularly at the more sophisticated colloquies of Erasmus.

The humanists' own formal education was in fact scholastic. And their pedagogical works may be seen as elaborations of inherited forms. Didactic simplicity, which had always been considered a virtue in elementary books, was sometimes compromised by a humanist writer's professional training, his

15. L. Massebieau, *Les Colloques scolaires du seizième siècle et leurs auteurs (1480–1570)* (Paris, 1878), pp. 54f.

awareness of a professional audience, or his desire to rival Cicero. Erasmus raised the teaching of grammar and rhetoric by dialogue to the summit of moral sensitivity, but this was made possible in part by his youthful training in and rejection of formal logic and the *modi significandi.* In their school-dialogues the humanists cast a wealth of learned material in the same question-and-answer mold in which the scholastics cast grammatical precepts. This general adherence to scholastic form may also be found in university humanists, such as Melanchthon, who believed that a university without a carefully organized system of disputations was unworthy of the name of "schola."[16]

The study of the new *colloquia* and *dialogi* of Erasmus, Vives, Cordier, and Castellion, to name the most widely read, had two aims. One was to change that harlot Medieval Latin into a Roman vestal; the other, to bring the schoolroom in touch with the life and thought of the outside world, but this in the language, within limits, of Terence and Cicero.[17] Obviously both aims admit the question of degree; not everyone found the language so foul or the schoolroom so unreal. Old schools, predictably, did not rush to embrace the humanists' grammatical textbooks. It has been said that Henry VIII substituted Lily for Donatus by force,[18] but the prevailing method was anything but dead. John Stanbridge, the vigorous informator of Magdalen School from 1488 to 1494, produced a book of "phrases of common occurrence in the vulgar tongue," to be translated into Latin.[19]

16. William Harrison Woodward, *Studies in Education during the Renaissance, 1400–1600* (Cambridge, England, 1924), p. 231.

17. See Beatrice White, ed., *The Vulgaria of John Stanbridge and the Vulgaria of Robert Whittinton,* E.E.T.S., Orig. Series, no. 187 (London, 1932), pp. lv–lvi; cited hereafter as "White." See also Foster Watson, *The English Grammar Schools to 1660: Their Curriculum and Practice* (Cambridge, England, 1908), pp. 325–48.

18. White, p. xxxix. On the royal injunctions, see J. B. Mullinger, *The University of Cambridge,* 3 vols. (Cambridge, England, 1873–1911), I, 629f., and M. L. Clarke, *Classical Education in Britain 1500–1900* (Cambridge, England, 1959), pp. 30f.

19. White, p. xviii. The date of the first edition is not known, perhaps 1509, before Stanbridge's death; see *STC* 2 23195.5.

Another *Vulgaria* was compiled by his pupil and successor Robert Whittinton, whose controversy in print with Lily of St. Paul's and Horman of Eton exploded with exuberant vituperation.[20] Whittinton's and Horman's vulgars have been condemned as "so arbitrary and unclassical," the sort of thing Ascham was fighting against.[21] But Whittinton's works have survived in at least one hundred and fifty editions.[22] Unclassical but not unpopular!

There was in fact nothing retrograde about the *vulgaria.* They served equally the boy who would pursue humanistic studies and him who desired to survive the scholastic examinations of the university, and often this was the same boy. The extent to which they became part and parcel of ordinary grammar school training is suggested by some of the precepts from the *Ludus Literarius, or the Grammar School,* which John Brinsley, writing in the tradition of Ascham, published in 1612. According to Brinsley, "the surest course for entring young schollars to speake Latine" was, among other exercises: "Daily practice of Grammaticall translations; chiefly reading bookes of Dialogues out of English into Latine"; "To talke together in the wordes of the Dialogues, each sentence first in English, then Latine"; and "Daily practice in disputing."[23]

It is true that sixteenth-century *vulgaria* look back to medieval collections of words and brief, practical dialogues, such as *A Book for Travellers,* a fourteenth-century French/Flemish compilation adapted by Caxton as a French/English book around 1483.[24] Probably the most important early prototype of the *vulgaria* is

20. For the *Antibossicon* controversy, see White, p. xxiv. Whittinton's *Vulgaria* was published in 1520, Horman's in 1519.

21. White, p. xliv.

22. H. S. Bennett, *English Books and Readers, 1475–1557 . . .* (Cambridge, England, 1952), p. 86. Bennett notes that all five of Stanbridge's works were printed and reprinted at least fifty times. See the unusually complete treatment of Stanbridge and Whittinton in *STC* 2.

23. Cited in White, pp. liii–liv.

24. *Dialogues in French and English,* ed. Henry Bradley, E.E.T.S., Extra Series, no. 79 (London, 1900).

the *Hermaneumata Pseudodositheana.*[25] At the same time, however, sixteenth-century *vulgaria* reveal the contemporary interest in rhetoric usually associated with the humanists.

In providing propaedeia in speaking Latin, *vulgaria* and colloquies led in turn to the oration. Yet this art would have been inconceivable without practice in logical disputation.[26] *Progymnasmata,* or written themes, had their oral counterpart in more advanced exercises known as "appositions" and "declamations." These were in fact *oratorical disputations.*[27] These curious hybrids, sprung from coexistent traditions, testify to the fertility of the school-dialogue form. Moreover, as an acute reader of Renaissance literature has observed, some of the exchanges in an Oxford *vulgaria* could almost have been acted out as "rudimentary playlets in the classroom"; they are not mere conversation but involve action and acting.[28] In a variety of ways

25. The text of the *Hermaneumata* underwent a complex series of accretions between the fourth and the ninth centuries; it is included, along with numerous other examples of bilingual colloquy, in the *Corpus Glossariorum Latinorum,* vol. 3, ed. George Goetz (Leipzig, 1892). For historical discussions of it, see Garmonsway and Lindsay, note 12 *supra.* Inclusion of short dialogues for drill in grammar was a device of Ælfric and his disciple Ælfric Bata; see Garmonsway, ed., *Ælfric's Colloquy,* and Stevenson, ed. cit., no. VI. This device was doubtless inspired by the *Ars Minor* of Donatus and its numerous recensions.

26. Vives's very popular *Linguae Latinae Exercitatio* (1539) includes a dialogue, "Schola," which describes a school disputation as an eyewitness account. The collection is translated by Foster Watson as *Tudor School-boy Life: The Dialogues of Juan Luis Vives* (London, 1908). Watson (p. x) quotes Vives's description of how young scholars used to dispute all the time. Vives's twenty-four precepts on education are given in a little dialogue reminiscent of Socrates' speech on Diotima's lesson in the *Symposium.*

27. White, p. lix. For a list of their typical subjects, see Foster Watson, *English Grammar Schools,* pp. 465f. Later textbooks on this subject include John Stockwood's *Quaestiones, & responsiones grammaticales* (1592) and John Clarke's *Formulae oratoriae* (1632). On appositions and declamations, see M. L. Clarke, *Classical Education in Britain,* pp. 8 and 16, and Watson, pp. 93–95.

28. William Nelson, ed., *A Fifteenth Century School Book* (Oxford, 1956), p. xxvi. Nelson finds the whole *vulgaria* striking in its dramatic quality, some speeches being imaginable as beautiful soliloquies. In the next generation Erasmus would write his *Colloquia.*

school-dialogues laid the groundwork for more mature dialogists by implying more elaborate forms.

They could also signal crisis. Early sixteenth-century school-dialogues and educational treatises show varying degrees of consciousness of the forces—such as ambition for professional status, interest in new learning and hope of curricular change, and the influence of educational ideologists—which motivate their authors. Richard Pace's *De Fructu qui ex Doctrina Percipitur* (1517) illustrates these mixed motives in the near schizophrenia of its conception of both form and audience.[29] The work is essentially a children's book on pedagogy. Pace shines as one of the first Tudor authors to articulate the new humanist theories of education, and thus he anticipates Ascham (p. xx). But in its style the *De Fructu* reveals imbalanced aspirations. As Pace's modern editors remark: "Although he certainly writes for the boys of St. Paul's school, he is nevertheless trying to impress the great with a display of sparkling virtuosity." Unfortunately this perfectly usual combination gets out of his control. As the editors further point out, Pace's book with its off-color humor and unconscious undermining of learning would have been unsuitable for use in St. Paul's school. The picture of humanism it paints is disconcerting, at times unattractive. In the wrangling of the seven liberal arts, Grammar and Rhetoric are, like all the others, "pompous asses, more concerned with their own prestige than with the value of the humane disciplines which they are supposed to represent." The fact that "highly colloquial dialogue continually interrupts a respectable Ciceronian eloquence" points to an author who vitiates both styles rather than mediates between them. Blurred form indicates Pace's original but ambivalent understanding of the forces in conflict around him.

On the whole and with enormous variety, elementary dia-

29. Richard Pace, *De Fructu qui ex Doctrina Percipitur (The Benefit of a Liberal Education)*, ed. and trans. Frank Manley and Richard S. Sylvester (New York, 1967). Quotations in this paragraph are from the editors' introduction, pp. xix–xxv.

logues in the sixteenth century express the response to humanist theories by the incumbent teaching population, namely, a renascence of what might be called primary scholastic rhetoric. Colloquies and *vulgaria,* in laying the foundations of grammar and logic, gave a scholastic strength if not a scholastic structure to the larger patterns of humanist rhetoric. Scholasticism itself had of course long possessed a complete rhetoric, the rhetoric of logic, with its own persuasive powers. It was now for the schoolmasters, their trivium confronted with a changing philosophy of language, to provide in their dialogues and treatises a logic of rhetoric.

IV

Let us consider the rationale of humanist rhetoric. If, as Kristeller has declared, the humanists were no philosophers, the *élan* of their dialogues may be traced ultimately to a passionate philosophical need. The humanists needed to engage in moral instruction, and for this task they imagined no greater instrument than *bonae litterae.* Their didactic prose literature stands as it were on the fringes of the more familiar discussion by Renaissance theorists of the purer art of poetry. The history of literary criticism of the Italian Renaissance points to the importance of literary theory for the whole age. Bernard Weinberg finds its importance to consist in several elements:

> the necessity to justify the art of poetry against all objections, past and present; the desire to discover the factors which make for differences of judgment between good works and bad works, past and present; and the determination to find those precepts and devices that would assure the Italian poet, present and future, of success in his pursuit of the poetic art. In short, the nature of the art, its criteria, and its rules.[30]

In the Renaissance, Weinberg argues, the formulation of rules betokened the need to justify the art of poetry as a part of moral philosophy. In seeking after moral ends, in the person and in

30. *A History of Literary Criticism in the Italian Renaissance,* p. 797. Cf. Chapter 5 *infra.*

the state, poetry (as moral instruction) had to be included. Thus, for Renaissance theorists, "poetry was by its nature an imitation or representation of reality, made to conform as nearly as possible to that reality in order to produce moral effects desirable both for the individual and for the state" (p. 801).

The dialogues in which the humanists practised moral instruction seemingly needed no aesthetic justification. If they were mere didactic treatises, they were critically *hors de combat.* This is why many of them sleep today in footnotes as "sources" of Renaissance poetry. While they shared the literary preoccupation of the age with moral usefulness, humanist dialogues were not strictly poetic. Their art was rhetorical, and their proliferation attested to the growing importance of rhetoric. As Weinberg observes, "what becomes increasingly clear, as one studies the criteria evolved by Renaissance theorists, is that they take on, progressively, more of a rhetorical than of a poetic cast" (p. 805). Weinberg perceives the ascendancy even in poetic theory of the supremely pragmatic art of rhetoric. Rhetoric had always been defined as an art with ulterior aims, and this coincided perfectly with the fact that dialogue sought to produce moral effects.

Thus in its ideal form Renaissance dialogue might wield the rhetorical power of the ancients more directly than poetry. The reason for imitating Cicero was to move the audience to action; the knowledge which made a wise man was a deed. The later humanist Sidney would elevate the *poet* over the philosopher because "mooving is of a higher degree then teaching":

> For as Aristotle saith, it is not [*gnosis*], but [*praxis*] must be the frute [of moral doctrine].[31]

But Sidney is only appropriating the ideal which throughout the earlier Renaissance had been placed in the orator. As counselor or courtier, the humanists valued him as the supreme philosopher.

31. *The Defence of Poesie* (finished 1581), ed. Albert Feuillerat, *The Prose Works of Sir Philip Sidney*, 4 vols. (Cambridge, England, 1962), III, 19. *Ethica Nicomachea*, I.i.

The themes of humanist dialogues are too numerous to treat in exhaustive detail, but they may be represented by a brief look at three important authors, Ficino, Bembo, and Erasmus. Their dialogues display the main interests of the humanists, philosophy, elite culture, and language. Ficino is occupied with the life of the mind in its most exalted states, but his work also embraces the worldly concerns of political philosophy and ethics. Bembo will here represent the humanist literature of sentiment, a body of edifying literature often seasoned with pagan or courtly attitudes. Avowedly cultist, such works as Bembo's *Gli Asolani* were written in the vernacular for a genteel coterie. Erasmus's dialogues are concerned essentially with education, and they take up the problem of expression and the benefits of philological learning.

Marsilio Ficino, founder of the Platonic Academy of Florence, remained in many ways an Aristotelian. He stands out as the coalescence of humanist interests and medieval methods which is characteristic of the period, and not in Italy alone. He was the first to present the complete works of Plato, many of which had only recently become available, in Latin translation. His analysis of the *Symposium*, the dialogue *De Amore*, not only embodied the aesthetic sensitivity and intellectual freedom which the humanists revered in Plato but also, as a commentary in *questiones*, was profoundly medieval in its metaphysical terminology and method of argumentation.[32] Ficino's contribution may be summed up as a new vision of Plato. To stress just one dimension of his impact, this vision was registered in the transformation of dialogue during the Renaissance. For Ficino opened up the spirit of Plato, which brought a fresh impulse to

32. Paul Oskar Kristeller, *The Philosophy of Marsilio Ficino*, trans. Virginia Conant (New York, 1943), p. 14. See also his "Florentine Platonism and Its Relations with Humanism and Scholasticism," *Church History*, 8 (1939), 201–11, and "The Aristotelian Tradition," in *Renaissance Thought: The Classic, Scholastic, and Humanist Strains* (New York, 1961), p. 33; Sears Reynolds Jayne, ed. and trans., *Marsilio Ficino's Commentary on Plato's "Symposium"* (Columbia, Missouri, 1944), pp. 25–27; and Ficino's *Commentaire sur le Banquet de Platon*, ed. and trans. Raymond Marcel (Paris, 1956), pp. 11–131.

the scholastic form of disputation. This cannot be called a Platonic revolution since the old methods of disputation were not discarded, but it was a compelling new perspective. Like other powerful intellectual systems (Copernican cosmology, Darwinism, Marxism), Italian Platonism touched the culture in unexpected places.

"I believe," wrote Ficino in the preface to his *Theologia Platonica,* ". . . that it was decided by divine Providence that even the perverse minds of many people who do not easily give in to the authority of divine law should at least acquiesce to the Platonic reasons which come to the aid of religion."[33] Medieval scholastics had sought to confirm doctrines based on ecclesiastical tradition, that is, on the *auctoritas* of the Bible and of the Fathers, by means of *ratio,* independent philosophical reflection. In his use of Plato to further this aim Ficino was guided both by the scientific theologians in the line of Aquinas and Scotus and by the authors of more popular devotional literature beginning with Augustine.[34] It was, significantly, in a dialogue that Ficino gave Plato's authority a value comparable to that of the Bible. The *De Amore* looks back to the tradition of *auctoritas* in patristic dialogues and forward to the revival of Platonic method in dialogues such as Elyot's *Of the Knowledge Which Maketh a Wise Man.* Though the harmonizing of Plato and Christianity by Ficino, and by Pico, did not last long but broke down even in their own lifetimes,[35] the influence especially upon the written and visual arts endured in intellectual life. The adoption by Ficino of Platonic dialogue in theological and philosophical debate became a new though not a universal standard.

In the *De Amore* Ficino shows a total command of the dialogue form. First of all, he imitates the *Symposium* itself in substituting for interlocution the sequential exposition of views which

33. Trans. Kristeller/Conant, in *The Philosophy of Marsilio Ficino,* p. 321.

34. Ibid., p. 12. Pontano's similar debt to Augustine is discussed by Francesco Tateo in *Umanesimo etico di Giovanni Pontano* (Lecce, 1972), pp. 189–210.

35. Ernst Cassirer, *The Platonic Renaissance in England,* trans. James P. Pettegrove (Edinburgh, 1953), p. 9.

characterizes the dialogues Plato composed after he had given up teaching eristic. Yet Ficino is able to involve the reader by having a speaker address you directly as if you were the lover under discussion. "What are you to do, poor wretch? . . . you seek your self outside yourself, you cling to your captor so that you may recover your captured self."[36] Here in Tommaso Benci's speech Ficino is engaging the reader in a new type of dialectic, that between two selves in love. Perhaps the fullest implications for the interpersonal dialectic between writer and reader in dialogue are expressed in Antonio Agli, bishop of Fiesole's analysis of Pausanias's speech on the two Venuses and the nature of reciprocal love.

> The truth must rather be that each [lover] has himself and has the other, too. A has himself, but in B; and B also has himself, but in A. When you love me, you contemplate me, and as I love you, I find myself in your contemplation of me; I recover myself, lost in the first place by [my] own neglect of myself, in you, who preserve me. You do exactly the same in me. And then this, too, is remarkable: that after I have lost myself, if I recover myself through you, I have myself through you, and if I have myself through you, I have you sooner and to a greater degree than I have myself. I am therefore closer to you than I am to myself, since I keep a grasp on myself only through you as a mediary.[37]

As the reader in reading participates in this reasoning, Ficino reveals stage after stage in the meaning of the loss and recovery of the self through love of another. He expands the text just quoted to show that the dialectic of love leads to contemplation and thence to self-recognition, ultimately to the overcoming of death and a kind of resurrection. The dialogue between the writer and the reader mirrors the reciprocity between the lover and the beloved.

In Bishop Agli's speech we have a species of rhetorical reasoning which may be termed *humanist logic,* and it is by no means uncommon in dialogue. The speech avoids technical (scholastic) terminology, and disputation is replaced here by a

36. Jayne, trans., p. 202.

37. Ibid., pp. 144f. The passage is echoed in Erasmus's *Praise of Folly;* see Clarence H. Miller, ed. and trans. (New Haven and London, 1979), p. 136.

single speaker assembling the links of an argument. Usually the writer observes the decorum of plain expository prose, though sometimes, as in the example below, the logic adopts figurative language. Perhaps the idea of a humanist logic may help to exculpate the humanists from the antiphilosophical prejudice in which many scholars have imagined them immured.[38]

The humanists' attention to the logical structure of rhetoric is on occasion rewarded by the attainment of eloquence. In his comment in the *De Amore* on the speech of Aristophanes, the poet Cristoforo Landino fashions the metaphor of a feast (Jayne, trans., p. 162). Thus Ficino, who is in his commentary reenacting a symposium (banquet), has a speaker describe the heavenly symposium at which each lover of God is given a seat, ambrosia, and nectar "forever without satiety." This endless feast becomes in turn a metaphor for the reciprocal love between God and man, love as the highest appetite endlessly fulfilled. No one comments on the metaphor after Landino's speech, yet we feel the flourish of eloquence in the construction of a speech which rivals Aristophanes' original in Plato. To make sense beautifully, to be "apt" and "fitting," is the aim of humanist logic. This sort of metaphor-within-a-metaphor in dialogue never seems to lose its power to charge the imagination. One remembers Lady Jane Grey reading a Platonic dialogue in Ascham's *Toxophilus*, and Erasmus's allusions to himself and his works in his own *Colloquies* still bring a smile.

In the genteel vernacular dialogues called *Gli Asolani* Pietro Bembo made a deliberate attempt to popularize the Platonic studies which the Florentine Academy had made a generation earlier.[39] The Italian dialogues are very pretty; it is easy to see

38. E.g., J.-C. Margolin, "La Critique humaniste de la Dialectique médiévale," in *La Dialectique*, Actes du XIVe Congrès des Sociétés de Philosophie de Langue française (Paris, 1969), pp. 29–33, and Pierre Mesnard, ed., *Dialogus Ciceronianus, Opera omnia* [*Erasmi*], *ordo* I, tome 2 (Amsterdam, 1971), p. 664n.

39. Pietro Bembo, *Gli Asolani* (1505), trans. Rudolf B. Gottfried (Bloomington, 1954). Information and quotations in this paragraph are taken from the translator's introduction, pp. xviiff.

how they could run through at least twenty-two editions before 1600. Gottfried rightly regards their Platonism as literary rather than philosophical. "From his study of [Plato's] *Dialogues* . . . Bembo gained not merely the arguments of Lavinello's hermit or an occasional reference like Gismondo's to the myth that every pair of lovers was at first a single creature, but a perception of what might be done with the dialogue as a literary form." It is not so much for the arguments of the hermit as for the use of the figure himself, modeled upon Diotima, to produce an almost supernatural climax that Bembo is indebted to Plato. Thus *Gli Asolani* is "the artistic rather than the intellectual fruit" of the Ficinian Academy.[40]

Gli Asolani provides a clear picture of the state of humanist dialogue at the turn of the century. First, it reveals a basic literary debt to Plato. Second, it carries vestiges of scholastic argument, as in Lavinello's critique (pp. 153ff.) of the reasoning of the preceding two discourses. That Bembo is impatient with this method is confirmed by the hermit's (the Diotima figure's) remark to Lavinello (p. 175): ". . . I would not reason or dispute with you as closely as with school philosophers. . . ." Third, the garden setting is adopted from classical dialogue and extensively elaborated. For this the primary model is Cicero, but Bembo gives the Tusculan garden a number of piquant embellishments; e.g., the participants include women, one of whom trails her hand in a fountain; and the queen who joins the party in the garden sits not on the grass but on two pillows. Fourth, the dramatic moments are sentimental; e.g., Perottino, moved by his own speech in the first dialogue, weeps. This technique will be more fully exploited by Castiglione. Both the dramatic focus on psychological character and the elaboration of the garden setting are prominent elements in *Utopia,* written a decade later. And fifth, a growing predilection for the resources of rhetoric and poetry may be seen in Bembo's mingling of poems

40. Burckhardt was an enthusiastic admirer of *Gli Asolani;* in the Italian style of these dialogues, he declares, "a classical perfection was reached" (*The Civilization of the Renaissance,* ed. cit., p. 145).

with dialogue. His influence in England begins with Wyatt's translation of the poem "Voi mi ponese in foco" from *Gli Asolani;*[41] and in Sidney's *Arcadia,* dialogue punctuated with verse becomes a structuring principle of didactic romance. On the other hand, the extreme contrast between *Arcadia* and the dialogues culminating in poems by Boethius suggests how subversive of philosophy the rhetorical use of poetry can be.

De Amore and *Gli Asolani* throw up another important question: Were these and other humanist dialogues, as their authors often claim, records of actual debates? Kristeller believes that dialogues "deviate" much further from conversations that actually took place than is the case with orations or letters, and that in many cases they are pure fiction. "Since a specific occasion for writing a commentary, an oration, or even a letter, was lacking in the case of the dialogue," he concludes, "it must thus be assumed in most cases that an author wrote a treatise or dialogue on his own, in order to state openly his views on specific themes."[42] While this is doubtless true in many cases, the situation is more complex than Kristeller allows.

We know that the dialogues of the Fathers, who chose contemporary characters for their Christian apologies, often reflected actual debates of the times.[43] There is considerable evidence, as Raymond Marcel shows in his edition of the *De Amore,* that Ficino's dialogue is based on a historical banquet. With Erasmus and More we feel historical characters and events slide into fiction. The interplay can be very subtle. One of Ascham's

41. Sir Thomas Wyatt, *Collected Poems,* ed. Kenneth Muir (London, 1949), pp. 93f.

42. "The Scholar and His Public in the Late Middle Ages and the Renaissance," in *Medieval Aspects of Renaissance Learning,* ed. and trans. Edward P. Mahoney, Duke Monographs in Medieval and Renaissance Studies, no. 1 (Durham, North Carolina, 1974), pp. 3–25, p. 13.

43. For examples from Jerome (*PL,* 23, 155–82 and 495–590) and others, see Robert J. Menner, ed., *The Poetical Dialogues of Solomon and Saturn* (1941; repr. New York, 1973), pp. 54–56. And Alcuin in a letter to Charlemagne, as Menner notes, reports that in his youth he heard a debate between a Jew and Master Peter of Pavia (*PL,* 100, 313).

sources for *Toxophilus*, for example, is the *Dialogus de Milite Peregrino* (1543) by Petrus Nannius, which was in fact a version of an actual debate between Louis of Flanders ("Xenophon") and the Duke of Aerschot ("Olympius").[44] We would like to know more about the rules and management of such contests.

This much is clear: humanist dialogists did not merely refurbish classical dialogues; they also wrote down performances which were themselves imitations or re-creations of ancient events. These dialogues are transcript evidence of a cultural phenomenon, literary precipitates of the new education which introduced classical disputation first into academies, then secondary schools, and finally universities. One may speculate on the phenomenon as a series of projections. Beginning with its introduction into the school curriculum, classical dialogue was projected into more advanced student debates concomitantly with scholastic forms. These exercises gave rise to actual debates among learned men, which in turn inspired the composition of literary versions. The latter became subjects of further study and debate. Written dialogues thus stand in a relation to actual oral practice similar to that between written and oral disputations. Dialogues testify to the humanists' belief in *praxis* rather than *gnosis* as the definition of wisdom.

As readers of English Renaissance dialogues, our critical concern often centers on the degree of "deviation" of a written dialogue from an actual conversation or from historical reality. At times, when the actual events already possess an aesthetic unity, the degree of deviation is slight, as in the interrogations of Thomas More as recorded by Roper or the trial and execution of Latimer and Ridley as recorded by Foxe. Contemporary historical events exert an inescapable influence on the projection of a classical literary model, and this is the key to reading the humanists' dialogues. There are a few cases, as in Roper and Foxe, where history assumes the shape of art, and then dialogue need only report the interlocution. More usually, dialogue

44. Alvin Vos, "The Humanism of Toxophilus: A New Source," *English Literary Renaissance*, 6 (1976), 198 n. 25.

fictionalizes in subtle ways the *real actions* of men, and the result is a strange half-art.[45]

Erasmus amply represents the humanist problem of expression. His use of classical literary forms was frankly eclectic, characteristically lacking in generic consistency. His dialogue *De pueris instituendis* was in fact a "declamation" tricked out in the guise of ancient dialogue.[46] In his great experiment in irony, Folly's monologue, Erasmus achieved an eclecticism of tone that continues to make sport of scholars. The *Colloquies,* as Craig Thompson has shown, evolved from sets of formulae for schoolboys in the first edition (1518) to longer dialogues in later editions, such as *The Godly Feast* (*Convivium religiosum*), that appealed to adults. Gradually realizing the serious possibilities of the *Colloquies,* which had first been published without his permission, Erasmus transformed his book of exercises into real colloquies; and these provided models of writing as well as speech.[47] Above all, the smiling spirit of these conversations caught an ideal toward which a whole generation of dialogists aspired. The charming setting of *The Godly Feast* recalls that of More's *Utopia,* just as the journey-motif in Elyot's dialogue *Of the Knowledge Which Maketh a Wise Man* reminds us of *The Pilgrim-*

45. The first half of the seventeenth century in France saw the development of the *entretien,* a form which sometimes recorded real *viva voce* conversations, sometimes incarnated attitudes or positions. In contrast to intimacy with the self in the *essai,* the *entretien* analyzed intimacy in relation to another. Jean-Louis Guez de Balzac, *Les Entretiens* (1657), ed. B. Beugnot (Paris, 1972), pp. xxxii–xxxv. Beugnot concludes: "L'entretien est à l'image d'une société qui privilégie les relations humaines et personnelles, qui aspire à une culture soeur de l'aisance et de la grâce, qui cherche à multiplier à l'infini 'le plus grand plaisir de la vie, et presque le seul' au dire de Mlle de Montpensier, la conversation." Is Mlle de Montpensier alluding to Folly's remark that the chief solace in life is uninhibited garrulousness?

46. Written in 1506–9, published 1529. See Jean-Claude Margolin, ed., *Opera omnia, ordo* I, tome 2 (Amsterdam, 1971), p. 5.

47. *The Colloquies of Erasmus,* ed. and trans. Craig R. Thompson (Chicago and London, 1965), p. xxv.

age for Religion's Sake (*Peregrinatio religionis ergo*). "The whole Renaissance," wrote Johan Huizinga, "cherished that wish of reposeful, blithe, and yet serious intercourse of good and wise friends in the cool shade of a house under trees, where serenity and harmony would dwell."[48]

Pierre Mesnard, in a penetrating essay, his last writing before his death, calls attention to the fact that Erasmus balances a variety of modes of dialogue in the *Dialogus Ciceronianus* (1528).[49] First (p. 593) is the strict dialogue between protagonists, but this occurs only when Erasmus wants to get past a stage in the dialectic, in order to reach a conclusion. Mesnard refers to these confrontations between adversaries as "rounds"—the same term Ryle (*Plato's Progress*, p. 202) uses for the dramatized eristic in Plato. Second, in the *Ciceronianus* one of the principal characters usually has the floor for a long period—the procedure we recognize as peirastic. And third, says Mesnard, though the dialoguing parties are direct descendants from the *Colloquies*, from which they take their life and movement, the doctrinal expositions make one think rather of the *Praise of Folly* and the divers diatribes of Erasmus. Mesnard's analysis allows us to see the *Ciceronianus* as an almost symbolic example of dialogue appealing to both audiences of fifteenth- and sixteenth-century scholarly literature, scholastic and humanistic.

Renaissance literary theorists, as we have seen, were anxious to justify poetry as part of philosophy. For them the art of poetry consisted in the imitation or representation of reality. In terms of Platonic idealism the thing imitated ought to be of a high order, but in terms of poetry the representation itself, the poet's own style, ought to strive for perfection. Now on the whole, the humanists were not poets but pedagogues; for them the theoretical problem focused on the issue of Ciceronian imitation. In the *Ciceronianus* Erasmus inquired into the two concerns of the writer of prose which also preoccupied the poetic theorists: the source of inspiration and the nature of genius.

48. *Erasmus*, trans. F. Hopman (London, 1952), p. 104; cited by Thompson, *Colloquies*, p. 46.

49. In Erasmus, *Opera omnia, ordo* I, tome 2 (Amsterdam, 1971), pp. 583–96.

Mesnard puts the case well. He observes that Erasmus's view of imitation is that one must follow one's natural talent, which may or may not be Tullian. To imitate Cicero truly, one should express oneself in one's own originality; otherwise imitation is a lie. How then can literary education influence character? Erasmus's thought profited from the doctrine of Quintilian. The latter, after admitting the possibility that a tutor can know and use the character, *ingenium,* of his student (*Inst.* 1, 3, 1), defines the pedagogy which follows from that assumption: one must respect these innate differences and direct the instruction in such a way that favors the natural tendency of the intelligence (2, 8, 1–3). Quite naturally one finds this advice transposed into rhetorical terms. No matter what perfection the authors we wish to imitate have reached, we must avoid going in a sense opposed to our own personal genius (10, 2, 19–21). Moreover, we must preserve the vigor of our personal inspiration even as we attempt to surpass the greatest of our ancestors. It is only at this cost that one can become a "perfectus orator." The whole second part of the *Ciceronianus,* Mesnard concludes, is a methodical application of this doctrine.[50]

In the *Ciceronianus* Erasmus attempted to annihilate a cloud of perverse, confused opinions regarding imitation. Between them and the model Cicero his new dialogue mediated by adopting the pedagogy of Quintilian. Perhaps the greatest significance of the work lies in Erasmus's elucidation of the purpose of humanist rhetoric. Valla had revitalized the antique argument that the aim of rhetoric was to persuade one's audience. But Erasmus, taking this practical aim for granted, penetrated to a deeper level of motivation. Our tendency to regard the humanists as public performers is precisely the habit which obscures our perception of their inner life. Erasmus grasped the inner purpose of humanist rhetoric: to find one's personal genius. Surprisingly, this purpose has little to do with changing the world or oneself; it is a writer's goal, to invent a style. The ability of rhetoric, or poetry, to change character must remain doubtful, yet both can

50. Ibid, pp. 589 and 648n.

give expression to the beauty and truth of one's individual humanity. A dialogue may show the private strength behind apparent public failure. Recognizing with Erasmus the true ideal in the pedagogical aim of pure, pagan Ciceronianism, humanists such as More and Elyot were able to draw the final analogy between finding one's genius and attaining personal sanctity.

4

Plato and Elyot: Knowledge as Action

I

It is not hard to imagine the Tudor dialogists as an academic procession, a line of black gowns moving down Broad Street or King's Parade, the picture of a common purpose. Yet if we were to pick out one of those learned worthies, and follow him home, how long before, observing his willful individualism or isolation, we realized how incompletely he shared with that procession the fictions of a corporate campaign and communal responsibility? We tend to forget that his affirmations, his published teachings, are the result of a fundamental, continuous dialectic between strengths, such as initiative and integrity, and weaknesses, such as the sense of inferiority and despair. In whatever forms it takes, he must mediate the inevitable conflict, which arises in the course of personal development, between self-absorption and concern for the world. And so in selecting a limited number of cases for analysis we are examining the dilemma of a class, self-conscious and intellectual, without of course pretending to do justice to all aspects of the dilemma or to draw a general conclusion.

Young Thomas Elyot (?1490–1546) pursued a legal rather than an academic career. His father, Sir Richard Elyot (?1450–1522), was judge of assize on the Western Circuit, and Thomas served as clerk of this court from ca. 1510 to ca. 1526. With Wolsey's help he received a junior clerkship to the Privy Council from ca. 1523 until the cardinal's death in 1530.[1] Elyot also possessed a fine education in Greek and Latin authors, his interest centering on classical political thought, the theory of education, and medicine. In order to describe the form of a just public weal in *The Book Named the Governor* (1531), his first published work, Elyot set forth a method for educating those destined to hold authority in it. This great work has been called "the very Magna Carta of our education."[2] *The Doctrinal of Princes* (1533?), a translation of Isocrates, and *The Education or Bringing up of Children* (1533?), a translation of Plutarch, extended Elyot's view that education should impart civic duty. *The Image of Governance,* "compiled of the actes and sentences notable, of the most noble Emperour Alexander Severus," was another translation from Greek, probably written during this period but not published until 1541. *Pasquil the Plain* and *Of the Knowledge Which Maketh a Wise Man* were both published in 1533, Elyot's *annus mirabilis;* the first of these satirical dialogues concerned court slander, the second the necessity of speaking out against tyranny. Another dialogue of political satire was *The Defence of Good Women,* published in 1540. Elyot's medical interests came to fruition with the publication of his encyclopedic *Castle of Health,* probably in 1536, followed by two more editions in his lifetime. Perhaps his su-

1. See K. J. Wilson, ed., *The Letters of Sir Thomas Elyot,* "Texts and Studies, 1976," *Studies in Philology,* 73, no. 5 (Chapel Hill, 1976), 11–12; hereafter cited as "*Letters.*" Stanford E. Lehmberg's biography, *Sir Thomas Elyot, Tudor Humanist* (Austin, 1960), provides much useful information (but see R. S. Sylvester's review in *Renaissance News,* 14 [1961], 178–81). Biographical studies, as well as texts and criticism of Elyot, are surveyed by Jerome S. Dees in "Recent Studies in Elyot," *English Literary Renaissance,* 5 (1976), 336–44.

2. Paul Elmer More, *Aristocracy and Justice* (New York, 1915), p. 55; cited by Robert Carl Pinckert, "Sir Thomas Elyot's *The Image of Governance* (1541): A Critical Edition," Ph.D. dissertation, Columbia University, 1964, p. xiv.

preme achievement was the Latin-English *Dictionary,* partially compiled in the king's library and published in 1538, enlarged in 1542. His contributions to moral education were rounded out by four devotional works: *A Sermon of St. Cyprian on the Mortality of Man,* published together with a translation of Pico della Mirandola's *Rules of a Christian Life* in 1534; a florilegium from the Fathers, *The Banquet of Sapience* (1534?); and his last work, a meditation entitled *A Preservative against Death* (1545).

The combination of a principled, classical perspective on the Tudor court and the unsettling effect of erratic, delayed patronage from the king, Wolsey, and Cromwell, gradually imbued Elyot's ambition with a peculiar bittersweet ambivalence. On the one hand was the classicist's need to provide moral instruction. It can be said of him, as John Oakesmith said of Plutarch, that "the dominating principle of his teaching" was "the paramount necessity of finding a sanction and an inspiration for conduct in what the wisdom of the past had already provided. . . ."[3] Just as Plutarch's work is governed by the "desire of making the wisdom and tradition of the past available for ethical usefulness," so is Elyot's. In such works as *The Governor, Pasquil, The Defence of Good Women,* and the dialogue of *Knowledge,* Elyot adheres to the rhetorical and legal dictum that one's words count as actions for which one is responsible. Yet on the other hand, Elyot had to confront the corruption and indifference of the world. "Will I or no," he wrote to Cromwell, "I am inforcid to be cruciate in my poure mynde. . . ."[4] In this chapter I would like to argue that Elyot's finest eloquence rises from the well of his ambivalence, and that this dialectic takes its most natural form in a dialogue concerning self-knowledge.

Elyot's dialogue *Of the Knowledge Which Maketh a Wise Man* exhibits two types of mediation. The first is the interpretation of antiquity to his own age, which often characterizes humanist literary endeavor; the second is the record of internal tensions between his own aspirations and his failures, which often

3. *The Religion of Plutarch . . .* (London, 1902), pp. xixf.

4. *Letters,* p. 12.

characterizes humanist civic endeavor. As in each of the early Tudor dialogues examined in the following pages, the published work must be weighed, as far as possible, against its personal cost. In Elyot's case the dialogue of *Knowledge* supplies a revealing balance sheet of public values and subjective experience.

Elyot failed to become a royal counselor, only to succeed as a civic scholar, because he was too virtuous a machiavel. The complex evolution of his lifelong obsession with reputation (and its eventual satisfaction) is recorded in Elyot's letters to Cromwell and his dedicatory epistles to Cromwell or Henry VIII, and the theme is intricately involved in his literary works. Elyot's private desire for recognition and authority coincided with the public necessity that the governor's authority be recognized. In his first book he attempted to resolve the tension in his own attitude toward authority and experience precisely by determining their proper balance in the governor. As a reward perhaps for that book Elyot was sent in 1531 as Henry VIII's ambassador to the migratory court of Charles V to sound out the emperor's opinion concerning the king's divorce. But from the tangle of Hapsburg diplomatic ceremony an academic amateur proved incapable of extracting support for the cause, and in January, 1532, he was summarily replaced by Thomas Cranmer.[5] The main chance missed, burdened with new debts, Elyot wrote the dialogue *Of the Knowledge Which Maketh a Wise Man:* a symbolic enactment of the same theme he had treated in *The Governor.* Let us begin with the opposition between authority and experience, since this problem, as an element of Elyot's character, troubles all his writings.

Such a dichotomy is a familiar trope in medieval storytelling. In the prologue to her tale, Chaucer's Wife of Bath would have her experience count as *authoritee.* It is tempting to see Elyot as reversing her claim, making scholarly authority a substitute for experience. The overriding concern of *The Governor* is justice. Elyot explores not only its public but also its private standards.

5. *Letters,* pp. xi–xii.

He argues from two bases, personal experience and historical authority (usually classical or scriptural). Like the *Tale* of the Wife of Bath, *The Governor* expresses its narrator's deepest preoccupations.

The governor himself cannot remain fixed in the study of authorities. But if experience enhances his understanding of them, authorities may well find practical application. The commentaries of Julius Caesar, says Elyot (I, 87–89), comprise a book which "is studiously to be radde of the princes of this realme of Englande and their counsaillors; considering that thereof maye be taken necessary instructions concernynge the warres agayne Irisshe men or Scottes, who be of the same rudeness and wilde disposition that the Suises and Britons were in the time of Cesar"![6] But Elyot himself harbored a far different attitude toward authority and experience; somewhat indefinite in *The Governor,* this attitude gradually developed into a firm belief, as his subsequent works reveal.

Let us look at Elyot at work in the lines following his assessment of Caesar's commentaries:

> Also there be dyvers orations, as well in *all the bokes of the saide autors as in the historie of Cornelius Tacitus whiche be very delectable,* and for counsayles very expedient to be had in memorie. And in good faythe I have often thought that the consultations and orations wryten by Tacitus do importe a majestie with a compendious eloquence therin contained.
>
> . . . .
>
> Surely if a noble man do thus *seriously and diligently rede* histories, I dare affirme *there is no studie or science for him of equal commoditie and pleasure, havyinge regarde to every tyme and age.* (emphasis added)

What emerges from these lines on histories, as from the first book as a whole, is Elyot's allegiance to classical authorities and his love of learning *per se.* What value might the governor, the

6. *The Boke Named the Gouernour,* ed. Henry Herbert Stephen Croft, 2 vols. (London, 1883; repr. New York, 1967). References to volume and page numbers of Croft's edition appear in the text. Abbreviations in all quotations from Elyot are silently expanded, and spelling is modernized with respect to *u/v, i/j,* and long *s.*

author, and we assign to the experiences related by those authorities? Can one discern in Elyot's love of old authors a reluctance toward experience in the world?

In 1530–31 he had not yet traveled on the Continent. He writes in Book I of *The Governor* (I, 77f.) that all the world is painted in the old maps of Ptolemy:

> All be it there is none so good lernynge as the demonstration of cosmographie. . . . And surely this lesson is bothe pleasant and necessary.

The inward eye is fixed on an authority now; the mind takes its pleasure.

> For what pleasure is it, in one houre, to beholde those realmes, cities, sees, ryvers, and mountaynes, that uneth in an olde mannes life can nat be journaide and pursued: what incredible delite is taken in beholding the diversities of people, beastis, foules, fisshes, trees, frutes, and herbes . . .

These things Elyot *beholds,* and the desired end of the exercise is:

> to knowe the sondry maners and conditions of people, and the varietie of their natures, and that in a warme studie or perler, without perill of the see, or daunger of longe and paynfull journayes . . .

For him the journey of incredible delight is study. He concludes this single compendious sentence in a tone of utter satisfaction:

> I can nat tell what more pleasure shulde happen to a gentil witte, than to beholde in his owne house every thynge that with in all the worlde is contained.

Revealing as these lines are, they remain susceptible to misinterpretation. Elyot was a private scholar to the degree that reading is a solitary occupation and one which he relished. On the other hand, such thoughts are as little reclusive and as highly sociable as one could wish in a scholar. How can we measure the value of the experiences related by the old cosmographers? Elyot answers first for the benefit of the governor:

> The commoditie therof knewe the great kynge Alexander, as some writars do remembre. For he caused the countrayes wherunto he purposed any enterprise, diligently and counningly to be discribed and

paynted, that, beholdynge the picture, he mought perceyve whiche places were most daungerous: and where he and his host mought have most easy and covenable passage.

More examples of this commodity follow. Thus while Elyot reveals, almost parenthetically, his private reservations about experience and his passion for study for its own sake, he specifically introduces cosmography in order to demonstrate its utility to a governor. The historical examples found in authorities such as Caesar, Sallust, or the cosmographers are vicarious experiences for governors. For Elyot, they are, or at least eventually will become, an end in themselves. In *The Governor* the primacy of either authority or experience remains in question. Knowledge itself is not yet recognized as an action.

Once we have differentiated Elyot's response to classical authors from the response of his readers destined to become governors, we discover an interesting incidental transformation in the concept of experience. Here is Elyot early in Book I (Ch. 9): "Also by a cruell and irous maister the wittes of children be dulled; and that thinge for the whiche children be often tymes beaten is to them ever after fastidious: wherof we nede no better autor for witnes than daily experience." Instead of "daily experience" he might have said Quintilian. The clause hardly matters, a mere formula, yet it provides a channel into Elyot's mind. Somehow for him daily experience is measured on a par with old authors, at least when he is in search of authority. By the time he writes Book III, experience itself has evolved, as it evolves for us all, into a kind of authority:

Concernynge that parte of fidelitie which concerneth the kepynge of promise or covenauntes experience declareth howe litle it is now had in regarde; to the notable rebuke of all of us whiche do professe Christes religion. (II, 246)

Here *experience* is used exactly like a classical authority to ratify an argument of Elyot's. Experience *declareth*, and, like Caesar or Tacitus, *rebukes* us. So strong is Elyot's attachment to learning that his way of validating the examples of daily experience is to handle them exactly as he handled ancient authorities. He elevates experience to the stature of authority, although experience rarely serves alone.

In the mind of a man for whom contact with ancient authorities is a daily experience it is understandable that the two could become equivalent. This in turn affects his perception of the contemporary world. It were better to have a constant enemy than an inconstant friend, Elyot writes. "Wherof I my self have had sufficient *experience.* But nowe to declare some *experience* of constance, wherby the reders may be the more therto provoked, I will reherce some examples therof out of olde histories, as I shall happen to remembre them" (II, 321f.). Let us consider these two uses of the word *experience.* Elyot's preference here for historical "experience" doubtless stems from tact; but it is also clear that personal experience is seen as arising from those "olde histories," that is, from authority. Thus in subsequent pages we find Elyot saying, for instance (II, 328), "This vertue [moderation] shall best be perceived by rehersinge of examples shewed by noble men, whiche is in effecte but dayly experience." Or later (II, 439): "I will declare a notable experience *which I late hapned to rede.*"

The course of Elyot's attitude toward authority and experience in the first two books of *The Governor* may be seen as a vacillating adherence to one or the other. In Book III he defines experience. "Experience wherof commeth wysedome" consists in part in "actes committed or done by other men, wherof profite or damage succedynge, we may, (in knowynge or beholding it), be therby instructed to apprehende the thing which to the publike weale, or to our owne persones, may be commodious; and exchue that thing, which either in the begynnyng or in the conclusion, appereth noisome and vicious" (II, 383f.). This is a rhetorically wrought and *enjoyed* definition. Note the exquisite care of the parenthetical phrase: experience is something the effects of which one "knows" or "beholds." Elyot's defining powers grow sharper as he proceeds: "The knowledge of this Experience is called Example, and is expressed by historie, whiche of Tulli is called the life of memorie." Wisdom comes, Elyot is arguing, from nothing less than an experiencing of history. Such a claim compels a defense of historical writing, and to this defense Elyot applies all the force of his most personal style. "And therfore to suche persones as do contemne auncient histories, reputing them amonge leasinges and fantises (these be their wordes of reproche), it may be sayd, that in contemnynge histories they frustrate Experience. . . . And that shall they perceyve manifestly if they will a litle while laye a parte their accustomed obstinacies, and suffre to be distilled in to their eares two or three dropes of the sweete oyle of remembraunce." For, Elyot is emboldened to say, "there is no doctrine, be it eyther divine or humaine, that is nat eyther all expresssed in historie or at the leste mixte with historie." With absolute conviction he concludes: "Finally, so large is the compase of that whiche is named historie, that it comprehendeth all thynge that is necessary to be put in memorie."

We find the narrative "I" everywhere in *The Governor;* the whole exposition involves us in asides, incidental judgments, digressions, and a vast repertoire of Elyot's moods. What brings the reader back to the work of an author who dryly announces, "I wyll ordinately treate of the two partes of a publike weale, wherof the one shall be named Due Administration, the other Necessary Occupation, whiche shall be devided in to two volumes," is the sense Elyot conveys that, despite his ponderous intention to be ordinate, he knows himself still to be in the process of perfecting his judgment. It is not surprising perhaps that Elyot is willing to pose Socratic challenges to his premises late in the argument (e.g., Book III, Ch. 24, par. 1). But would one have expected the spare, somber quotation from Lactantius with which Elyot concludes Chapter 25 of Book III? "Thou must nedes perysshe if thou knowe nat what is to thy life profitable, that thou maiste seke for it, and what is daungerous, that thou mayste flee and exchue it." The knowledge of what is profitable to a man's life Elyot would seek in a Platonic dialogue, printed two years later. Here he simply appends to Lactantius's dictum:

"Whiche I dare affirme may come soonest to passe by redynge of histories, and retayninge them in continuell remembraunce."

In *The Governor* Elyot attempts to teach an ability he possesses—to live in history. Practical experience he recognizes as indispensable to the governor, but he is more familiar with historical experience acquired through the study of classical examples. He desires the governor to profit from the lessons of history by applying them in practical experience; and yet as we observe Elyot's method in *The Governor* and accumulate glimpses of his preoccupations, we come to see that for himself he charted another course.

The ground of Elyot's method in *The Governor* may be derived from Chapter 23 of Book III, "*Of Sapience, and the definition therof.*" Searching for apophthegms in an effort to define this fugitive concept, he recalls the verses of Lucius Afranius which were set over the porch of the temple where the senate of Rome commonly assembled:

> Usus me genuit, mater peperit memoria.
> Sophiam me Graii vocant, vos Sapientiam.

Which in englysshe maye be in this wyse translated:—

> Memorye hyght my mother, my father experience.
> Grekes calle me Sophi, but ye name me Sapience.[7]

These verses together with Elyot's explication sum up both his ideal for the governor and his own method as a writer.

> By use or experience in these versis expressed the poete intended as well those actes whiche we our selfe dayly do practyse, as also them whiche beynge done by other in tyme passed. . . . And the cause why that the poete conjoyneth experience and memorie together, as it were

7. II, 367. Elyot himself realized the aptness of the lines, for a few pages later when he asserts, "The knowledge of this Experience [i.e., acts done by other men] is called Example, and is expressed by historie, whiche of Tulli is called the life of memorie," he adds: "And so it agreeth well with the versis of Affranius by me late declared." Ascham employs the first verse in *The Scholemaster,* ed. William Aldis Wright, *English Works of Roger Ascham* (1904; repr. Cambridge, England, 1970), p. 195. Cf. Aulus Gellius, *Noctes Atticae,* XIII, vii, 3.

in a lefull matrimony, experience bigettynge, and memorye alwaye producynge that incomparable frute called Sapience, is for that memorie in her operation proprely succedeth experyence. For that which is presently done we perceyve, that which is to come we conjecte or divine, but that whiche is passed onely we have in our memorie.

According to the genealogy of sapience, experience, consisting of both daily and historical aspects, is wed to Mater Memoria. Sapience is engendered when "memorie in her operation proprely succedeth experyence." Memory is thus the fertile *mediary,* a stage in which, it is important to note, all things are in the past. For Elyot, experience—daily as well as historical—is transformed, *anteriorized,* by its commerce with memory which thereby produces sapience. And sapience, or wisdom, as Elyot repeatedly emphasizes, is the ultimate authority.

II

In the dialogue *Of the Knowledge Which Maketh a Wise Man* the zealot of classical culture very nearly baptizes Plato. Elyot's *Dictionary* calls Plato "the Prynce and chiefe of all philosophers, as welle in wysdome and counnynge, as in good lyvynge and eloquence"; and *The Governor* (I, 93) asserts that "above all other, the warkes of Plato wolde be most studiously radde when the jugement of a man is come to perfection. . . ." What more natural "allective" or enticement to the study of the great philosopher, what better introduction, since "the jugement of a man. . .is instructed in the fourme of speakynge that philosophers used," than this "disputacion Platonike," as Elyot later subtitled his dialogue? Elyot offers not a translation of a Platonic dialogue but a Tudor Plato. In the opening lines the mists of centuries and a strange language are brushed away:

> Who is this man / whom I perceyve commynge hitherwarde? . . .
> Plato / thou art wel founden againe in this contray.
> Gramercie Aristippus.[8]

8. I use Edwin Johnston Howard's page-for-page reprint (Oxford, Ohio, 1946) of the first edition, *STC* 7668. Page references are to the numbers in brackets added by Howard.

In *The Governor* (II, 96) Elyot had asserted that "in every discipline example is the beste instructour," and so in his straightforward way he produced a didactic example of dialogue. It was not enough simply to read Plato: Elyot had a particular conception of the purpose of Plato's dialogues. When near the conclusion of *The Governor* Elyot says that "the ende of all doctrine and studie is good counsayle," he adds that this fact "shall appere to them that will rede the bokes of the noble Plato"; moreover, in these books, "every investigacion [of Socrates'] . . . is in fourme of a consultation . . ." (II, 433f.). "Consultation" is Elyot's term for Socratic dialectic, and the dialogue as a whole can be denoted by his term "counsel," the process as well as the end of all doctrine and study. Socratic consultation, in Plato's dialogues as in Elyot's, is a form of *dispute;* and this word too has a characteristic significance for Elyot. We derive an idea of the resonance which the subtitle "A disputacion Platonike" has for Elyot from his definition of *disputare* in the 1538 edition of his *Dictionary:* "to dispute, to make plaine to be understande," to which he adds in 1545, "to rayson." Elyot conceives of Plato and, to a lesser degree, Cicero as counselors. Their works embodied the best methods of consultation, and this lesson Elyot undertakes to teach in his Platonic dialogue.

Elyot's concept of arriving at counsel through disputatious consultation coincides with Socrates' description of the right way to form a judgment or opinion:

> I mean the conversation which the soul holds with herself in considering of anything. I speak of what I scarcely understand; but the soul when thinking appears to me to be just talking—asking questions of herself and answering them, affirming and denying. And when she has arrived at a decision, either gradually or by a sudden impulse, and has at last agreed, and does not doubt, this is called her opinion. I say, then, that to form an opinion is to speak, and opinion is a word spoken,—I mean, to oneself and in silence, not aloud or to another. . . .[9]

Elyot cannot have failed to realize that this interior process is

9. *Theaetetus,* 190A, *The Dialogues of Plato,* trans. Benjamin Jowett, 3d rev. ed. (Oxford, 1892).

imitated when one reads dialogue and thus that a literary consultation could serve to train the mind.

Of the Knowledge Which Maketh a Wise Man is a continuous, five-part dialogue whose subject is the nature of wisdom. Its occasion is Plato's explanation to his old rival, the Cyrenaic philosopher Aristippus, of his cruel treatment by King Dionysius of Sicily.[10] As the work begins, Aristippus, *solus,* wonders whether it is Plato whom he sees approaching; there is no indication of scene. Although Aristippus and Plato allude to the fact that each of them is accompanied by a servant, neither servant has any role. The language of interlocution is spare, indeed plain; its structure, subtle. What interests Elyot is the form of consultation—the qualifying of assertions and jockeying for position in dialogue. The consciousness that he is Platonizing produces in his speakers a self-critical attitude which exceeds anything of the sort in Plato.

> PLA. . . . But nowe Aristippus, for as moche as longe disputation provoketh tediousenes, me semeth / if we broughte in some varietie or chaunge in the order of our communication, it shulde refresshe both our wittes.
>
> ARISTIP. What menest thou therby? Take hede that we runne not out of our matter. (52f.)

There is a certain awkwardness, for example at the outset, in having speakers who have met by chance arbitrarily assume they are in for a formal disputation ("we shall speke more therof

10. The Plato-Dionysius story is found in Diogenes Laertius's life of Plato, and this anecdote, as Elyot relates in his preface, inspired the present dialogue. Elyot may have been drawn to the story by Thomas More's reference to it in *Utopia;* see Edward Surtz, S. J., and J. H. Hexter, eds., *The Yale Edition of the Complete Works of St. Thomas More,* vol. 4 (New Haven and London, 1965), p. 86. On Aristippus of Cyrene and the hedonist school of knowledge, see Eduard Zeller, *Outlines of the History of Greek Philosophy,* trans. L. R. Palmer, 13th rev. ed. (London, 1931), pp. 112–15, and Theodore Gomperz, *Greek Thinkers. . . ,* trans. G. G. Berry (London, 1905), II, pp. 209–45. See also Diogenes Laertius's life of Aristippus, which Elyot seems not to have known; at least he appropriates nothing of the Oscar Wilde–like character preserved in this biography.

hereafter"). And when in the second dialogue Plato refers to a remark of Aristippus's as "thy fyrst division," i.e., rhetorical partition, we realize then if we have not already that they have all along been engaging in formal debate. One further example of the extensive internal critique of the form:

> PLA. Lette it not be tediouse unto the to have some thinges repeted, which thou hast spoken.
>
> Fyrst if thou remembre thy selfe, thou woldest not denie, but that wisedome was knowledge. After warde thou grauntiddest also, that Ignoraunce was none other thynge but lacke of knowlege, whiche concluded, that Ignoraunce could be no wisedome. And than dyddest thou raison / that the diversitie betwene man and beast was onely ignorance. And that Ignoraunce dyddest thou suppose to be the lacke of knowlege of them selfes / and other in the diversitie of theyr kyndes. This was very well gathered of the, in myne opinion. And the raison that folowed by the example that thou dyddeste putte of thy horse / the bee / and the spaynell [i.e., spaniel], was not unfitte to the purpose, if thou woldest have abyden well by it. But by our mery digression in to Pythagoras regenerations / thou were brought from that argument / soner than thou shuldest have ben. . . . (76–78)

Elyot includes a number of stations such as this in the dialogue, points of summary and evaluation. The seams are made to show. Plato then proceeds like an Oxford master to connect the deficiency in Aristippus's reasoning powers with the inadequacy of the Cyrenaic philosophy—with capital success, especially cumulatively:

> whiche hapned unto the / as it doeth ever to them, whiche lyke unto the / do folowe the concupiscence and pleasaunt affects of the body. For lyke as they be unstable, so the folowers and lovers of them be ever inconstant: as well in their opinions as in their actes. But if thou being sometyme the herer of Socrates as well as I was, haddest folowed directly his doctrine / accordyng as he spake it / and also practised it by his example of lyvyng / and haddest not as a truant pycked out of his argumentes suche matter as thou supposiddest mought only maynteine thy sensuall appetite / thou shuldest have perceyved what thou thy selfe haddest mente, whiche thou doest not nowe / it varieth so

moche from thy profession. And peradventure the knowledge that we nowe seke for, shuld never have comen betwene us two in question.

Plato is trying to draw him from his "wanton affections and fantasyes," confident that Aristippus will "finde [his own "professed opinion"] otherwise, or [ere] we be at an ende of our communication . . ." (94). A good consultation, by teaching, can cure a mind "nosilled in carnall affections" (111). The characteristic mark of Elyot's Plato is a humble *chivalric faith* in the power of dialogue. "I will helpe the forthe / as well as I can," he says to Aristippus (111). Elyot's language is suddenly alive with Malory's meter and rhyme yet tempered with the humble piety of an Arthurian knight. "All be it I know wel inough I shall not brynge these thinges in order sufficiently. The providence of god is so inscrutable that it can nat all be comprehended by mans imagination / not withstandynge by my demaundynge and thyne aunswerynge / I truste we shall fynde therin matter competent ynough to help us to that thing that we go about, that is to saye, to fynde oute knowledge / wherin wysedom lieth hydde."

Aristippus's crippled philosophy turns out to be a very real obstacle, the irrational blocking the rational, which forces Plato to move by slow degrees and indirection. The work of the first dialogue is to define ignorance as a kind of dark background on which to paint the image of knowledge. Were it not for Aristippus's philosophy, Plato says in the second dialogue (78f.), "peradventure the knowledge that we nowe seke for, shuld never have comen betwene us two in question. But it shulde have suffised to have told to the, what I sayde to kynge Dionise, and howe he delte with me." Such a direct approach to the known truth is not possible. Plato sees "the sedes of Socrates doctrine / which remayne in the, but they wyll not springe) in such wyse as thou mayste see them / except I do water them with my declaration" (79). Thus we have neither disinterested debate nor didactic exposition but instead the consultation between a resistant, ill-equipped philosopher and a patient, persistent one.

Their relation corresponds to that between the reader and Elyot.

The eristic tours de force of the second dialogue leave both Aristippus and the reader confused. "I doubt me what I shall say," he begs; "I can not remembre." And so Plato's point strikes home:

> It is no mervayle, thy wyttes be so involved in carnal affections, that this clene and pure doctrine canne not entre in to them without great difficultie, and whan they be ones in, they can not longe abide / thy memorie is so occupied about wanton and beastly fantasy. But yet wyl I ones agayne reherce unto the that, whiche thou haste so shortly forgotten. (85)

The method of Elyot's Plato—like the method of dialogue described in the seventh epistle of the historical Plato—calls for good will on both sides.

> Wherfore Aristip. I praye the as thou has done hitherto / here me patiently, and whan I shall demande of the any question, answere me simply without cavillation. (96)

Thus the remainder of the second dialogue and all of the third proceed in the manner of an examination-argument. "Dyd not I say?" "What meaneste thou therby?" "Diddest not thou declare?" There is also courtesy and reinforcement in Plato's interrogation. "But nowe remembre welle what thou haste spoken." "I can the thanke, thou art nowe of a good remembrance." "Ergo we be agreed . . ." (105–9). The reason for Plato's care in laying this groundwork becomes apparent in the fourth dialogue. It is of prime importance that the memory be trained, for this function holds knowledge present before the conscious mind. He urges the striving soul to "put Wyll in to the prison of Drede / under the streyte custodie of Remembraunce and Rayson" (130). This task Elyot set himself.

The effect of Plato's single-minded chastening by patient criticism is a noticeable cure. Mutual good will and a certain skill at dialectic are reconstructing the castle of health. "Well, though there were some debate betwene us in Sicile," Aristippus murmurs in his first speech, "yet wyll I salute him / and desire him to shew to me the state of all his affaires." And with a free familiarity permitted between old acquaintances Plato can begin with the plain remark: "But now wyll I recite the my storie." Under this therapy Aristippus begins to improve in the second dialogue.

Lo, see, howe by our longe communing thou art drawen from thy wanton affections and fantasyes / whereby the sparkis of wysedome, that thou gatist of Socrates lessons / lyke as fyre hydde under askes and deed cooles, whan they be removed is found sindrynge in lytel imbres: so thyn affections beinge withdrawen wysedom doth begyn to glyter and shew / whiche if it wold abide kendlyng, and not like unto imbres remove and fle awai with everi puffe of winde, I doubte not but for the sharpnes of thy wit, of all Socrates scolers thou shuldist be at the last one of the most wisest and excellent. (93f.)

One may count this encouragement merely as an expression of Plato's optimism. It appears nonetheless that Aristippus does improve—in his power of memory. His speeches lengthen, but although his reasoning is better than at the outset, it is still imperfect, requiring as in the foregoing speech Plato's reinforced care as the third dialogue draws to a close.

The fourth dialogue discovers memory as the medium of the knowledge which makes a wise man. Repetition, first of all, receives strong praise, even from Aristippus. "I thanke the hartly Plato for this repetition: wherby thou haste well revived my remembrance" (122). Plato responds with what anyone familiar with *The Governor* will recognize as a credo in the pedagogic benefits of repetition.

I knowe well inoughe Aristippus, that in matter of great importaunce / to men that be sensuall, havinge their myndes ingrossed with carnall affections, there is required a plaine and sensible forme of raisoning, broken nowe and than with often repetitions: which all though to froward herers it seemeth to make the matter tediouse, yet if they can abide it / they shal therby retain some sedes of knowledge . . . .

Aristippus's reply is pure balm; he becomes the perfect student:

Go to now Plato I have al my hole mynde setlyd and prepared to here the, and I shall not wyllyngly let one worde that passeth from thy mouthe / eskape me.

This luxurious sublimation of Elyot's, while it out-Glaucons Glaucon, has also a judicious thematic function; for it is essential to the revelation of the knowledge which makes a wise man that Aristippus be drawn from his pernicious and irrational position. The sensationalist is locked perforce in a present existence, while the Socratic philosopher, or simply *the man who remembers,* has access to a fuller and, it is argued, a truer world. Thus Plato reasons that in a man such as Aristippus, "his affections deceyved by his sences do falsely perswade hym" (125). Remembrance becomes a virtue, forgetfulness a peril (127).

What is to be remembered? Man, particularly a man such as Aristippus, should remember that he is "mortall and passible [i.e., transitory] and no god / but the ymage of god by understandynge" (130). This is at once a deflating and an enlivening truth. Full of metaphoric power here, the admonitory Elyot achieves a moralist's eloquence.

In the grene banke lyeth the serpente hidde / redy with his trembling tunge to stryke mortally them whiche doo approche hym. The scorpion wounden in the grene grasse / lyeth watching with his forked tail in a redynes to styng them / which loke not down to their fete. The bodi infected or wounded, findeth in pain and anguishe his owne propre ignoraunce / in that / that he so moche estemed dilectation and plesure / which in so short a momente vanysshed awaye. Also sens a lyttel herbe / whiche is inanimate, maye chaunge pleasure in to peyne / and helthe into syckenes / or a lyttel vile worme at one stroke may bireve hym of all dilectation and pleasure, and fylle hym with so moche anguysshe and dolour, that the life / whiche he desyred ever to continue, becommeth to hym tedious and lothesome / he shall therby not onely remembre / that he is passible / and therefore no god, but also perceyve and consyder of how lyttell importance or valour is than his strength / auctoritie / or puissance, were he never so myghty a champion or so puisant a kynge or Emperour. (127f.)

The sturdy exhortation, savoring of the controversial religious writing of Elyot's age and reminiscent of the preoccupation with authority which burdens Elyot's letters and prologues, remains essentially Platonic.[11] For if a man remembers that he is indeed "the ymage of god by understandynge," that is, by virtue of his rational faculties, then he need not fall headlong into the bottomless pit of ignorance, provided "the soule have understanding alway at her elbowe, whiche shall bydde raison correcte Wylle . . ." (126, 130f.).

The long admonition just quoted exemplifies the double perspective through which Elyot often directs his reader's vision. The topic of life's brevity looks back to medieval Christian writers and as a justification of philosophy leads us to Seneca. But it also figured commonly in contemporary religious polemics. In Elyot's dialogue the remembrance of mortality evokes in the present not only a specific Christian feeling but also a pagan thought (in the *Phaedo* and reiterated by Boethius in the *Consolation*) that all knowledge is remembered knowledge. In creating Christian piety in his Plato Elyot exercises the *binocular vision* which is fundamental to humanist mediation. In the moral realm such dual, or multiple, perspectives supplement rather than contradict each other, and from this fusion comes a new sense of solidity.[12]

Stretching the thews of reason generates new energy in the fourth dialogue. We hear the voice of the schoolmaster.

> How sayst thou, Aristippus? doest thou beare away and perceyve what I have al this whyle spoken? Ye that I do Plato, all thoughe hit be mervayllous. . . . (131)

For the first time Aristippus questions Plato sincerely rather than automatically defending himself. He wonders at the necessity of all men's "kepynge Wyll (as I moughte use thy words) within the precinct prescribed to hir by understandying . . ."

11. Cf. *Letters*, pp. xvii and xxviii.

12. I interpolate the term "binocular vision" and borrow other words from the interesting essay on Cervantes by Joseph Wood Krutch in his *Five Masters: A Study in the Mutations of the Novel* (New York, 1930). "Sancho Panza and Don Quixote are the names of the two eyes through which he looked forth" (pp. 99f.).

(133). Having been encouraged to advance a *responsio,* he is learning to speak Plato's language.

Even while attacking the irrationality of an old hedonist, Plato demonstrates care for this body-centered man in offering comfort for human adversity. The idea the "siknesse, adversitie, and dethe if they happen to a good man be good"[13] requires some dilation, but Plato is anxious to avoid the machinery of academic method. "I wyll sette out a more plaine profe in applieng my raysons to the examples and similitudes / which I have alredy induced" (171f.). The carnally engrossed mind especially needs a plain and sensible form of reasoning. There is no need to review Plato's meditation on this subject; perhaps its most striking characteristic is the delicacy with which Plato's comfortable words are allegorically infused with Christian consolation. It is God's love which empowers us to endure all the "littell incommodities / incident to mortalitie," or rather God's love in conjunction with man's rational nature, which is the image of God.

> . . . who so ever . . . hereafter beinge brought where he shal prove his strength agaynst puissaunte and mighty adversaries / that is to say anguisshe and peine / sharpe and perillouse sickenes / cruel adversitie in any thing that fortune semeth to rule / losse of children / frendes / or favour of princis / prisonment / or exile / and like other tourmentes / and vexations of body and mynde: if he valiantli do resist and with fortitude whiche is the strengthe of the mind, do subdue and vanquisshe those adversaries, he shall have the rewarde that belongeth to good men / . . . that incomparable price, which is promysed to them that shall be so happy to gette the victorye. . . . (173–75)

As Plato continues, we observe a gradual and highly significant modulation in style. In applying consolation he is drawn, as Elyot was to be drawn finally and irresistibly in the *Dictionary* and other late writings, to aphorism.

> Adversitie is not so grevous, bycause it is oute of the body, and nothynge compelleth us to suffre but our own wylles. . . . Thou recey-

13. The theme of the *Tusculan Disputations* to which Elyot also alludes in a Latin epistle to Cromwell (*Letters,* p. 34). Like the Tusculan dialogues, Elyot's are divided into five parts.

veste of thy father this comfort, that no man lyveth so poorely in the worlde as he came into hit. And he hathe nede of a lyttell that measureth aboundance by natures necessitie / and not by superfluitie of ambicious desyre. Grefe shall dissolve or elles be dissolved. Fortune hath not so sharpe a weapon that it may byte on the soule. (178–80)

Something has happened—the dialoguing impulse has broken down. In Elyot's letters and prefaces this kind of narrowing or heated focusing is always a sign of intense personal feeling. As the long speech proceeds, Plato directs comfort not so much to Aristippus as to himself. Plato indeed is the fallen man, an ancient mariner. Thomas Elyot had just sailed home in humiliation from his unsuccessful embassy to the emperor's court. "Fortune hathe taken frome the that, whiche she had lent to the," says Plato; ". . . those be veri goodes that be within us gyven by raison. For they be sure and durynge / nor can not decaye or minisshe for any occasion. They that be without us / lent onely by fortune they be good by opinion onely" (183f.). It is the exile in rags who declares to Aristippus:

Stonde boldly agayne sickenes and fortune, the one is natural, the other is casualle / In the fyrste is necessitie / whiche wylle thou or not, thou muste suffre: If thou doest hit wyllyngely, thou knoweste the price / If thou addest to angre / thou doubleste thy peyne. In the second is no necessitie, for thou moughteste alwaye refuse hit, as welle whanne it was prosperous, knowynge it to be unstable / and burdaynous / as also whanne hit is adverse or contrarious, consyderynge that hit was never soo moche thyne owne / that thou haddeste any ryghte to reteyne hit: sens it was ordeyned for other as well as for the. And Fortune whiche is the disposer therof / never made bargayne with the / that thou shuldeste stylle kepe hit: And if she dydde / brynge forthe thy recordes. She lackethe not wytnesses innumerable to prove that she hathe bene ever inconstant. Defye hir malyce: for whanne she hathe doone hir warste, yet shalte thou have more than thou broughteste with the. (186f.)

Plato's monologue against tribulation provides a kind of self-recovery for him, and for Elyot.[14] If in the fourth dialogue Plato

14. Cf. Elyot's letter to Cromwell (*Letters,* pp. 22–24) which may have accompanied a presentation copy of the dialogue.

has introduced comfortable knowledge, he has also planted in Aristippus the seeds of conversion to reason. The fifth dialogue will be undertaken in the two miles left to ride. Although much remains to be settled, Aristippus confesses at the conclusion of the fourth, "In dede thou haste almost made me chaunge myne olde opinion."

III

The temporary breakdown of dialogue is now rigorously corrected. As the fifth dialogue begins, Plato reviews the ground of "our disputation" and requires Aristippus and us to reexamine the whole argument. The reassertion of the dialogue form coincides with a recapitulation of the elements of knowledge so far ascertained. Plato and Aristippus are now in phase; they work swiftly, wasting no arguments. In the course of their previous dialogues it was shown that knowledge of the goodness and providence of God is essential to wisdom. Now Plato declares:

> knowledge is secrete and bryngeth forth no frute but by operation. . . . Than if I were a wise man / it ought to be declared by operation. . . . Wherefore all though wisedome be knowledge, yet by knowledge onely none may be called a wise man, but operation of that whiche is in knowledge called wysedome / expressynge the wysedome, maketh the user or exercisar therof to be justly named a wyse man. (195–97)

Plato summarizes in "a short epilogation" the steps in his reasoning which have brought them to this stage, then devotes the remainder of the dialogue to clarifying his conception of wisdom.

When we first met on the road, Plato now reminds Aristippus, "thou beheldest me in this pore astate and apparaylle, the occasion wherof I declared to the in the forme of a story. . ." (192). The crux of this story, which intrigued Elyot in reading Diogenes Laertius, was Plato's reply to Dionysius that his words savored of tyranny, for which he was sold as a slave and narrowly escaped death. This example, Plato's own experience, now emerges as the embodiment of wisdom; for in replying to Dionysius Plato joined knowledge and operation.

This act is most striking in its symbolic meaning. It provokes in the reader a growing awareness of correlations. The reader may recall that the exchange in Sicily was itself a dialogue. In response to Dionysius's command to delineate the state of a king, Plato "set out and expressed"

> suche a man, in whom the soule had intiere and ful auctorite over the sensis, and alway kept the affectis in due rule and obedience, folowyng only the counsayle of Understanding, and by that governaunce was moste like unto god. (206)

By contrast he described a tyrant, "whose soule rulith not. . . and by that transformation, she loseth also Understandynge. . . ." These words, said Dionysius, were idle and foolish, whence followed Plato's reply that Dionysius's speech savored of tyranny. That dialogue, Plato now gives Aristippus to understand, expressed the knowledge which is wisdom. For that reply, which cost him so dearly, represented the operation of knowledge: the act of speaking truth. The present dialogue thus concerns a dialogue. At one remove, in the dialogue with Aristippus, Plato explicates his own speech, reenacts his earlier operation. The present dialectical operation contrasts consecutively knowledge and ignorance, soul and body, king and tyrant, *each pair standing in ratio to each.* It becomes apparent that the five dialogues of *Knowledge* comprise a new apology by Plato.

Elyot's *Knowledge* is not merely an exegesis of the anecdote from the *Life of Plato* but a reconsideration of a broad vein in Platonic thought. To establish a relation between knowledge and wisdom in the state, and to do so by means of good counsel, is a fundamental concern in the *Republic.*[15] The problem of creat-

15. See, e.g., Book IV, 428. For a concise discussion of Plato's conception of wisdom, see Robert E. Cushman, *Therapeia: Plato's Conception of Philosophy* (Chapel Hill, 1958), pp. 187–295. The masterwork on this subject is F. M. Cornford, *Plato's Theory of Knowledge* (London, 1935). The idea that wisdom is an acquirable human virtue is studied in relation to Elyot's dialogue of *Knowledge* by Eugene F. Rice, Jr., *The Renaissance Idea of Wisdom* (Cambridge, Mass., 1958), pp. 85–89.

ing a world in which wisdom and the wise have authority is central both in the *Republic* and the *Laws*. The problem holds special interest for Elyot, and his writings take it up again and again. The very title of his dialogue seems to be taken from a speech by Socrates in the fourth book (429A) of the *Republic*. It is not surprising that the knowledge which makes a wise man has affinities with the wisdom of Plato's guardian.[16] The guardian is a governor, and he is engaged in the practice or operation of ruling. For him, exactly as for Elyot's governor, knowledge—of essence and existence—is the precondition for virtue. The nature of his wisdom is necessarily both cognitive and ethical. In the dialogue of *Knowledge* Elyot gives us an example of a wise man practising knowledge. Elyot wanted, one might say, to try it out, in several senses to "imitate" Plato. He conveys his belief, through a plain, English Plato, that the ideal of the wise man of the *Republic* is at least approximable.

The aims of Elyot's dialogue also reflect his conception of the aims of education. Primary among these is the ideal of *familiar learning*. Elyot takes wonderful pains to reduce to a minimum the historical apparatus surrounding the anecdote; it seems unnecessary to know precisely where or when the dialogue occurs. The emphasis in this "Introduction to Plato" falls on those aspects of Plato's thought which are accessible to and assimilable by a sixteenth-century student. Elyot's ideal of familiar learning is related to Plato through the analogy (in the *Sophist*, 227–29) between ignorance and disease or deformity. Ignorance, says the Stranger, like disease must be purified. The solicitude with which Elyot attends to the ignorant mind resembles the physician's care for the sick. The pedagogical ideal—celebrated in *The Governor* and sought in the dialogue of *Knowledge*—is to give the student the experience of antiquity and its authorities. Moreover, just as Elyot establishes in *The Governor* that sapience is the ultimate authority, so in the dialogue he attempts to delineate the most authoritative form of sapience. Elyot himself wanted to experience the Plato-Dionysius story as personally as

16. The connection is controversial; see John M. Major, *Sir Thomas Elyot and Renaissance Humanism* (Lincoln, Nebraska, 1964), p. 194 n. 48.

possible and thereby "ratify" and "consolidate" the conception of knowledge which it signified to him.

Elyot's dialogue originates in a complex of personal desires and aesthetic, imaginative goals. If he idealized familiar learning as a gift to his readers, he also idealized its value for himself. In this "dialogue of the dead," this revivified scene from antiquity, Elyot could make Plato his own Plato. Elyot understood this special use of imitation—it allowed him to possess the authority. The same notion prevailed in contemporary theory regarding the teaching of Latin and Greek grammar and rhetoric: the student learns by imitating. Such a theory implies that what the student ultimately imitates, and by imitating possesses, is the wisdom and authority of the ancients. True Ciceronianism, as Erasmus argues, is mastery of the spirit, not the style, of Cicero.[17]

Thus Elyot's desire to grasp Plato is more urgent than has been hitherto realized. Once we have perceived this in his other books and letters, the private interiors of the dialogue of *Knowledge* begin to unfold. His ability to make a little room an everywhere, to live in history mentally, has already been noted. The absorbing intensity of this gift is perhaps what set him apart from others, what made him seem at times—as in Holbein's portrait—*ailleurs.* But beyond his historical penetration and his attraction to the inner life of the mind Elyot was fascinated by the story of Plato and Aristippus for more particularly personal reasons.

Knowledge vividly exemplifies Tasso's definition of dialogue as the imitation of reasoning. In his conviction, adduced from the old anecdote, that wisdom is the operation or action of knowledge, Elyot sought a representational form in which *l'azione è quasi giunta de' ragionamenti,* a dialogue, that is, in which the action is joined to reasoning. The attempt to represent reason in action was an imaginative, artistic venture. Just as Tasso recognized that the good dialogist occupies a position between the dialectician and the poet, so Elyot understood that even perfect

17. See Bulephorus's last long speech in the *Ciceronianus.*

logic may require the art of rhetoric to persuade. Elyot's use of the metaphor of painting as a way of talking about the dialogue form strikes us as natural and appropriate. In the first dialogue (67) Plato begins by defining ignorance as a dark background against which to contrast knowledge—as Aristippus says, "a good grounde on thy table to set out thyne ymage." Socrates' conception of thought as the mind's dialogue with itself is perhaps the source of this conception of dialogue as an explicit *image* of reason.

The image of reason, the imitation of reasoning, is created out of a subjective state which Elyot is willing to probe. In the dialogue of *Knowledge* he debates with himself whether wisdom can ever be proved. Behind the debate lie the longing for recognition and authority and the green memory of ambassadorial recall. The philosophical problem, because it involves ideals, is a personal one—and this fact too affects the form. For it is the nature of a philosophical problem that it has no real empirical or factual solution; it is not solved, but rather, once the confusion (usually verbal) which it causes is disentangled, it "dissolves."[18] Precisely this result is achieved in Elyot's dialogue once Plato rationalizes his behavior and obtains agreement from Aristippus. We shall return to Elyot's desire to eliminate verbal confusion.

Here it should be observed that dialogue is always a problem-dissolving form. While it is possible to regard all artistic creation as sublimation providing a kind of relief or dissolution, the dialogue form is doubly equipped in that, as dialectic, its ostensible purpose is the resolution of a philosophical problem, while simultaneously as an imitation of a human action, i.e., reasoning,

18. See Alice Ambrose, "Philosophy, Language, and Illusion," in *Psychoanalysis and Philosophy*, ed. Charles Hanly and Morris Lazerowitz (New York, 1970), p. 17: "The extremely unorthodox conception of a philosophical problem as one not requiring solution but, to use Wittgenstein's word, dissolution, a problem which, like a neurotic symptom, is dissolved by insight into what produces it, can only be appreciated if seen in historical perspective." This study correlates (1) the elimination of a pathological entanglement with words through insight into the linguistic structure of a philosophical problem with (2) the cure of neurotic symptoms through insight into their determinants. Grief, says Elyot, "shall dissolve or elles be dissolved" (*Knowledge*, p. 180).

dialogue seeks the revelation of knowledge and catharsis. However, while it is true that in the dialogue of *Knowledge* Elyot seeks to solve a philosophical problem which itself is laden with personal meanings, the latter never obscure his social interest. "Not onely we two shulde agree in our opinions and forme of living," Plato says to Aristippus (31f.),

> For all men that knowe us bothe by the unitie of oure doctrine shulde be brought to insue [i.e., pursue] one conformitie of lyvinge, or at the leste convayte to followe it / wherin shuld be a perfecte harmony. The hole quiar synging in one tune.

Thus Elyot brings to the dialogue conflicts to be balanced—authority with experience, knowledge with action—recognizing in these conflicts a public, universal applicability. By the time the reader reaches the fifth dialogue, a pattern of analogues has been created: soul, king, and knowledge of wisdom interact with body, tyrant, and ignorance. These Elyot must disentangle. Plato comes to speak of the wisdom of the king and the understanding of the soul as contrasted with the ignorance of the tyrant and the tyranny of the senses. Once the problem and its components are defined, Aristippus, at last understanding, is ready to assent. Plato's definitions *are* his rationale.

Let us recall the definition of a king, on which so much depends. Plato reiterates for Aristippus the description of a king which he made to Dionysius (206):

> . . . such a man, in whom the soule had intiere and ful auctorite over the sensis, and alway kept the affectis in due rule and obedience, folowyng only the counsayle of Understanding, and by that governaunce was moste like unto god. This man I called a kyng / although he had no more in his possession than had Crates the Theban.

Aristippus grasps the truth that in speaking these words to Dionysius Plato put his knowledge in operation. "For me semeth that thy description of a kynge was wonderful true and necessarye," he says, "and also therin was the knowledge wherof thou haste treated compendiously / and playnely declared" (223). And Plato concurs (227):

> . . . my description of a kynge by his definition / and also by comparyng

hym to his contrarye [the ignorant tyrant] / conteyned that knowledge, wherin is wysedome. . . .

In the course of the dialogue analogues cross and recross. The king whom Plato defines is a man—any man, even the poorest—who has achieved a balance in his own dualistic nature, a consensus with himself, which is analogous to the harmonious sense of formal closure we feel in the final speeches of the dialogue.

Plato concludes that "this kynge by that knowledge that he hath of hym self, he also knoweth other men" (207). Elyot had previously considered the far-reaching implications of this idea in Book III, Chapter 3, of *The Governor,* entitled *"The thre noble counsayles of reason, societie, and knowledge."* In the dialogue of *Knowledge* he returns to *nosce te ipsum* with a deeper conviction. The conclusion he reaches, through a form involving two reasoners, is that the primary object of knowledge is the self, or in his idiom (229 and 226): "the very man which is the soule . . . by whose operation I was called a wyse man." *Nosce te ipsum* is itself a reflexive dualism whose conflict and eventual harmony Elyot here represents in dialogue.

The dialogue between Plato and Dionysius was, as noted above, a form of counsel. "And for that benefite soo soone offred," Plato asks (225), "was I not worthy a great gramercy?"[19] "Yes if he wold have so taken it," replies Aristippus, who later affirms that "by thy counsaile [thou] shuldist have ben to hym so royall a tresure. . . ."[20] Plato's desire for recognition completes the pattern of the dialogue whose conflicts are analogues of the author's own. We discover in this pattern a two-way meaning;

19. Aristippus's sentiment "That kindenesse or benefite that is most prompt or sonist employed, is to be chieffely estemed" (224) crops up more forcefully in the quotation from Seneca with which Elyot begins the preface to the 1539 octavo edition of *The Castle of Health* addressed to Cromwell: "HE GIVETH twise that gyveth quyckly . . ." (*Letters,* p. 55).

20. P. 231. Note the same coda in the final paragraph of Elyot's translation, *The Doctrinal of Princes* (*STC* 14277), where Isocrates admonishes Nicocles that a good counselor "is of all other treasure the most roiall and profitable. . . ." See *Letters,* pp. xiv–xv.

not that the speakers say one thing and mean another, but that what they pronounce publicly may have an interior meaning for the author. Elyot, a man of subtle play, can convey allegorical meanings, as in the much disputed passages which suggest that Dionysius and Plato correspond to Henry VIII and Thomas More, without needing to sharpen his meanings beyond suggestion. There are few more successful Socratic ironies than the maddening doubt Elyot sows whether he intends a political allegory. Every writer plays innumerable private games. But it is distinctive of Elyot's dialogue that the private and public analogues are so exquisitely balanced. To take another example, Elyot's personal desire for doctrine and authority coincides with the necessity, according to Plato's argument, that the ruler be wise and authoritative. Moreover, Elyot's relation to his work exemplifies the Platonic belief that what is necessary for the individual, i.e., the union of knowledge and virtue, is necessary for society, the *polis.* The historical Plato declared (*Epis.* 7, 355D) that this correspondence *should* have existed between Dionysius and his own kingdom:

> He possessed great power, and if in his empire philosophy and political power had really been united in the same man, its glory would have shone forth among all men, Greek and barbarian, and would in itself have brought home to them the true belief, namely, that neither city nor individual can attain happiness except through a life wisely conducted under the rule of justice. . . .

Elyot's Plato imagines "the hole quiar synging in one tune."

The publication date of the dialogue of *Knowledge,* 1533, provides one further indication that the Plato-Dionysius story and the dialogue it engendered represent a version of Elyot. For according to the preface to *The Image of Governance* (1541), Elyot composed that work, a life of the emperor Alexander Severus, in 1532 ("about .ix. yeres passed"), i.e., just after the publication of *The Governor.* However, instead of printing *The Image of Governance* forthwith as a sequel to *The Governor,* Elyot, heeding Horace, kept his manuscript nine years, and chose to present an alternative image, *Of the Knowledge Which Maketh a Wise Man.* The dialogue was for a variety of reasons a truer sequel. It undertook to resolve many of the philosophical problems left by *The Governor.* It satisfied in its method a number of Elyot's pedagogical aims. Its form imaged forth under the rein of reason many of Elyot's personal dilemmas, which had been or could be but dimly adumbrated in *The Governor* or the life of Alexander Severus. And not least important, unlike *The Image of Governance* the dialogue subordinated the image of the ideal king to a portrait of the model counselor. If, as I suspect, Elyot considered his dialogue a fit extension to *The Governor,* it was not until he was finally confident of his role as a scholar-statesman, eight years later, that he chose to print his *Image* of the model king for all the nobility of England.

Elyot could look upon *Knowledge* as a sequel to *The Governor* with a measure of satisfaction. He wrote to Cromwell that not only might it be "profitable to theim which will reade or heere it" but also that it had provided "comfort of my self."[21] Having written the dialogue, he seems to have felt the sense of an ending, of having had his say.[22] And yet this sense of dissolution and assent was but temporary and provisional. "Wel Plato in such experience of wysdome I wyl not folow the," says Aristippus. The closing speeches remain open.

PLA. Grammercy Aristippus for thy gentylle audience: nowe be we come to the towne / and have made a good ende bothe of our journaye and also of oure communication.

AR. Farewell Plato, and for my parte I wolde not have lacked it for the horse that I ryde on. And to say the truth it hath made me to change some what of myn olde opinion.

21. *Letters,* p. 22.

22. It is possible that Elyot was referring to the dialogue of *Knowledge* when he wrote to Cromwell: ". . . this is the last Englissh booke which I purpose ever to make, onelass the desyre of some speciall frende do compelle me" (*Letters,* p. 23). In a sense Elyot's remark proved true; for of the books following the dialogue *The Castle of Health* might be excluded as a florilegium, the *Dictionary* as only partly English, *The Image of Governance* as a translation, and *The Defence of Good Women* and *A Preservative against Death* as works written for special friends.

PLA. The nexte tyme that we mete I wyl make the to change all / if thou wylt here and abide rayson.

Even when we have noted the conventions of modest conclusions and scholarly restraint, we must admit that the dialogue falls short of the satisfaction of a total conversion. The form, as we know from reading Plato's peirastic dialogues and Cicero's, accepted the inaccessibility of certainty. In the dialogue of *Knowledge* Elyot experienced the limits of dialectic so far as he was able. In his subsequent writings he is driven increasingly by the desire to define knowledge with certainty. The speculations of dialogue give place to more static forms.

In the preface to *The Image of Governance*—a companion, in a sense we have just seen, to the dialogue of *Knowledge*—Elyot reflects on the broad question of the stature of learning.

Moreover many being ignorant of good letters, do universally reprove all them that be studiouse in lerninge, alleginge this commune proverbe, The grettest clarkes be not the wisest men: affirming, that they be founden negligent about their own profit, and consequently unapt to the ministration of thinges of waighty importance. How untrue their allegations be, and on how feble a foundation they are buylded, it shall in this wise appere unto wise men. First the sayd proverb semeth by him which lacked lerninge, to be devised, sens that he preferrith ignorance before kunninge: whiche arrogance declared hym to be a very foole, and unwitty: consideringe that by knowledge most chiefly, a man excelleth all other mortall creatures, and therby is moste like unto god.

In a tone remarkable for its restraint Elyot, his *Dictionary* now in the revising stage, is prepared to offer his definition of learning, a definition which in fact governed his entire career:

And lerninge is none other thinge, but an aggregation of many mens sentences and actes to the augmentation of knowledge.

All of Elyot's writings are gatherings from other writers; they are translations, collections, compendiums, dictionaries—all except the dialogues. *Of the Knowledge Which Maketh a Wise Man* and *Pasquil the Plain* were his nearest approximations to a fictional form. Perhaps the experience they provide, somewhere between the discursive and the aesthetic, expresses the way Elyot was perceiving the process of his life. In any case, the dialogues stand by virtue of their subject within the main current of his writing: the definition of knowledge. "Suppose not them to be wise men, that sharpely can talke of small thinges and trifles," says Isocrates in the *Doctrinal* (sig. B6^{v}), "but those that can substancially reason in matters of weighty importance." Such perhaps is the moral of the dialogue of *Knowledge.* It was only in the *Dictionary* that Elyot could devote himself purely to tending the definer's fire; and in that task he defined a life which had so long seemed incapable of definition. There the need to eliminate verbal confusion could be met head-on. It was a book on the meanings of words, the act of a scholar in retirement, and, above all, itself an authority.

All of Elyot's work circles back upon *The Governor* and its dictum that "the ende of all doctrine and studie is good counsayle. . . ." A speech by Isocrates prefigures the career of *The Governor*'s author:

> . . .they that labour in the studie of P[h]ilosophy, concernyng the exercise of myndes, be of sondriė opinions, some saiying that men become wiser by muche disputyng and reasonyng, other affirme that it hapneth by exercise in polityke governance, or civill causes, divers suppose it to come of other doctrines: but finally thei all doe confesse, that he whiche is well brought up, may by every of the saide studies gather mater sufficient to geve good counsaile.[23]

Isocrates included among the "actes" of the governor "knowlageyng and myndyng." Nearly a decade later, in his own person, in the preface to *The Image of Governance* Elyot continued to refine his definition.

> lerning is the augmentation of knowlege which the more that it is, the more maye be perceived what shalbe most necessary in thinges which happe in consultation. And the more that it is perceyved, the better and more aptly may it be ministred and executed.

23. *Doctrinal,* sig. C1^{v}.
24. *Doctrinal:* Elyot's "Addicion, to fill up vacant pages," sig. C4.

His Platonic dialogue was an experiment in knowledging and minding: actions of "wisedome, that bringeth all good thynges with it, [which] Salomon praied for, that she shulde alwaie bee assistent to his Throne, as a moste faithfull and trusty counsailour."[24]

5

Roger Ascham: Ciceronian Archery

I

Roger Ascham's dialogue *Toxophilus* is a book made of books. Ascham himself indicated the importance of classical sources to his "schole of shootinge" by providing an apparatus of marginal references in *Toxophilus*.[1] In its substance his dialogue of expert knowledge envisioned the old learning, drawing upon its forms in a new imaginative style. It is remarkable that for his use and conception of classical learning Ascham always had a model. He admired the great teachers Cheke and Sturm,[2]

1. First ed.: London, 1545 (*STC* 837). Lawrence V. Ryan, in *Roger Ascham* (Stanford and London, 1963; cited hereafter as "Ryan"), provides a bibliographical summary for this book (p. 49) and devotes considerable space to its analogues and progeny. The standard Ascham bibliography is Samuel A. and Dorothy R. Tannenbaum, *Roger Ascham: A Concise Bibliography*, Elizabethan Bibliographies, no. 34 (New York, 1946). I use William Aldis Wright's one-volume edition of the *English Works of Roger Ascham* (1904; repr. Cambridge, England, 1970) for all quotations (noting page numbers only) from *Toxophilus, A Report of the Affaires and State of Germany* and *The Scholemaster.* Abbreviations have been silently expanded, and modern typographical conventions adopted in respect to the use of *i/j, u/v,* and long *s.*

2. Ascham corresponded for nearly twenty years with the classical scholar and teacher of Strassburg, Johann Sturm, whom he never met. Ascham's corre-

and his writing abounds in judgments and appreciations of other classical scholars of his time. But his model for his relation to the literary past was Cicero. Not Cicero the master orator but Cicero the student of the ancient Greeks. "If truly I should desire to become another Cicero," he wrote in his last letter to Sturm, "(and indeed that is hardly a sinful thought), whom sooner should I summon to myself for counsel in becoming and in the planning to become than Cicero himself?"[3] For Cicero had perfect propriety in Latin but his speech was born in Greece, that is, in the study of Greek. Greek was to Cicero writing Latin as Latin was to Ascham writing English.

The triumph of Cicero in Ascham's mind and work does not mean a preference for Roman over Greek oratory or thought but means rather that Ascham was overwhelmingly committed to the ideal of Cicero's own assimilation and transformation of Greek culture as well as to the humanistic ideal of relating Greek to Roman culture. His dialogue, like all his writing, displays his continual effort to imitate Cicero by using the past in this way. Ascham tended, however, to veer away from the Continental humanists' practice of Latin imitation, preferring instead the uncharted goal of vernacular eloquence. In this he followed More and Elyot, though it seems he had a more scholarly sense of the sort of standard of vernacular style that might be achieved than they. If he departed in this respect from the Continental

---

spondence, in Latin, is collected by J. A. Giles, ed., in *The Whole Works of Roger Ascham*, 3 vols. in 4 (London, 1864–65), and translated into English by Maurice A. Hatch, "The Ascham Letters: An Annotated Translation of the Latin Correspondence Contained in the Giles Edition of Ascham's Works," Ph.D. dissertation, Cornell University, 1948; cited hereafter as "Giles" and "Hatch."

3. December 1568. Hatch, p. 879. Giles, II, 181: "Si vero optarem ipse fieri alter CICERO, (et optare quidem nefas non est,) ut fierem, et qua ratione fierem, quem potius ad consilium mihi adhiberem, quam ipsum CICERONEM?" Two useful discussions of Ascham's Ciceronianism are Alvin Vos, "The Formation of Roger Ascham's Prose Style," *Studies in Philology*, 61 (1974), 344–70, and Marion Trousdale, "Recurrence and Renaissance: Rhetorical Imitation in Ascham and Sturm," *English Literary Renaissance*, 6 (1976), 156–79.

humanists (and his friends among them would have been mostly unable to appreciate his vernacular writing), his *Scholemaster* contributed nevertheless to classical studies. In *Toxophilus*, as Ascham's eighteenth-century biographer remarks, "He designed. . .to give an example of diction more natural and more truly *English* than was used by the common writers of that age. . . ."[4]

It has been said that *Toxophilus* often seems to be not so much a treatise on shooting as a treatise on learning any skill or body of knowledge.[5] This is the thrust of Toxophilus's instruction of Philologus. To the latter's declaration, "If you can teache me so well to handle these instrumentes as you have described them, I suppose I shalbe an archer good ynough," the former responds with the characteristically generalized "To learne any thing . . . ," (p. 97) before proceeding with specific details. If, however, the reader places himself in the position of Toxophilus, learning from Philologus, the orientation of the entire dialogue is recast. In the field of rhetoric it is the bow-lover who is the amateur. Reading in this new light, we discover an important difference in the values of the two young men. Throughout Part A, when the skillful Toxophilus repeatedly insists on *excellence* in shooting, the rhetorician Philologus seeks the knowledge of *perfection* in shooting. Part A ends with a dispute on this point. Toxophilus has maintained that the end of shooting is hitting the mark. But, Philologus argues, there is a perfect end, unattainable perhaps, for which one must strive. "I wyll tell you," he says, "every crafte and science standeth in two thynges: in Knowing of his crafte, and Working of his crafte: For perfyte knowlege bringeth a man to perfyte workyng" (p. 66). When Toxophilus continues to balk at the "folie" of teaching a man to strive for the unattainable, Philologus recurs to his own discipline:

4. "Life of Roger Ascham" [attributed to Samuel Johnson], in *The English Works of Roger Ascham*, ed. James Bennet (London, 1761), p. vi.

5. See the suggestive essay by Thomas M. Greene, "Roger Ascham: The Perfect End of Shooting," *ELH*, 36 (1969), 609–25.

But where as you thynke that it were fondnesse to teache a man to shoote, in lokying at the most perfitnesse in it, but rather woulde have a manne go some other way to worke, I trust no wyse man wyl discommend that way, except he thincke himselfe wyser than Tullye, whiche doeth playnlye saye, that yf he teached any maner of crafte as he dyd Rhetorike he would labor to bringe a man to knowlege of the moost perfitnesse of it, whyche knowlege should ever more leade and gyde a manne to do that thynge well whiche he went aboute. Whych waye in al maner of learnyng to be best, Plato dothe also declare in Euthydemus, of whome Tullie learned it as he dyd many other thynges mo. (p. 67)

Philologus is insisting that they portray the perfect shooter just as Cicero had attempted to portray the perfect orator.[6] It is not enough merely to "look on them which shoot best"; for, says Philologus, in an effort to synthesize their values, "in every crafte, there is a perfite excellencie, which may be better knowen in a mannes mynde, then folowed in a mannes dede" (pp. 63 and 66).

Once Part B is under way Philologus's analogy between shooting and eloquence acquires full currency. In contrast with Elyot's struggling interlocutors in the dialogue *Of the Knowledge Which Maketh a Wise Man*, Ascham's appear not only to accept each other's ideas but actually to adopt and use them. Toxophilus, nodding to Philologus in the parentheses, applies his fellow's analogy to his own exposition of the types and handling of arrows.

Now howe big, how small, how hevye, how lyght, how longe, how short, a shafte shoulde be particularlye for everye man (seynge we must taulke of the generall nature of shootyng) can not be toulde no more than you Rhethoricians can appoynt any one kynde of wordes, of sentences, of fygures fyt for every matter, but even as the man and the matter requyreth so the fyttest to be used. (pp. 84f.)

The rhetorician, like the shooter, aims at balanced restraint; Toxophilus turns the analogy toward his own reflections on the nature of all skill:

6. A description of the ideal model of perfect eloquence is sought in the *Orator* (2, 7–8), *De Optimo Genere Oratorum* (1, 3), and *De Oratore* (1, 118).

Yet yf a man happen to offende in any of the extremes it is better to offend in want and scantnesse, than in to muche and outragiouse excedynge . . . , whiche thyng is not onely trewlye sayde in shootynge, but in all other thynges that ever man goeth aboute, as in eatynge, taulkynge, and all other thynges lyke, whych matter was onse excellentlye disputed upon, in the Scooles, you knowe when.[7]

Thus the dialogue has been guided to teach the art of shooting as Cicero and Plato taught the art of rhetoric. While Toxophilus is intent on the exposition of and apology for shooting, Philologus is no less assiduous in relating its principles to eloquence, both recognizing the double meaning of their words.

In thinking about shooting and rhetoric as types of "skill" or "art," we need to bear in mind the extremely problematical meaning of these terms. The study of rhetoric in antiquity and the Middle Ages was plagued by uncertainty as to the proper category under which to inquire into its nature. It was variously defined as an "art," a "study," or a "science" admissible to philosophical discussion; or it was dismissed as a "knack" (one meaning of *skill*) or as merely a natural "gift."[8] It seems probable that shooting appealed to a man of Ascham's interests in part because it provided a practical subject matter upon which speculation on correlative subjects could be based. The idea of relating rhetoric to shooting may have occurred to him as an expansion of the classical commonplace that words are weapons. Moreover, as Ryan has noted, Ascham was aware of the affinity between the principles of rhetoric, such as those which were to appear in *The Arte of Rhetorique* of his friend Thomas Wilson, and the structure of earlier works on sport.[9] Philologus the rhetori-

7. P. 85. It is doubtful that a particular debate is referred to here; the matter might pertain to a work by Ockham or Scotus. The reference reminds the reader of the academic curriculum, with its daily practice in logic and rhetoric (from which the present dialogue is a respite!).

8. See H. M. Hubbell, trans., *Cicero: De Inventione . . .* , Loeb Classical Library (Cambridge, Mass., and London, 1949), p. 4.

9. P. 73. Ryan suggests a parallel between Wilson's triads of topics and the three divisions typical of a treatise on sport. These divisions are traceable to Xenophon, the father of the practical treatise, whom Cheke had taught Ascham to admire; see Ryan, p. 69.

cian sees shooting as comparable to "every crafte and science"; thus, attaining perfection in shooting involves the same problems as those of the best kind of orator. His dialogue with Toxophilus explores the relation between art and skill.

II

The communication between the school of shooting and the art of rhetoric displays the elegant simplicity of which Ascham's style is capable. The manipulation of classical sources and the successful double meaning resulting from their synthesis with his own purposes are extraordinary achievements within the dialogue form. To understand the significance of this communication, and its aesthetic quality uniquely Ascham's, it is necessary to return to his interest in Plato. Though some scholars have noted Ascham's allusions to certain dialogues of Plato in *Toxophilus*, no estimation of their role has been offered. The Platonic dialogue which figures prominently in Ascham's work is the *Phaedrus*. It is not a model for *Toxophilus* in the usual sense in which we understand that term; yet the *Phaedrus* contributes subtly and complexly to both the structure and the content of the later dialogue.

The *Phaedrus* frames *Toxophilus*. At the beginning of Ascham's dialogue, when Philologus happens upon Toxophilus, he finds him absorbed in *"Phedro Platonis,"* reading of the nature of the soul. The dialogue concludes with Toxophilus's request that Philologus meet with him here some other day, for the purpose of "entreatinge the question *De origine animae*,. . .that I maye knowe howe far Plato, Aristotle, and the Stoiicians have waded in it." Though it is possible that Toxophilus may be referring here to the *Phaedo*,[10] the full phrase "the question *De origine*

10. See Ascham's first letter to Sturm (Hatch, p. 329; Giles, I, 187), where he links the *Phaedo* with Aristotle's *De Anima*. The latter work, in the Latin translation of James of Venice revised by William of Moerbeke, was required reading of Oxford determiners. The expression "waded in" is borrowed perhaps from More, who uses it in the same sense in the *Dialogue Concerning Heresies* (1529), II, 7 (end).

animae, and the joynyng of it with the bodye," strongly indicates that he has in mind the discussion of the relation between the soul and body and the origination of the soul within the body as presented in the *Phaedrus.* Toxophilus's request is a witticism too, for, as we shall see, Philologus's comments on the art of rhetoric and the point of view of the dialogue as a whole are based on the theory of the soul's relation to the rhetorical work of art which Socrates expounded. In other words, they have already entreated that question! Thus the dialogue evidently opens and closes with a reference to the *Phaedrus.*

The framing device is more elaborate still. It has been noticed that not only is Toxophilus reading Plato as the dialogue opens, Ascham has even borrowed the setting of the *Phaedrus.*[11] It is more than a literary invention that the source of the scene should also be a prop in it. For by introducing the *Phaedrus* at this conspicuous moment Ascham at once creates a tone of relaxed inquiry and sets his stage with its theme of excellence in the art of rhetoric. Interestingly, an anonymous critic writing in *The Retrospective Review* notes the similarity of the opening of *Toxophilus* with the celebrated interview between Ascham and Lady Jane Grey when he visited her at Brodegate in Leicestershire before quitting England on his travels in Germany.[12] The scholar found the young pupil reading a dialogue of Plato's (the *Phaedo*) in Greek. Although the interview took place in 1550 and could not therefore have influenced the writing of *Toxophilus,* such a similarity reminds us that a life, like a work of art, has its themes. Literary biography must show how the subjects of a writer's work correspond to the themes of his life. The structural use of the *Phaedrus* in *Toxophilus* is but the first indication of Ascham's deep interest in its subject.

In the opening scene with its reference to the *Phaedrus* Ryan sees a skillfully devised *exordium* in which "opening pleasant-

11. Alfred Hettler, *Roger Ascham: sein Stil und seine Beziehung zur Antike* (Elberfeld, 1915), pp. 28ff.; cited and supported by Ryan, pp. 75f.

12. Vol. 4 (1821), 80. The incident is recorded in *The Scholemaster* and in a letter to Sturm (see Ryan, p. 313 n. 2).

ries" are linked with the "serious business" of the dialogue (p. 79). Plato's dialogue, however, plays a far more fundamental role than introducing feathered arrows by way of feathered souls. Let us consider the initial reference to Plato more closely. Toxophilus says (p. 1) that he has just now been reading "in *Phedro Platonis,* a place that entretes wonderfullie of the nature of soules. . . ." While it is true that his head aches "with loking on it," and he is glad of the interruption by Philologus, he voices the highest praise for this "place" which "whether it were for the passynge eloquence of Plato, and the Greke tongue, or for the hyghe and godlie description of the matter, kept my mynde so occupied, that it had no leisure to loke to my feete." He then indicates more precisely the part of the book which has so impressed him: "For I was reding howe some soules being well fethered, flewe alwayes about heaven and heavenlie matters, other some havinge their fethers mowted awaye, and droupinge, sanke downe into earthlie thinges." It is evident that Toxophilus refers to the following speech by Socrates: "Thus when [a soul] is perfect and winged it journeys on high and controls the whole world, but one that has shed its wings sinks down until it can fasten on something solid, and settling there it takes to itself an earthy body. . . ."[13] Now it is important to locate with precision the place of the reference, for at this point Socrates has just introduced the extraordinary simile for the soul—the team of winged steeds and their winged charioteer—and it is this which has struck Toxophilus. The task of the charioteer is difficult and troublesome, for he must control the pair of steeds, one noble and good, and other of opposite character. In this three-part image of the soul, the charioteer who fails to control both steeds loses for the soul its natural immortality and perfection. The task of the disinherited mortal is then to regain that lost perfection, a process which Socrates equates with learning. The relearning of perfection, or the recollection of truth, is the

13. Toxophilus refers to *Phaedrus,* 246C, not, as Ryan notes, to the passage "246E." With one exception, I use Edith Hamilton and Huntington Cairns's edition, *The Collected Dialogues of Plato including the Letters* (Princeton, 1961).

goal for which the soul is always eager. In *Toxophilus* this notion underlies Philologus's thirst for the perfect knowledge of shooting rather than excellence in the skill. Toxophilus's acceptance of this goal of the "idea" of shooting, as well as his initial impression from reading Plato's dialogue, shows that the speakers share a common ground in their understanding of the nature of man and the ultimate aim of education.

Plato's passionate study of perfection in the *Phaedrus* makes sense of Ascham's intense expenditure of energy on the subject of the perfect end of shooting. It is not necessary to identify Toxophilus with Ascham, as Ryan does (for in so doing we would exclude the philological side of the author of *The Scholemaster*), to grasp the importance of the idea of perfection for a humanist scholar. As Socrates tells Phaedrus (249B–C), only the soul of the philosopher, once she has beheld truth, may recover her wings: "he and he alone becomes truly perfect."

We need to recall, however, that the *Phaedrus,* like Ascham's plainer dialogue, insists on applied knowledge. In the *Phaedrus* the knowledge of the soul is applied directly to the art of oratory. "Since the function of oratory is in fact to influence men's souls," says Socrates (271D), "the intending orator must know what types of soul there are." He must know "what type of man is susceptible to what kind of discourse. . . ." When the orator has perfectly coordinated his speech with the soul of his listener, he may be said, to borrow Ascham's term, to have hit the mark.

In *Toxophilus,* then, we have a model for the attainment of perfection in an art which possesses the richest affinities with the art of rhetoric. Moreover, in composing his dialogue Ascham followed the formal procedure indicated in Socrates' two-part definition of the art of speech writing (277B):

> First, you must know the truth about the subject that you speak or write about; that is to say, you must be able to isolate it in definition, and having so defined it you must next understand how to divide it into kinds, until you reach the limit of division. . .

Division, as Ryle has said, "is only a preparation for dialectic" (*Plato's Progress,* p. 141). A glance at the paradigmatic tables of contents of *Toxophilus* reveals that in the first book Ascham, reviewing the history and uses of shooting and thereby demarcating its "kinds," gradually isolates his subject in definition. The schematic "Table conteyning the seconde booke" begins with that definition, "Hittyng the marke," and proceeds by degrees to the limits of division. As a precondition for the divisions according to (1) the things and (2) the handling of the things belonging to shooting, we find that Ascham has included some arrestingly "human" categories in his table: things "Proper for every sere [i.e., individual] mannes use" and "General to all men" and handling or technique "without a man" and "within a man." The apparent necessity of this precondition for division strongly suggests that Ascham is illustrating the second requirement of the formal procedure outlined in the *Phaedrus* (277C):

> . . .secondly, you must have a corresponding discernment of the nature of the soul, discover the type of speech appropriate to each nature, and order and arrange your discourse accordingly, addressing a variegated soul in a variegated style that ranges over the whole gamut of tones, and a simple soul in a simple style.

Thus *The schole of shootinge* epitomizes the art of rhetoric; the master of either must meet the conditions defined in the *Phaedrus.* "Until he has accomplished all this," Socrates asserts, "he will be unable to handle arguments according to rules of art, as far as their nature allows them to be subjected to art, either for the purpose of teaching or persuading;—such is the view which is implied in the whole preceding argument."[14]

The view that *Toxophilus* advances certain aesthetic standards both by precept and by example is further supported by Ascham's own account of his book to Sir William Paget shortly after its composition. "I have also written and dedicated to the king's majesty a book, which is now in the press, *On the art of shooting,*" wrote Ascham,

> and in which I have shown how well it is fitted for Englishmen, both at home and abroad, and how certain rules of art may be laid down to

14. Jowett's rendering of this sentence.

ensure its being learnt thoroughly by all our fellow-countrymen. This book, I hope, will be published before the king's departure [for France], and will be no doub[t]ful sign of my love to my country, or mean memorial of my humble learning.[15]

III

If knowledge of the soul may be applied toward the perfection of the art of rhetoric, that art itself serves an ideal end. For, as Socrates says at the conclusion of the *Phaedrus* (277E–278A), the proper goal of discourse is not mere persuasion, but justice. It should be the purpose of discourse, "for the sake of instruction," to expound lessons in justice. This moral of the *Phaedrus* allows us to perceive the philosophical aim of *Toxophilus,* which is as it were the extreme limit of its subject. Ascham considers shooting first as a physical and mental pastime, then as a skill, and finally as an art bearing affinities to the art of rhetoric. The concluding note of the *Phaedrus* reminds us that a good art, skill, or pastime aims ultimately at the perfection of judgment. What, we may ask, do Ascham's "rules of art" teach? One answer may be found in an observation by Crassus on a similar question in *De Oratore* (2, 232): An art of eloquence?. . .

> A practice indeed there is, . . . of observing sundry conventions serviceable to speakers, but, if this practice could impart eloquence, who would fail to be eloquent?. . . However I hold the virtue and benefit of these maxims to lie in this: we do not discover what to say by artificial devices, but after we have learned a true standard of comparison, they assure us of the soundness, or reveal to us the weakness, of whatever resources we attain by native talent, study or practice.

Crassus is hard to understand, for the thought is almost a paradox.[16] Soundness of judgment is both the goal of the orator

15. Giles's translation, I, xl; the Latin is found in I, 52. Ascham calls his book literally *"de re Sagittaria."* Edward Grant, in his "Oratio de Vita et Obitu Rogeri Aschami . . ." (1576), repr. in Giles, III, 317, calls it *"De arte sagittaria."*

16. "Observatio quaedam est, . . . earum rerum, quae in dicendo valent; quae si eloquentes facere posset, quis esset non eloquens? . . . Sed ego in his praeceptis hanc vim et hanc utilitatem esse arbitror, non ut ad reperiendum, quid di-

and the continually developing means to that goal. For Cicero and Ascham, only by knowing the true standard of excellence can one perfect one's skill. As Toxophilus says: "any man whiche will wisely begynne, and constantlye perserver in this trade of learnyng to shote, shall attayne to perfectness therin."[17]

In making bold to assert the attainability of perfection in shooting, Toxophilus relies upon the doctrine, found in the *Phaedrus* and in Cicero's oratorical works, of the redemptive power of human judgment on human nature. His comments on the perfection of shooting in this passage (pp. 98f.) may allude specifically to Cicero's comment on the gradual perfection of his own art of oratory in the *Brutus.* Just as the young Phaedrus had taken Lysias's speech to Socrates for criticism, Cicero betook himself to Rhodes to the distinguished orator and critic Molo. The rules of art which he learned from him, we recall, claim a perfection very like that which Toxophilus lays before Philologus. Of Molo Cicero says: "He made it his task to repress if possible the redundance and excess of my style, which was marked by a youthful impetuousness and lack of restraint, and to check it so to speak from overflowing its banks." "It is better," says Toxophilus (p. 85), "to offend in want and scantnesse, than in to muche and outragiouse excedynge. . . , which thyng is not onely trewlye sayde in shootynge, but in all other thynges that ever man goeth aboute. . . ." At last, says Cicero, "Thus I came back after two years' absence not only better trained, but almost transformed."[18] For Ascham too, the exercise of judgment transforms a man. "And hereby you may see," says Toxophilus of his

---

camus, arte ducamur, sed ut ea quae natura, quae studio, quae exercitatione consequimur, aut recta esse confidamus aut prava intellegamus, cum, quo referenda sint, didicerimus."

17. P. 99. Cf. *De Oratore,* 1, 149–51.

18. Gertrude E. Noyes, in "A Study of Roger Ascham's Literary Citations with Particular Reference to His Knowledge of the Classics," Ph.D. dissertation, Yale University, 1937, p. 247, notes that this passage in *Brutus* (xci, 316) is echoed in *Toxophilus* (p. 98).

lesson in shooting, "that this is true whiche Cicero sayeth, that a man by use, may be broughte to a newe nature." In practice a man may not only achieve perfect skill; he finds his nature altered. In "covetinge to come nighest a moost perfite ende," the shooter and the orator aim at virtue.

In providing a model for the cultivation of judgment, *The schole of shootinge* also promotes good counsel. Although Ascham does not emphasize this practical, patriotic application of a perfected virtue—shooting in itself is amply "profitable" for the use of gentlemen and yeomen in both war and peace—it is fitting that he should at least draw the connection and thereby acknowledge his debt to Sir Thomas Elyot, whose works represent good counsel as the noblest endeavor of man.[19] Toxophilus, in an interesting simile, compares a good bow with good counsel:

> A good bowe is knowen, much what as good counsayle is knowen, by the ende and proofe of it, and yet bothe a bowe and good counsell, maye be made bothe better and worse, by well or yll handlynge of them: as oftentymes chaunceth. And as a man both muste and wyll take counsell, of a wyse and honeste man, though he se not the ende of it, so must a shooter of necessitie, truste an honest and good bowyer for a bowe, afore he knowe the proofe of it. And as a wyse man wyll take plentye of counsel afore hand whatsoever need, so a shooter shoulde have alwayes .iii. or .iiii. bowes, in store, what so ever chaunce. (p. 75)

As the bowyer furnishes a bow to the shooter, so the counselor

19. Elyot is often regarded as Ascham's direct source for the subject of shooting. In the final chapter of Book I of *The Governor* (ed. H. H. S. Croft [1883; repr. New York, 1967], I, 286 and 305), Elyot asserts *"That shotyng in a longe bowe is principall of all other exercises,"* concluding that "it incomparably excelleth all other exercise, passetyme, or solace." Elyot appears in Ascham's dialogue (p. 53) as an acquaintance of Toxophilus's who is cited as an authority for the origin of shooting in England. Ascham is perhaps invoking the authority of Elyot when he says in the preface to *Toxophilus* (p. xv): "If any man woulde blame me, eyther for takynge such a matter in hande, or els for writing it in the Englyshe tongue, this answere I maye make hym, that when the beste of the realme thinke it honest for them to use, I one of the meanest sorte, ought not to suppose it vile for me to write. . . ."

furnishes counsel to the governor. But of either a bow or counsel one's knowledge is uncertain; initially one can only go on one's judgment. Toxophilus's simile leads with flawless logic to a hard paradox in human life—that the uncertainty of the "ende and proofe" (of either a bow or counsel) necessitates trust. We govern our lives according to our judgments in situations involving "both muste and wyll." The shooter and the governor alike understand this necessity; they understand their relation to the bowyer and the counselor. This significance in the simile makes clear why models of perfection are so important to Ascham, for these alone guide the cultivation of sound judgment, which is the basis of trust. For the counselor there is also an implicit *political* usefulness in such models, though this is more apparent in—to take an example with which Elizabeth's tutor would have been familiar—Erasmus's careful description of the ideal king in the *Institutio principis Christiani,* itself a model of princely counsel.[20] Philologus's response to Toxophilus's simile is touchingly human in its self-interest: "But if I truste bowyers always, sometyme I am lyke to be deceyved." The reply is tempered, patient, Socratic: "Therefore shall I tell you some tokens in a bowe, that you shall be the seeldomer deceyved."[21] The necessity of the shooter's trust in the bowyer applies, by extension, to the relation between the reader and Ascham; for the dialogue continually draws the parallel between the bow and the book.

Whom did Ascham conceive of as his reader? One might start with "Ascham's avowed intention," as Ryan observes (p. 73), "to persuade his readers to take up archery. . . ." We know from the dedication and preface, as well as from letters which have been cited, that Ascham had many intentions in composing his dialogue. Conspicuous among these is his desire to lay down certain rules of art to ensure that shooting is learned thoroughly by his countrymen, thereby showing his love of his country and

20. See, e.g., *The Education of a Christian Prince,* trans. Lester K. Born (1936; repr. New York, 1968), pp. 162–72.

21. The importance of the theme of trust is further emphasized by the dramatic placement of Philologus's one-line response (just cited) between two lengthy speeches by Toxophilus.

memorializing his own learning. It is his hope, as his dedication and correspondence indicate, to win the favor and patronage of the king. To these intentions should be added the pursuit of more abstract subject matter. The avowed motive is evidently too restrictive, ignoring the content of this subject matter, such as Ascham's reflections in Part B on the psychology and morality of the archer. Moreover, the "intention to persuade" is itself rather doubtful. For the king and many of the gentlemen to whom the book is addressed were already persuaded of the value of archery. Like most literary apologies and defenses, *Toxophilus* was written for a convinced audience. Those readers were interested in a moralization and indeed—to use an awkward critical term—an aestheticization of this skill. These terms summarize our earlier argument that the dialogue treats philosophical subjects beneath a didactic surface.

In a sense, Ascham's dialogue has less in common with the polemical literature of persuasion popular in his age than with displays of wit such as Elyot's *Defence of Good Women.* It belongs to the ancient, shameless category of epideictic oratory. On one occasion (p. xv), Ascham speaks of "this lytle treatise," in a flash of Sidneyan *sprezzatura,* as a practice shot. "And therefore did I take this little matter in hande," he continues, "to assaye my selfe, and hereafter by the grace of God, if the judgement of wyse men, that looke on, thinke that I can do any good, I maye perchaunce caste my shafte amonge other, for better game." But the tone of the effortless courtier is not habitual with him. His work displays erudition before wit; "its real object is to show the learning of the author," writes the Victorian compiler Henry Craik, "and his power of managing a dialogue in the Platonic manner."[22]

IV

We have been analyzing so far the relation between form and subject in Ascham's dialogue. But it is questionable whether a local analysis of style, with its interest in avowed and latent

22. *English Prose: Selections,* 4 vols. (New York and London, 1893–95), I, 269.

intentions and themes, can yield a conclusive estimate of the literary value of the work. There is no very satisfactory term for the critical key we need, as commentators on Tudor prose have sensed. To A. W. Reed's historical introduction and philological notes for More's *Dialogue Concerning Heresies* W. E. Campbell added an essay on "the spirit" and doctrine of the dialogue. And J. H. Hexter's introduction to the historical milieu of *Utopia* is complemented by Father Surtz's essay on *Utopia* as a work of literary art. Our *experience* of *Toxophilus* as readers seems to be a function not only of the aspects of its style but also of the "world view" of the work as a whole.[23] In order to formulate the spirit or world view of Ascham's dialogue, we need to ask what the aesthetic purpose of *Toxophilus* is and whether it succeeds.

Toxophilus seeks to convey the image of perfection in shooting. This image, like Zeuxis's painting of Helen, must be conceived in the mind. It is such a process that Ascham intends by "imagination." Philologus asks Toxophilus, "I praye you as I sayde before teatche me to shoote as fayre, and welfavouredly as you can imagen" (p. 100). It is never a question of Toxophilus offering *his own* shooting as the example but rather a question of imagined perfection. Indeed, he elaborates most of "the discommodities whiche ill custome hath graffed in archers" (pp. 101–3). "Of these faultes I have verie many my selfe, but I talke not of my shootynge, but of the generall nature of shootynge. Nowe ymagin an Archer that is cleane wythout al these faultes and I am sure everye man would be delyted to se hym shoote." Regardless of its ultimate practical application (to shooting or, in the case of the ideal in *De Oratore,* to eloquence), the initial perception of the image of perfection is an aesthetic experience. Now the aesthetic object, the object of experience, is not the image of the perfect shooter; that image exists, like Zeuxis's

23. René Wellek and Austin Warren argue the value of distinguishing "the world view which emerges from the work . . . [from] the view didactically stated by the author within or without the work" (*Theory of Literature,* 3d ed. [New York, 1962], pp. 245f.). I have borrowed several terms from their chapter "Evaluation."

Helen, only in the mind. The aesthetic object is the dialogue itself, a thing of language. Thus Dr. Johnson's appraisal of Ascham's dialogue takes on new meaning: "He designed not only to teach the art of shooting, but to give an example of diction. . . ." For in reading *Toxophilus* we are moved to imagine or contemplate perfection by eloquence.

The purpose of the aesthetic object is to create the aesthetic experience; in this case, language conveys the image. Hence the primary importance of eloquence to perfect shooting. Ascham states this conceptual relation with admirable clarity in his preface:

> Yet in writing this booke, some man wyll marvayle perchaunce, why that I beyng an unperfyte shoter, shoulde take in hande to write of makyng a perfyte archer: the same man peradventure wyll marvayle, howe a whettestone whiche is blunte, can make the edge of a knife sharpe: I woulde the same man shulde consider also, that in goying about anye matter, there be .iiii. thinges to be considered, doyng, saying, thinking and perfectnesse: Firste there is no man that doth so wel, but he can saye better, or elles summe men, whiche be now starke nought, shuld be to good: Agayne no man can utter wyth his tong, so wel as he is able to imagin with his minde, and yet perfectnesse it selfe is farre above all thinking. Than seing that saying is one steppe nerer perfectnesse than doyng, let every man leve marvaylyng why my woorde shall rather expresse, than my dede shall perfourme perfect shootinge. (pp. xv–xvi)

The order of the schema is instructive. Perfectness may be approached in ascending steps of doing, saying, and thinking. Between the action of shooting and the mind's imagining of perfect shooting is saying, i.e., utterance or speech. Ascham emphasizes in this preface that he offers not a deed, perfectly performed or even thought, but an "expressive word." We see that the dialogue aims in two directions—toward the doing or performance of shooting, on the one hand, and toward conceiving a mental image of perfect shooting, on the other. It is clear that, in order to achieve both aims, the perfect performance of the perfect image, the dialogue must accurately "express" or *mean* what it says.[24] To say what one means, we conclude, is the perfect end of eloquence and the aesthetic purpose of Ascham's dialogue. As Toxophilus puts it (p. 106), "hyttynge of the marke, the ende both of shootyng and also of thys our communication."

Hitting the mark, then, whether in shooting or in expression, represents the correct relation between the image of perfection and actual operation.[25] The relation is analogous to (if not directly inspired by) Elyot's conception of wisdom as knowledge in operation. Ascham himself noted Aristotle's analogy between shooting and virtue, that both can be perfected toward an ideal end. Nor is the dialogue unaware that "hamartia" is "missing the mark." (The Greek term is also found in St. Paul, who at the end of his Epistle to the Romans salutes a certain Philologus.) For Ascham, hitting the mark has not only practical and moral dimensions; it has also an aesthetic appeal, in his word, a "comeliness." In all his works he values comeliness, or human beauty, as the aesthetic quality which can change our nature and move us to action.[26]

24. This congruency is high in Ascham's scale of perfection. In *A Report and Discourse of the Affaires and State of Germany* he expresses admiration for Albert, Margrave of Brandenburg: "when he talketh he so frameth hys toung to agree with hart, as speakyng and meanyng seemeth to be alwayes at one in hym" (p. 147). Maurice, Duke of Saxony, is likewise praised for his belief that "wordes should be so framed with the toung, as they be alwayes ment in the hart" (p. 155).

25. Greene, "Roger Ascham: The Perfect End of Shooting," p. 620, remarks that the skill of shooting "possesses a moral dimension as well. But the skill is discerned in operation, not in mere potentiality: it is determined by hitting the mark."

26. Greene, pp. 620f., has illustrated the depth of meaning in Ascham's use of this word in *Toxophilus.* Several more far-reaching aspects of "comeliness" should be recorded. Ascham maintains in the "Euphues" section of *The Scholemaster* (pp. 194f.) that comeliness in the speaking voice, and even in the human face, enhances eloquence, gives power to what is taught: ". . . surelie, a cumlie countenance, with a goodlie stature, geveth credit to learning, and authoritie to the person. . . ." Ascham was constantly sensitive to the didactic application of aesthetic beauty. To John Aylmer, Lady Jane Grey's tutor and later bishop of London, Ascham wrote of the eloquence of the countenance of his pupil, Princess Elizabeth. "I teach her words," he said, "and she teaches me

In the field of shooting, comeliness is equivalent to athletic "form"; it is thus an aesthetic standard by which Toxophilus measures the operation of perfection. In viewing the world, Ascham's dialogue, as well as *The Scholemaster,* assumes that one can recognize, if not the mind's construction in the face, the *mens pulchra in corpore pulchro.* "And vertue it self," says the rhetorician Philologus, "is nothynge eles but cumlynesse, as al Philosophers do agree" (p. 100).[27] When the image of perfect shooting is set into operation, or when speaking is aligned with meaning, the result—hitting the mark—is a sublime beauty. In the *Report of Germany* Ascham returns to the scheme of perfection with which he justified his dialogue. Here he imagines a model in which the heart, look, tongue, and hands, respectively, "so alwayes agreeying together in thinkyng, pretendyng [i.e., expressing], and speakyng, and doying, as no one of these foure should at any tyme be at jarre with an other" (p. 147). This is a most exalted comeliness; "which agreeyng together in their right tune, do make a pleasaunt melody in all mens eares both sweetest and loudest, called in English (honor) and most fitly in *Greeke* [*Timē*], the price and prayse of vertue."[28]

Such is the joy of perfection, of which a dialogue can offer only the image. Toxophilus teaches that an act may be improved by imagining the image of its perfect execution. An interesting example of this is *holding* the drawn bowstring, which, according to Toxophilus (p. 105), "must not be longe, for it bothe putteth a bowe in jeopardy, and also marreth a mans shoote, it

---

things. I teach her the tongues to speak, and her modest and maidenly looks teach me works to do. . . ." Cited by Hartley Coleridge, "Memoir of Roger Ascham," *Northern Worthies* (1833), repr. in John E. B. Mayor, ed., *The Scholemaster* (London, 1934), p. 18.

27. See Plato, *Republic,* IV, 444E; V, 452E; *Symposium,* 201C *et seq.*, 204E *et seq.*

28. Cf. Elyot's "hole quiar synging in one tune" (*Of the Knowledge Which Maketh a Wise Man,* ed. Edwin Johnston Howard [Oxford, Ohio, 1946], p. 32). In neither Ascham nor Elyot do we find the possibility of a duplicitous comeliness in the figure of honor, which Spenser would exploit in the cases of Guyon and Philotime and Arthur and Prays-desire.

must be so lytle that it maye be perceyved better in a mans mynde when it is done, than seene with a mans eyes when it is in doyng." Here Toxophilus stresses the importance of rehearsing the ideal act in the mind. For one compares each shot against an image of the ideal in preparation for the next shot. In this example the reason that sound judgment is necessary becomes, almost startlingly, clear: no two shots are the same. Nor are we confronted in life with any two absolutely identical ethical situations.

In the *Phaedrus* Socrates showed that the universal necessity of making judgments could be developed into an art, the art of eloquence. Part of the aesthetic purpose of *Toxophilus* is to teach how judgments in shooting, and judgments generally, are made. For this purpose the dialogue form is specially qualified. It teaches by way of dialectic—question and answer, statement and counterstatement. Dialogue is the imitation of reasoning, a picture of the mind's attempt to reconcile contraries and to find the "meane betwixt bothe," which is the "best in al thynges."[29] On the other hand, the more evenly matched the contraries are and hence the more honest the contention of the dialectic is, the more formally the dialogue shows that judgment is always, at best, a compromise, an imperfect approximation.

Thus the literary form of *Toxophilus* qualifies the goal of hitting the mark; for in representing judgment as an adjustment between "thinking" and "doing," between the image of perfection and operation, the dialogue makes its peace with imperfection. Such a resolution is rather uncommon in humanist thought, in which—to speak generally—we observe that the tendency to think in terms of dualisms often leads to a factitious claim of synthesis (to hold up two and say one). Ascham's dialogue sim-

29. See pp. 85 and 105. Early in the dialogue Toxophilus asserts that "Comparisons . . . make playne matters" (p. 22), and later he equates comparison with "honeste contention" or what we would call competition, which leads to victory, pleasure, and excellence (p. 57). The discussion of shooting as a heteropathic medicine (pp. 30f.) is further evidence of Ascham's thoroughgoing belief in the efficacy of contraries.

ply admits the possibility of *not* hitting the mark. In taking as his example an athletic skill, in which deception is usually impossible,[30] Ascham must come to terms with the fact of imperfection.

V

In *Toxophilus* there are two kinds of imperfection. One is inevitable and natural, and for this Toxophilus offers consolation. "Good shooters also, that can not whan they would hit the marke, wil labour to come as nigh as they can. All thinges in this worlde be unperfite and unconstant, therefore let every man acknowledge hys owne weakenesse, in all matters great and smal, weyghtye and merye, and glorifie him, in whome only perfyte perfitnesse is" (p. 107). The imperfection of human judgment is such that not only does it fall short of, but often it willfully rejects, the ideals encountered in books. "It is pitie that mans nature is such," writes Ascham in the *Report of Germany* (p. 131), "as will commonlie commend good thynges in readyng and yet will as commonly follow ill thynges in doying." This nature he acknowledges in himself to John Astley who he is sure is not "so unfrendly to looke for so much from me": "to know perfectly by reading and to performe perfectly in doyng" (*Report,* p. 127). The second kind of imperfection, however, is avoidable, for it is the result of ignorance; and upon this kind Toxophilus unleashes a torrent of indignation. It is worth looking at his diatribe closely, for the implicit values and world view which underlie his position evidently inform all of Ascham's work.

The passage (pp. 109–11) centers on what every archer "must knowe"; a knowledge of which bow and shaft are fittest for him and which season and time of day are best for him is essential. Indeed, Toxophilus continues, in *all* things it is most commend-

30. Intellectual imperfection is easier to conceal. Ascham heatedly contrasts shooting in broad daylight with the deceitful play with cards and dice in dark corners. The surprising vehemence of his attack on this vice no doubt arises in part from the fact that it involves deliberate deception of the judgment.

able and profitable for a man to "knowe perfitly for what matter and for what tyme he is moost apte and fit." Toxophilus values most what in fact every man must have: self-knowledge. "Yf men woulde go about matters whych they should do and be fit for, and not suche thynges whyche wylfullye they desyre and yet be unfit for, verely greater matters in the common welthe than shootyng shoulde be in better case than they be." The absence of this knowledge, says Toxophilus (the *indignatio* of the passage expressing a cold rage), is the grossest "ignorancie," which causes

> some to desire to be in the Courte, whiche be borne and be fitter rather for the carte. Somme to be maysters and rule other, whiche never yet began to rule them selfe: some alwayes to jangle and taulke, whych rather shoulde heare and kepe silence. Some to teache, which rather should learne. Some to be prestes, whiche were fytter to be clerkes.[31]

This ignorance, "when men mesure them selfe a misse," results in that imperfection unworthy of consolation, the "perverse judgement of the world. . . ." Missing the mark is but a trifling symbol of a greater danger. Misjudgment, Toxophilus is arguing, brings in the reign of misorder. Imperfect judgment

> bringeth muche mysorder and greate unsemelynesse to the hole body of the common wealth, as yf a manne should were his hoose upon his head, or a woman go wyth a sworde and a buckeler every man would take it as a great uncumlynesse although it be but a tryfle in respect of the other.

The Platonic identity of comeliness and virtue, which Philologus expounded earlier, Toxophilus now holds up against that of uncomeliness and vice. The danger to the commonwealth is that through perverse judgment a father, if he have two sons, will set to learning the one who is "impotent, weke, sickly, lispynge, stuttynge, and stammerynge, or havynge any misshape in hys bodye" rather than the one who has "a countenaunce full of

31. Cf. *Ne sutor ultra crepidam* ("Shoemaker, stick to your last") in Erasmus, *Adagia;* More's youthful poem "A Mery Gest" is also based on this wisdom. Ascham alludes to the adage later in this speech.

cumlynesse to allure good menne, a bodye ful of manlye authoritie to feare ill men, a witte apte for al learnynge with tongue and voyce, able to perswade all men." This perverse judgment of fathers, ignorant of the nature of their own children, "causeth the common wealth [to] have many unfit ministers": the "outcastes," "the rifraffe of the world," "the great deformitie of the common wealthe." When judgment fails, ideal thought is operationally deformed, and the social result is misorder in the commonwealth.[32]

It is important to see that the danger to the commonwealth is the externalization of an internal misorder. I know of only two other occasions on which Ascham becomes so vehement as he does in this passage: his vituperation against the Turk, into whose habits of "beastlye blynde barbarousness" Englishmen by their "contemnying of knowledge and learnynge" are in danger of falling (*Toxophilus*, pp. 48–50), and his famous attack against the Italianate Englishman with which the first book of *The Scholemaster* ends. In both passages, as in the one now at hand, his scorn is directed against the corruption of judgment by willful ignorance. The heat of oratory can reveal, perhaps better than cool reason, that at the heart of the dialogue, grounded on a philosophical outlook found in Plato and Cicero, is Ascham's belief in the power of judgment to work change in human nature. This disorder in the commonwealth

> myght be sone wyped awaye, if fathers would bestow their children on that thing alwayes, wherunto nature hath ordeined them most apte and fit. . . . Whan this is done, than muste every man beginne to be more ready to amend hym self, than to checke another, measuryng their matters with that wise proverbe of Apollo, *Know thy selfe:* that is to

32. In *The Scholemaster*, pp. 202ff., Ascham compares the schoolmaster, the governor, and the father—"*Praeceptore, Paedagogo, Parente.*" On p. 220 he warns the "great ones in the Court" that they are responsible for "all misorders in Religion. . . ." He goes so far as to assert that he who cannot like "*Tullie* in Rhetoricke and Eloquence" will probably presume to mislike "greater matters: that is either in Religion, to have a dissentious head, or in the common wealth to have a factious hart" (pp. 243f.)

say, learne to know what thou arte able, fitte, and apte unto, and folowe that. (pp. 110f.)

The responses of Philologus and Toxophilus to this inspired departure from the latter's present subject of the "handlyng of the wether" are both characteristic and instructive. The rhetorician is "well pleased" with the speculations of this expansive speech, "For these things touched of you by chaunse, and by the waye, be farre above the matter it self, by whose occasion the other were brought in." Toxophilus, covered with exaggerated Socratic modesty, scoffs at his own eloquence; such "weyghtye matters" are "fit bothe in an other place to be spoken: and of an other man than I am, to be handled. And bycause meane men must meddle wyth meane matters, I wyl go forwarde in descrybyng the wether, as concernynge shooting. . . ." But Toxophilus's handling of the problem of judgment is not quite over. The critically celebrated passage which follows—his observation of the wind—can best be understood as a continuation, a vivid example taken from personal experience, of the subject of judgment and the forces of misorder it opposes.

"To se the wynde, with a man his eyes, it is unpossible, the nature of it is so fyne, and subtile, yet this experience of the wynde had I ones my selfe. . . ." So begins the description by Toxophilus (pp. 112f.) of the motions of the winter wind which he was able to observe one clear morning as it carried the snow in flying streams over the Yorkshire fields. What "great delyte and pleasure" was it to behold, as he rode on the "hye waye betwixt Topcliffe upon Swale, and Borowe bridge," the whole "nature of the wynde. . .so variable in blowynge."

And that whych was the moost mervayle of al, at one tyme .ii. driftes of snowe flewe, the one out of the West into the East, the other out of the North in to the East: And I saw .ii. windes by reason of the snow the one crosse over the other, as it had bene two hye wayes. And agayne I shoulde here the wynd blow in the ayre, when nothing was stirred at the ground. And when all was still where I rode, not verye far from me the snow should be lifted wonderfully.

Of the description as a whole Ryan has said that "it demonstrates why *Toxophilus* is regarded as one of the first triumphs of modern English prose" (p. 68), and Greene calls it, quite simply, "the most beautiful page Ascham ever wrote" (p. 622). Greene goes on to observe in Ascham's line "The more uncertaine and disceyvable the wynd is, the more hede must a wyse Archer gyve to know the gyles of it," a "triumphant moral" in which he sees a "species of Humanist optimism." In this line, Greene writes, "There is never any thought, here or elsewhere in Ascham, that the guiles of a windy nature are beyond the wisdom of the artist." With this view we may agree, for it assumes that there is an artistic component in "knowing the guiles" of the wind. We have seen in the idea of "comeliness" how nearly the dialogue equates aesthetic response with reasoned judgment. But the meaning of the description of the wind can be brought still more sharply into focus. Toxophilus has had, as he began his description by emphasizing, an "unpossible" experience: he has *seen* the wind. What does this mean? The loose snow allowed that "I myght se verye wel, the hole nature of the wynde as it blewe that daye." What is its nature? "Variable" and "unsensyble to oure nature." The wind is a perfect metaphor for uncertainty. Of course it is a real hindrance to shooting straight and "keeping a length," but the *nature* of the wind is uncertainty itself. And it is this which Toxophilus has unforgettably seen. "A good archer wyl. . .learne to knowe the nature of the wynde, and with wysedome, wyll measure in hys mynde, howe much it wyll alter his shoote" (p. 107). And a good man will learn to know the nature of uncertainty and with wisdom will measure in his mind how much it will alter his acts. It is evident why Toxophilus's long closing speech rejoices in that "wonderfull worke of god," the human eye; for it is not only a masterful instrument of sight but it also symbolizes human judgment without whose vision "the mynde is blynde" (p. 118). In another man fate or mutability might arouse horror. Toxophilus recalls that "the moost mervayle of al" is to see two winds cross one another like two highways. Ascham's "most beautiful page" is devoted to a vision in which uncertainty is contemplated as a marvel.

The experience of the wind brings into focus the world view of *Toxophilus* as a whole. Many things could have been made of that experience of the wind upon the snowfields; yet the wind is observed, as Ascham must have observed much in life, for its lesson, moral as well as aesthetic. "The wind bloweth where it listeth," writes St. John, who is surely Ascham's unconscious inspiration, "and thou hearest the sound thereof, but canst not tell whence it cometh, and whither it goeth. . . ." In the course of the dialogue the reader becomes aware of one pervasive assumption—that all experience *teaches*. The humanists' love of learning is a commonplace, but *Toxophilus* reveals such a quality of mind extraordinarily.

Like all of Ascham's writing, his dialogue is the work of a teacher. His important correspondence with Johann Sturm was inaugurated and continued on the basis of their common pedagogical concerns. His most significant function during his life was probably his role as tutor of royalty. In his first letter to Sturm, Ascham praises Princess Elizabeth for her ability to recognize excellence in style and in doing so reveals his own values, which, incidentally, might be applied to the concluding episode in *Toxophilus* which we have just discussed.

She approves a style born from the subject, chaste from its suitability, and beautiful from its perspicuity. She admires uniquely modest metaphors and comparisons well collated and contrasting felicitously with one another. Her ears are sharpened as by the careful notice of these matters, nay, have been made so discriminating and so exact in judgment, that nothing occurs in Greek, Latin, or English composition, either loose and wandering on the one hand, or tight and well-defined on the other, or too diffuse or justly tempered, that she does not so scrupulously notice while reading as to reject it at once with great disgust or receive it with the greatest pleasure.[33]

33. April 4, 1550. Hatch, pp. 336f.; Giles, I, 192. The letter was written with a view to publication, so that its compliments may be suspected of self-interest. "Ascham was always on the alert for chances to benefit himself," Hatch notes

His earliest biographer, Grant, and Coleridge following him, characterize Ascham as above all a "praeceptor."[34] His historical significance is to be found largely in the continuation of that character apparent in *The Scholemaster,* published posthumously. In his lifetime, however, that purpose was already discernible in his dialogue. It is noteworthy that Ascham, at the close of a letter to Sturm on learning and eloquence, mentions that his wife, "because she knows that I love you, herself loves your wife, and sends 'in remembrance' [Greek] of her kindness, a gold ring in the form of an arrow, with the inscription, 'Donum Fidelis Amici.' "[35] Archery had become the Aschams' trademark, though it did not require a concrete form. From the "broken Jewelles" of antiquity Ascham distinguished his "fewe rude English wordes." These "rules," which adorn all his writing, he leaves "to other, and namelie to my Children: which tooles, if it please God, that an other day, they may be able to use rightlie, as I do wish and daylie pray, they may do, I shal be more glad, than if I were able to leave them a great quantitie of land."[36]

(p. 339), "but one can hardly believe that he was entirely selfish." The same might be said of his letter to Cheke, dated February 12, 1548 (Giles, I, 160–62; excerpted in English, lvi–lvii), which also praises Elizabeth.

34. Grant's full title is "Oratio de Vita et Obitu Rogeri Aschami, ad Adolescentulos Latinae Linguae Studiosos" (Giles, III, 294–355). In Coleridge's "Memoir" (in *The Scholemaster,* ed. Mayor) see especially pp. 9 and 38.

35. April 11, 1562. Hatch, p. 715; Giles, II, 67. The ring was carried by a mutual friend, Michael Schütz, who had adopted the name Toxites.

36. *The Scholemaster,* pp. 267f. Cf. Cato, *Disticha,* I.28:

> Cumtibi sint nati nec opes, tunc artibus illos
> Instrue, quo possint inopem defendere vitam.

6

Thomas More: The Transfiguration of Dialogue

I

In or about 1505 Thomas More translated a "saint's life" of Pico della Mirandola. The *Life* includes several scenes in which Pico gives spiritual advice to his young nephew John Francis, author of the original *Vita,* and More further develops the relationship between the saintly uncle and his favorite nephew by appending his translation of two familiar, homiletic letters from Pico to John Francis. *Utopia,* appearing in 1516, depicted an old traveler, Raphael Hythlodaeus, recounting his tale in dialogue with two bright, amiable young men, Peter Giles and Thomas More. Whether the commonwealth Raphael describes is a secular heaven or merely "the best Hell," he provides his interlocutors not only with political but with spiritual counsel. More had prepared the translation of the life of Pico for his friend, a nun, Joyeuce Leigh; and *Utopia* too was written for friends, on this occasion an international group of humanists whose luminous names guard the gates of *Utopia* like swords of fire. Good writing must be *for* someone, and More was habitually careful to address a specific audience. In 1528 he completed *A Dialogue Concerning Heresies,* a comprehensive assertion of Catholic orthodoxy written by commission of Bishop Cuthbert Tunstal, evidently intended for a popular audience, including the English clergy, to enable them to answer the assaults of Luther and Tyndale and their adherents. The dominant figure in this work is More in his invested public role as the king's councillor and chancellor of the duchy of Lancaster. In answering the doctrinal questions put by the intense young Messenger sent by an old friend of More's, More the Councillor speaks not only with the force of mature common sense but also with all the authority of high estate. In the preliminary "Letter of Credence" from the Messenger's master, More shows himself aware of the significance of this *kind* of dialogue. He dwells for a space on what the two speakers may expect of each other in the lengthy dialogue which follows. The Messenger, writes the master to More, is more than meanly learned, and what will also content you—he has "a very mery wytte. He is of nature nothynge tonge tayed." His master has warned him against being too ceremonious in disputation with More and bidden him to be bold, "more to mynde his matter / then his curtesye / . . .gyuynge no fote in dysputynge vnto your authorytye / but yf he be borne backe with reason."[1] The ground rules require that each be equally armed, and it is only charity to fight with sharpest weapons; but there is never any doubt that the older man is undertaking to enlighten the younger. Last in the line we are tracing is Antony, the aged uncle in *A Dialogue of Comfort,* written in the Tower in 1534. In Antony, More universalized himself, for Antony is the titleless man, Everyman-at-the-last, to whom

1. *A Dialogue Concerning Heresies,* ed. Thomas M. C. Lawler, Germain Marc'hadour, and Richard C. Marius, The Yale Edition of the Complete Works of St. Thomas More, vol. 6 (New Haven and London, 1981), 25/30–26/2. The Yale edition of More's works is cited hereafter as "*CW,*" followed by the volume number; page and line numbers are separated by a slash.

his nephew Vincent comes for comfort against the day of tribulation at hand.

Amid the eclectic variety of More's writings one notices his recurrence to the figure of the old, or older, man. With this figure, in the examples mentioned and elsewhere, More commonly links its counterpart: the young friend, relation, disciple, servant. These two are the leading characters in his major dialogues. Again and again, throughout the thirty years of his literary career, More re-creates the primary Socratic situation.

Pico and John Francis; Hythloday, Giles, and More; the Councillor and the Messenger; Antony and Vincent—this situation, the wise older man addressing young friends, proved especially productive to More in treating moral questions. Perhaps every man's continuous dialogue with himself over moral questions involves this debate between the child and the man, the inner conflict, between one's instincts and the spiritual and rational faculties, which marks a mature person. The device of dialogue allows More, like Plato, to represent the conflict as two-sided. But if the situation More repeatedly adopts is dramatic, it is severely restricted to an elucidation of the dialectic. For in More's works, as opposed to the situation in *King Lear,* the old man is never confused; true maturity is identified with reason instructing ignorant or disorderly youth. More argues eloquently for man's essential rationality and spirituality, but he is never tragic.

Within the convention of the Socratic situation More freely develops the character of his interlocutors. In the *Dialogue Concerning Heresies* More, writing down the whole interchange for his friend, the Messenger's master, confesses a deep initial suspicion of the young man—"whether he were (as yonge scolers be somtyme prone to newe fantasyes) fallen in to luthers secte."[2] But More encourages him to "spare not to brynge forthe all that

2. *CW 6,* 34/29–30. The characters are related, according to Schuster, in an "alumnus-undergraduate opposition," i.e., a "basic posture of exchange between a conservative generation in middle age and a radical generation of youth" (*The Confutation of Tyndale's Answer,* ed. Louis A. Schuster et al., *CW 8,* 1141).

euer ye haue herde" (95/6); gradually he coaxes out the Messenger's objections to established doctrines and practices. By the middle of the first book More has brought the Messenger to voice, eloquently and honestly, the real doubts to which he has been driven despite his faith. The Messenger is no heretic, but, like many intellectuals for whom More was writing, he has found himself unable to articulate the orthodox position and thus defend his faith.[3] The Councillor's judgment on the Messenger's performance is a signature of More's own style.

> Surely quod I for my parte I can you very good thanke / for ye haue not fayntly defended your parte / as thoughe it were a corrupted aduocate / that wold by colusyon handell his clyentes matter febly for y[e] pleasure of his aduersary / but ye haue sayd therin / I can not tell whyther as moche as any man maye say / but certaynly I suppose as moche as ye eyther haue herde any man say or can your selfe say. And at the lest wyse / moche more than I haue herde of any man els / or coulde haue sayd of my selfe. (101/13–20)

The metaphor of the court of law reminds us of the Councillor's (and More's) position and the world of experience on which his authority in the present dialogue is based. The metaphor further points up the analogy between the dialogue and a courtroom debate. The *Dialogue Concerning Heresies* is indeed a trial; and in suggesting here that he and the Messenger are advocates, More implies that the reader sits as judge. Some of the first readers of the dialogue may actually have sat as judges in heresy trials.

In dramatizing the relation between More and the Messenger as a cultivated mutual understanding, not unlike the generous sympathy typical of Platonic dialogue,[4] More analyzes the two

3. On the audience of More's polemical writing, see W. E. Campbell, ed., *The Dialogue Concerning Tyndale by Sir Thomas More* (London, 1927), pp. 67f.; John M. Headley, ed., *Responsio ad Lutherum, CW 5*, 806; and Louis A. Schuster, ed., *The Confutation of Tyndale's Answer, CW 8*, 1264–68.

4. In his seventh epistle Plato speaks of the power of "benevolent disputation by the use of question and answer without jealousy" to produce understanding. *The Collected Dialogues of Plato*, ed. Edith Hamilton and Huntington Cairns (Princeton, 1961), *Epis.* 7, 344B.

impulses that underlie his problem, doubt and informed faith: "Doute on quod I bytwene vs twayne & spare not / nor let not to tell me what moueth you" (109/11–12). More, who by special dispensation had been permitted to peruse a spate of outlawed Lutheran books in order to prepare the official case against heresy, chose dialogue as a forum. Together his interlocutors represent, or fictionalize, the dialectic of religious doubt.

More goes to greater lengths to develop the character of the young interlocutor in *A Dialogue of Comfort*, though Vincent, like the Messenger, serves primarily to hold the subject of religious doubt in focus. By his opposition he, rather than Antony, sets the line of the dialogue. In both *Comfort* and *Heresies* we see dramatic conflict resolved by the gradual conforming of the antagonist to the protagonist. Yet we are given more than the functional minimum of characterization necessary to represent a troubled spirit. More's eristic pugnacity and didacticism are frequently tempered by a peirastic playfulness. The substantial individuality of his characters and the frequency with which he adverts to the setting are uncommon in the dialogues of the Tudor period. For More, while concentrating on heresies or temptations in the two dialogues, had the uncommon ability to reserve attention for his fiction. Dialogue was not simply the chosen method of exposition—it answered a variety of More's purposes.

The settings of More's dialogues reveal both classical influences and artful innovations upon earlier models. Elyot and Ascham were much less consistent and precise in their attention to this element of dialogue than More. He seems to have been satisfied with the Ciceronian solution, notably that of the *Tusculan Disputations.* In the first three *Disputations* (the last two dispense with scenic indications), the interlocutors wind up their dialogue with an agreement to meet on the morrow in the same place. The end of a day conveniently occasions the end of a dialogue, a device by which the dramatic unity of time had been observed in dialogues from the *Symposium* to More's own. Of this temporal and local indication in Cicero More makes a little convention, adding touches which tease it from a pastoral charm in the *Tusculans* into real domestic humanity. Situation is one measure of the distance between Cicero's dispassionate discussions of pain and the warm "confabulations" of the Tudor dialogist.

After exchanging the civilities which commonly pass at the first meeting of strangers, More writes in *Utopia,* he and Peter Giles took Raphael off to More's Antwerp dwelling: "There in the garden, on a bench covered with turfs of grass, we sat down to talk together."[5] Book I concludes with More's suggestion, " 'let us go in to dine. Afterwards we shall take up as much time as we like.' . . . So we went in and dined. We then returned to the same place, sat down on the same bench, and gave orders to the servants that we should not be interrupted" (109/29–34). In the punctilio toward time and place and in the afterglow of the meal in which a wise old man speaks, the Cicero of the *Tusculans* and the Plato of the *Symposium* are made to touch. At the end of Raphael's discourse More, abstaining from criticism, "taking him by the hand, led him in to supper" (245/32–33). May one venture to call this gesture Christian? It is certainly definite and particular; like the turf-covered bench, that clasp is an evocative sensuous detail characteristic of the setting in More's dialogues.

It is interesting that More retains this framing situation in the *Dialogue Concerning Heresies.* The heresy dialogue really has a double beginning—the Messenger's initial arrival when he delivers his message (Book I, Chapter 1), and his return next day to talk in earnest (Chapter 2):

> On the morow whan he was comen agayne somwhat before .vii. of the clocke (for so I appoynted hym) takynge hym with me into my study / and my seruauntys warned that yf any other sholde happen to

5. Ed. Edward Surtz, S. J., and J. H. Hexter, *CW* 4, 51/27–28. The verb is *confabulamur.* See Ambrosius Holbein's depiction of this scene (*CW* 4, Plate II). The *Tusculans* inaugurate a tradition of seated garden dialogues. For illustrations of "Turfed Mounds and Turf-Topped Benches Used for Seats," see Frank Crisp, *Medieval Gardens. . . , with Some Account of Tudor, Elizabethan and Stuart Gardens,* ed. Catherine Childs Paterson, 2 vols. (London, 1924).

desyre to speke with me (certayne except of whom I gaue them knowledge) they sholde dyfferre them tyll another leasour / *I set hym down with me / at a lytell table. And then I shewed vnto hym* / that where he had purposed on your byhalfe in short wordys / many longe thyngys / wherof the rehersall were losse of tyme / to hym y^t^ so well knewe them all redy / I wolde (all superfluous recapytulacyon set aparte) as bryefly as I conuenyently coude shewe hym my mynde in them all. (emphasis added)

One cannot but wonder about that little table. A relating bond like the grass-covered bench, it too is a device which indicates the literary bias of the present dialogue. For at the end of the first chapter More noted:

. . . I began to gather in mynde / the hole effecte as my remembraunce wolde serue me of all that he had purposed. And because I wold haue it the more redy at myne eye / so that I myght ye more fully and effectually answere it / leuynge no parte vntouched / in such ordre as he had purposed it / that is to wytte / after the maner that I haue aboue reherced / I bryefly commytted it to wrytynge.

It is apparent that the table at which More seats the Messenger and himself in his study can be nothing but a writing table, and that their morning dialogue begins not with conversation but with a mutual reading of More's written record of the preceding day. Literally, "then I shewed vnto hym" the plan of the whole disputation.[6] More undertakes to communicate with the Messenger in his study through writing, and this is of course his real relation to the reader.

In Book I the Messenger and More meet early in his study, and their conversation, which comprises an exposition of the heresies with which More means to contend, ends with an adjournment for dinner. Book II is set thus:

After dyner we walked in to the gardyne. And there shortely syttyng in an arber / began to go forth in our matter / desyrynge hym to shewe what thynge myght that be / that made our long forenone processe frustrat / and lefte vs as vncertayne as we beganne.

6. The outline is found in the second paragraph of Chapter 2.

One might offer many explanations of More's fondness for the meal and the garden. His house was indeed famous for the conviviality and intellectual variety at its board; and if a meal symbolizes some level of communion, the garden, partaking of an ancient sacred and poetic tradition, embodies a period of sweet security. More, like Marvell, assumes a tradition of associations in the reader's response to his briefest scenic indications.[7]

At the same time, More's use of time and place in the *Dialogue Concerning Heresies* is highly individual. At the close of Book II he neglects the convention he had taken trouble to invoke. The interlocutors simply depart until "another time." The third dialogue occurs, we are told, a fortnight later, but not until its conclusion, when they go to dinner, do we understand that like

7. The tradition of prose dialogues set in gardens begins perhaps with Plato's *Phaedrus,* by a stream, under a tree, continues with a meadow setting in Augustine's *De beata vita,* and is still flowering in *Gli Asolani,* written by Pietro Bembo. In the next decade follows More's *Utopia,* and in the next Erasmus's *Convivium religiosum.* Tudor examples include Roger Ascham, *Toxophilus* (*STC* 837), which opens in a field; O. B., *Questions of profitable and pleasant concernings . . . by two olde seniors . . . under an oake in Kenilworth Parke* (1054), which contains a retelling of Chaucer's orchard story of January and May; William Bullein, *A dialogue . . . against the fever pestilence* (4036), second and fifth scenes; John Coke, trans., *The debate betwene the heraldes of Englande and Fraunce* (5530), in a garden; Arthur Dent, *The plaine mans path-way to Heaven* (6626), a walk "in this pleasant meadow" after dinner on a May evening, then "a goodly arbor and handsome seats"; George Gifford, *A Dialogue concerning witches* (11850), scene shifts from streets to garden; Miles Hogarde, *A mirrour of loue* (13559), May morning in the fields; David Lindsay, *Ane dialog betuix experience and ane courteour* (15672), May morning in a park/garden; "Sophronistes," *A Dialogue, perswading the people to reuerence God* (22930), scene ii in a garden; F. T., *The debate betweene pride and lowlines* (23617), a verse dream of a May morning in a dale; Edmund Tilney, *The flower of friendshippe* (24076.3), gentlemen and ladies in an Italianate garden; Robert Vaughan, *A dyalogue defensyue for women* (24601), in a green arbor; Jean Veron, *The huntynge of purgatorye to death* (24683), dialogue iii in a garden; and Thomas Wilson, *A discourse vppon vsurye* (25807), in a "pleasant sweet arbor" after dinner. I am indebted for some of these references to Roger Lee Deakins's Harvard doctoral dissertation, "The Tudor Dialogue as a Literary Form" (1964). Thomas More's last work, *De Tristitia Christi,* re-creates the dialogue between Christ and his apostles in the garden of Gethsemane.

the first dialogue it must have been conducted in More's study. When the fourth dialogue begins after dinner, in the garden, in an arbor, it is clear that the setting is formulaic; and the final withdrawal to dinner is merely perfunctory. So, on the face of it, More found a good device but came to rely upon it complacently.

He relies, to be more precise, upon the reader, whose attention, More assumes, is focused increasingly on the content of the disputation. The same pattern is discernible in *A Dialogue of Comfort.* The situation in the first book presents Antony on his deathbed receiving a visit from his nephew, and the book closes with a farewell at day's end. Book II finds Antony, after several days, still on his deathbed, discoursing on the justice of tribulation, and ends with dinner being brought in. It may be that More's care in conveying the sense of leisure in the breaks between dialogues is very self-conscious. Writing in prison with complete awareness, as his letters show, of his mortal peril, More was actually hurried. Yet ceremoniously he gives Antony time for a nap! Although the third and final book begins after a lapse of but a few hours, More only hastens slowly to the end. The dialogue concludes with no other scenic indication than the remark that it is the end of the day.

We may observe in the situations in *Utopia,* the *Dialogue Concerning Heresies,* and *A Dialogue of Comfort* a progressive modification in a classical convention as More adapts the situation to personal needs and to the themes of his dialogues. We notice, for example, that the dialogue of *Utopia* is set entirely out-of-doors. Like Erasmus's *Convivium religiosum,* the *Dialogue Concerning Heresies* is divided between house and grounds; it moves twice from study to garden. That is, the work is situated half inside, half outside. *A Dialogue of Comfort* is set wholly indoors, in a single room. Surely there is a certain decorum in this. In a sense the deliberative mood of all peirastic dialogue conveys, like Manet's landscapes, an *interior* quality. In More's case the interiorizing of the setting corresponds to what we feel to be a gradual pressing in of the world upon the ambassador, the apologist, and the man destined to die. The movement inward is marked, as we have seen, by progressive abbreviation of scenic indications. The emphasis falls at such moments on climaxes in the dialectic. This effect is highly conspicuous at the conclusion of Cardinal Bembo's visionary speech in *The Courtier*, where the rapturous ascent of the dialectic is accompanied by a dematerialization of the setting. The situation of Castiglione's gorgeous interior dialogue fades as the attention of the company focuses into contemplation, and then Castiglione concludes with a brilliant dispersal scene. More's situations are far simpler, more classical; but like the moment at the end of Bembo's speech, the effect of withdrawing or de-emphasizing the conventional device enhances the mood of contemplation. There is finally, for the reader, nowhere to look but in.

The meaning of a situation need not be restricted to a single time and place. In *A Dialogue of Comfort* More's allusions to the danger of a Turkish invasion of Hungary not only create a situation which refers to the Lutheran inroads at home, they also operate, as Martz has rightly stressed, metaphorically.[8] Turkish persecution, argued John Fowler in the preface to his 1573 edition of *A Dialogue of Comfort*, encompasses all kinds of affliction and suffering to which Christian folk are subject. "It is a book of comfort," Martz continues, "against all kinds of tribulation, not only against that kind which Thomas More himself is suffering. . . at the hands of Henry VIII. . . . More is aware of larger issues than his own fate. He sees his plight as involved in mankind's universal condition." We observe then four levels of correspondence in the situation in the dialogue: the historical danger in Hungary, the religious upheaval in England, More's personal strait, and the tribulations of all Christians. Multiple reference is a distinguishing mark of many humanist dialogues.

8. *A Dialogue of Comfort against Tribulation*, ed. Louis L. Martz and Frank Manley, *CW 12*, lxvi–lxvii. Cited hereafter as "*CW 12*." Manley provides an account of the Turkish threat, *CW 12*, cxx–cxxv. See also R. J. Schoeck, "Thomas More's 'Dialogue of Comfort' and the Problem of the Real Grand Turk," *English Miscellany*, 20 (1969), 23–37.

In such works as Elyot's dialogue *Of the Knowledge Which Maketh a Wise Man*, Erasmus's one-sided dialogue *Encomium Moriae*, and *Utopia*, it can produce fierce irony. In More's polemical dialogues, too, a multivalent situation reflects not only his habit of guarded utterance (and the precaution of parable) but also a predilection for layers of meaning which the ironic mode makes possible.

More attempted artistically to solve the problem of speaking in one dialogue to an enormously complex audience by developing a precise decorum. According to this decorum, characters are arranged in suggestive, almost symbolic situations designed to express divergent points of view. "When your frende had thus declared his credence [i. e., read me your letter of recommendation] /" More writes to the Messenger's master in the *Dialogue Concerning Heresies*, clarifying the situation between the interlocutors and their relation to a third figure who represents the reader (32/25–30):

> . . . he desyred me bothe on your behalfe / and on his owne / in such thynges as were percase not well sayde [i. e., heretical opinions] / to take them as they were in dede / the mynde of other / whome ye woulde fayne answere / and satysfye with reason / whiche ye trusted to be the better able to doo / by myne answere. . . .

The Messenger is thus licensed to express his doubts, while More draws a picture of the other speaker as a plain-spoken honest layman responding to the challenge of the situation, and thereby validates the arguments against heresy. Always in the background to reinforce his authority are his office and title. In this way More legitimates all questioning but leaves no doubt as to the authority of the answers. Frequent repetition, with minute variation, of the Messenger's questions together with patient recapitulation of the argument in the Councillor's responses reveals More's effort to accommodate his dialogue to a diverse, troubled, and confused audience. *A Dialogue of Comfort* is similarly inclusive, Vincent and Antony expressing and responding to a whole range of human tribulations. Both the formal disputation of heresy and the persuasion to comfort—

arising as they do from the deliberate situating of the characters—adhere to the method which Cicero advocated in the *Tusculan Disputations:*

No need to wonder then that in the conduct of cases in court we do not always take up the same position (this is the term we apply to lines of argument in disputes), but we adapt the line we take to the occasion, to the character of the dispute, to the personality of the litigant; we act similarly in the alleviation of distress, for we have to consider what method of treatment is admissible in each particular case.[9]

II

The style of More's dialogues is created from a rhetoric of argumentation whose method serves two distinct purposes. In the *Dialogue Concerning Heresies* the argument is doctrinal and public; it aims at the control of reason over theological problems. In *A Dialogue of Comfort* the argument, however much it involves questions of state, remains essentially private.

The centrality of Scripture in all More's writing is confirmed in Marc'hadour's monumental study. Whether directed against heresy or toward comfort, the effect of Scripture upon his dialogues is to open a new dimension in the form. In buttressing arguments with scriptural quotations in the *Dialogue Concerning Heresies* he invariably translates his examples into English; this practice, like the choice of well-worn examples from the classics, lends a tone of unpretentious familiarity to the disputation. "Many chapters of his *Dialogue of Comfort* are mosaics of Scriptural texts. Where Boethius wrote a *Consolatio Philosophiae,* and Gerson a *Consolatio Theologiae,* More wrote a *Consolatio Scripturarum.*"[10] More's brilliant, often unexpected application of scriptural texts to human situations astonishes us in many

9. Trans. J. E. King, Loeb Classical Library, 3, 79: "Nimirum igitur, ut in causis non semper utimur eodem statu—sic enim appellamus controversiarum genera—, sed ad tempus, ad controversiae naturam, ad personam accommodamus, sic in aegritudine lenienda quam quisque curationem recipere possit videndum est."

10. Germain Marc'hadour, "St. Thomas More," *Month,* New Series, 29 (1963), 74.

places throughout his writing.[11] Instead of saddling the form with patristic exegesis and legalistic precedents (More has a taste for both), his use of scriptural authority introduces the element of faith into the intellectual process of dialogue.

The treatment of Scripture is in fact the most distinctive feature of the polemical method of the *Dialogue Concerning Heresies.* Here we confront a phalanx of critics of More's pretensions to theological competence. This is not the place to reassess the theological foundation of his polemics, which asserts the ultimate authority of Scripture as interpreted by the Church; the problem of the tradition of belief recurs throughout his polemical works.[12] Until the edition of his texts is complete, an accurate assessment of More's theology remains difficult. As Father Egan cautions: "Deficiencies in More's writing are deficiencies of method not of doctrinal content nor of analysis and argumentation."[13] No one was more aware of the limits of method than the author himself.

11. For illustrations, see André Prévost, *Thomas More et la crise de la pensée européenne* (Tours and Paris, 1969), pp. 49f., and Manley's excellent discussion in *CW 12,* cxlvii–clxiv.

12. For a discussion of contemporary sources of More's concept of *consensus* in the *Responsio ad Lutherum,* see Headley, *CW 5,* pt. ii, 744f. More's position recalls the *Commonitoria* or "Remembrancer for the Antiquity and Universality of the Catholic Faith against the Profane Novelties of All Heresies" of St. Vincent of Lérins. It was he who provided a general rule whereby to distinguish Catholic truth from heresy, writes his translator: "an appeal to that sense of Holy Scripture which is supported by universality, antiquity, and consent: by universality, when it is the faith of the whole Church; by antiquity, when it is that which has been held from the earliest times; by consent, when it has been the acknowledged belief of all, or of almost all, whose office and character gave authority to their determinations. This is the famous 'Quod ubique, quod semper, quod ab omnibus,' with which Vincentius's name is associated" (C. A. Heurtley, trans., *A Select Library of Nicene and Post-Nicene Fathers. . . ,* 2d ser., vol. 11 [1894; repr. Grand Rapids, 1964], p. 128). Compare *CW 12,* 98/24–99/2. More perhaps signals this Vincent in so naming the nephew in *A Dialogue of Comfort,* thereby uniting, with the name of Antony, the two great patristic lines—monastic and eremitic.

13. Willis J. Egan, S.J., *The Rule of Faith in St. Thomas More's Controversy with William Tyndale, 1528–1533* (Los Angeles, 1960). I quote from Marc'hadour's précis of this printed dissertation in *The Bible in the Works of Thomas More,* Part 4

In the *Dialogue Concerning Heresies* More could not escape adopting an adversary posture. In addition, his "defense of the old faith against Lutherans. . . inflicted on him the necessity of a drier, more intellectual approach to the sacred volumes" than that which he had in his youth.[14] But the method of the dialogue is a long way from the aridity of much anti-heretical writing. In one critic's view, "More's dialogue is as far removed as possible from previous attempts to halt heresy by means of scholastic logic."[15] For example, More breaks out of the chains of logic imposed by the scholastic style (as Fisher does not) by reaching back to a form of argumentation, as Pineas has noted, reminiscent of Augustine's dialogue *Contra academicos.* More's argument, like Augustine's, adopts a fiction, which is to have speakers *act out* a dialogue, a method which provoked Tyndale to refer to More's dialogue as "quod I, and quod he, and quod your frende."[16] But More's style reaches back still further, *ad fontes,* in search of materials for a new form. Platonic in its dramatic setting, Ciceronian in its oratorical rhetoric, More's dialogue of 1528 is a humanist synthesis.

Once he has created the Socratic situation, More adheres to the rhetoric of Cicero's orator. The seeds of this polemical style having been planted in the *Utopia,* in the *Dialogue Concerning Heresies* the orator's art flourishes. If More is at times guilty of twisting his opponent's words,[17] in so doing he is only following Cicero's advice. Even when his aim is not solely polemical, as in *A Dialogue of Comfort,* Ciceronian methods of oratory continue to

---

(Nieuwkoop, 1971), 193–96; the succeeding pages of Part 4 are also helpful. Cited hereafter as "Marc'hadour, *The Bible.*"

14. Marc'hadour, *The Bible,* Part 4, 121.

15. Rainer Pineas, "Thomas More's Use of the Dialogue Form as a Weapon of Religious Controversy," *Studies in the Renaissance,* 7 (1960), 198.

16. *The Practice of Popish Prelates,* in *The Whole Workes of W. Tyndall, Iohn Frith, and Doct. Barnes* (London, 1573), p. 364. See note 61 *infra.* On the adoption of the dialogue fiction, see *CW 6,* 32/25–32 and 62/25–63/3.

17. See Pineas, "More versus Tyndale: A Study of Controversial Technique," *Modern Language Quarterly,* 24 (1963), 144–50.

shape the dialogue. Antony methodically holds to the chosen topic, and though digressions are frequent, he is rigorous in pointing them out.[18] We notice in Antony's responses the care with which he repeats Vincent's objections, illustrating that he has listened and understood.[19] The manner of refutation is ostensibly formal, Antony's arguments being usually as systematic as those in the dialogue on heresies.[20]

Because More himself, like "this player here," has "the motive and the cue for passion," we are drawn to examine the personal situation in which the art of oratory is practiced. In writing of persecution and pain More is not arousing "morbid curiosity" nor building "suspense" by a titillating " 'cliff-hanger' technique."[21] More's art is quite unlike such cynical artifice. In the prolonged and highly elaborated oratorical treatment of persecution it is evident that More is gradually approaching the supreme problem of his own painful and shameful death. When Antony's oratory strikes us as cumbersome or tedious, it may be helpful to remember that More risks using rhetorical persuasion on the most difficult audience—himself. Socrates, Cicero, and Boethius provided precedents for the use of dialogic disputation in a situation of personal disgrace and danger. It was an organizing form for thought and language. In *A Dialogue of Comfort* More pits the form and its oratorical complement directly against this problem, with an incongruity between the subject and Antony's systematic treatment of it that is often shocking.

> . . . we will / I say / therfor begynne with the consideryng, what manner payne or incommoditie we shuld rekyn ymprisonment to be, of hym selfe & of his owne nature alone / And than in the course of our communicacion, you shall as you lyst encrease and aggreue the cause of your horrour, with the terrour of those paynfull accidentes / (256/21–26)

18. E.g., *CW 12*, 131.

19. E.g., Book I, Ch. 19, *CW 12*, 65ff.

20. An epitome of this manner is found in Book I, Chapter 16, where Antony numbers each point.

21. Leland Miles, "The Literary Artistry of Thomas More," *Studies in English Literature*, 6 (1966), 11.

If dialogue and oratory help to shape the exposition of so unwieldy a subject as that of the *Dialogue Concerning Heresies,* in *A Dialogue of Comfort* one is equally aware of tremendous tensions pulling the form apart, aware of the effort to maintain coherence.

Comfort is founded upon the inner dialogue of spiritual meditation, which is distinct from the inner dialectical conversation which Socrates says is thought (*dianoia*). In contrast with the succession of topics in the dialogue on heresy, the argument moves from station to station toward a center of pain where "spiritual causes of comfort" are needed. *A Dialogue of Comfort* begins *in medias res.*[22] As in a classical agon, the characters gradually reveal and exhaust their passions. As in a medieval allegory, their dialogue methodically unwinds the inner conflicts of one particular self. Thus the increasing role of Vincent, the quality of whose reasoning his uncle comes to commend, is undercut by a sense of his decreasing importance to Antony. Even from the first page, "Antony is shown as a man already on his way out."[23] Perhaps the repeated play on Vincent's name in the next to last chapter is meant to suggest that the vital comfort has been given and joyfully received.[24] There are in fact many pointers towards a mystical conclusion. But, as St. John of the Cross showed, the inner dialogue of spiritual meditation, however valid, is fraught with self-deceptions.[25] More is careful here, as in the dialogue on heresies, not to have his characters claim any direct revelation from God. His last dialogue attempts to use the "reasonings,

22. Marc'hadour, *The Bible,* Part 4, 129.

23. Ibid. Commendation intensifies in the last book, for example *CW 12,* 257/19: "This ys Cosyn well considerid of you / for in this you perceve well. . . ."

24. *CW 12,* 309/12–23: "*vincenti dabo edere de ligno vite* / To hym that ouercometh, I shall give hym to eate of the tree of lyfe. . . . *vincenti dabo manna absconditvm, & dabo illi calculum candidum. Et in calculo nomen nouum scriptum quod nemo scit nisi qui accipit* / To hym that ouercometh will I give manna secret & hid / & I will give hym a white suffrage, & in his suffrage a new name wrytten, which no man knowith but he that receyveth it /"

25. *Ascent of Mount Carmel,* ed. and trans. E. Allison Peers (London, 1935), II, xxix, pp. 209–15.

words, and conceptions" of the soul in scriptural meditation to obtain that most subtle comfort, the "genuine spiritual influence of the Holy Spirit. . . ."[26]

An analysis of the formal development from the *Dialogue Concerning Heresies* to *A Dialogue of Comfort* reinforces this conclusion. The dialogues may be contrasted with regard to their composition in two different periods in More's career. His resignation from the chancellorship (16 May 1532) marks the official end of his public career and the beginning of his retirement and preparation for death.[27] The *Dialogue Concerning Heresies* carries out to the letter the bishop of London's commission in a spirit of mixed personal and professional duty, while *A Dialogue of Comfort* professes to be the document of a private Christian. To take a longer perspective, the form developed in response to a gradual change in More's conception of the uses of disputation: between the youthful Pico, who offered to dispute his nine hundred questions with the clergy of Rome, and the aged Antony, who leans away from controversy, stands the disputation on heresies. In it More adopted dialogue for the purpose of theological argument.[28] In the Tower other needs sought satisfaction in the method of dialogue. The earlier, rather predictably correct use of a method adopted for argument contrasts with the later stage in which More made dialogue his own idiom for meditation, prayer, and transcendence.

That More elected the dialogue form in order to defend the Church suggests his conception of the nature of the heretical mind. A disorder in the right relation between faith and reason, heresy must have aroused a unique distaste in the author of *Utopia*. Etymologically,[29] a heretic was one who "chose" and pro-

26. Ibid.

27. G. R. Elton, "Sir Thomas More and the Opposition to Henry VIII," *Bulletin of the Institute of Historical Research*, 41 (1968), 19.

28. More had used the cumbersome technique of verbatim citation followed by point-by-point refutation in the *Responsio ad Lutherum* of 1523. See John M. Headley, ed., *CW* 5, 806–14.

29. From Greek *hairein*, to take for oneself, to choose.

fessed his unorthodox belief. Heresy thus implied willful error against reason, yet there remained hope that the method of rational dialectic might, if not overcome error, prevent the faithful from choosing it.

For a variety of reasons More vigorously opposed heresy in print. But it is difficult to read the language of opposition dispassionately, not least of all for modern academics, who can be as sensitive to opposition as heretics. We are told, for example, that "the gentle and sweet side of More's character, which so much attracted Erasmus on their first meeting, is not often evident in More's controversial writings," indeed that "More's vocabulary in discussing heresy exceeds in severity most other Renaissance polemic."[30] In general, More stayed well above the common level of dispute, for heretics indulged all too habitually in "railing." In *The Apologye of Sir Thomas More, Knight,* he says he would gladly reason with them if they would "write reason and leaue raylinge" but this he knows they will never do.[31] Much of what has been called More's "severity" and might be called his "railing" (especially toward Luther) is triumphant ridicule.[32] While they are not without harsh mockery, the restraint, not the invective, of his disputations is what surprises us. Nevertheless, the ugly lapses of polemical fury, relics of which can be found even in *A Dialogue of Comfort,* reveal those fears which continued to assail More's deepest hopes.

G. R. Elton has assembled evidence beyond the canon of More's writing in his case for the extreme vehemence of More's

30. Leland Miles, "Persecution and the *Dialogue of Comfort:* A Fresh Look at the Charges against Thomas More," *Journal of British Studies,* 5 (1965), 28.

31. *The workes . . . in the Englysh tonge,* ed. William Rastell (1557; facsimile London, 1978), sig. I_5v; cited hereafter as "*EW.*" See R. W. Chambers, *Thomas More* (1935; repr. London, 1963), p. 254; cited hereafter as "Chambers."

32. Prévost discusses the uses of humor in the *Dialogue Concerning Heresies* in *Thomas More et la crise de la pensée européenne,* pp. 188–91. See also Rainer Pineas, "Thomas More's Use of Humor as a Weapon of Religious Controversy," *Studies in Philology,* 58 (1961), 97–114. Schuster (*CW 8,* pt. iii, 1146–49) assesses the vilification of Luther in the *Responsio* which More moderated in his later, vernacular dialogues.

opposition. "All the evidence goes to show that More hated heresy with a real, even an exceptional passion."[33] Elton continues: "He dreaded heresy with a hatred that in so reasonable and balanced a man strikes one as a trifle abnormal," querying in a footnote: "Had More in his younger days ever experienced doubt about catholic orthodoxy?"[34] To this the only answer is, Who hasn't? Oddly, Elton, no less than the hagiographers, is unwilling to acknowledge More's right to hate the enemy, though it is permitted to the psalmist and even to the apostles.

Passionate hatred and abnormal dread do not ultimately characterize the dialogue on heresies. To say so would imply a triumph of irrationality, a loss of control, when it is these precisely which the formal language of opposition precludes. The critical reader who observes the deliberate harshness of the antiheretical rhetoric in the *Dialogue Concerning Heresies* should also notice the banter, the tranquil scene, and the leisurely pace which contribute to the image of reason in the dialogue.

It is interesting to recognize certain traces of the method of *Heresies* in *Comfort*. Reason still directs the argument. The dialogue begins by proposing to define tribulation, which "semeth generally to signifie nothyng els, but some kynd of grefe eyther payne of the body or hevynes of ⌈the⌉ mynd."[35] In its early preoccupation with definition the dialogue presents a logical partitioning or anatomy of melancholy. On the other hand, More scans the pagan philosophers and the Scriptures for rational reasons for joy in tribulation.[36] There are remnants of controversialist rhetoric in Vincent and Antony's early questions and answers, as for example in the opening speeches of Chapter 12.

But for More such rhetoric is no longer useful. *A Dialogue of Comfort* bespeaks an overwhelming desire to give up con-

33. "Sir Thomas More and the Opposition to Henry VIII," p. 22. To the evidence might be added More's own description of himself in his epitaph as grievous (*"molestus"*) to heretics.

34. Ibid., p. 33.

35. *CW 12*, 10/6–7; the definition continues to be refined to p. 50.

36. Especially Book I, Chs. 11, 13, and 20, and Book II, Ch. 7.

troversy. Vincent's reference in Chapter 12 to the heresies of no purgatory and salvation by faith alone only elicits from Antony the assurance that he takes comfort in the "good liklyhod" that the "variaunce in our beleve" shall reach "some good agrement to grow in one accord of our fayth" (37/25–38/5). On the challenged doctrine of the intercession of the saints, Antony replies simply, in contrast to the *Dialogue Concerning Heresies,* "Therefor will I let god worke & leve of contention. . . . Strive will I not with them for this matter now/"[37] The old disputant's renunciation is not untouched by irony.

> But cosyn as I told you the tother day before / In these maters with these new men I will not dispute / but surely for myn own part I can not well hold with them, for as far as myn owne pore wit can perceve, the holy scripture of god is very playne agaynst them / And the whole corps of cristendome in euery cristen region / and the very places in which they dwell them self, haue euer vnto their own dayes clerely belevid agaynst them / And all the old holy doctours haue euer more taught agaynst them / And all the old holy interpretours haue construed the scripture agaynst them. And therfor yf these men haue now percevid so late / that the scripture hath be misse vnderstanden all this while / and that of all those old holy doctours / no man could vnderstand yt / than am I to old at this age to begyn to study it now / (98/24–99/2)

As for disputing between the claims of the new men and the traditional interpretation of Scripture, says Antony (57/5–6), "I shall not nede to breke our brayne. . . ."

Yet, as his actions and writings after his retirement make clear, it was More's attitude toward controversy itself, not heresy, which changed. He grew more scrupulous, more sensitive to circumstances, in the years following the *Dialogue Concerning Heresies.* In Antony's words (173/5–8),

> Hard is it Cosyn in many maner thinges, to bid or forbede, afferm or

37. *CW 12,* 38/18, 39/19–20. Elsewhere Antony declares: "I will not dispute the mater here / . . . And bettre dare I iuberd my soule with the soule of saint Bernard, than with his that fyndeth that faut in his doctryne" (156/6–12).

denye, reprove or alow, a mater nakidly proponid & put forth / or presisely to say this thing is good or this thyng is nought, without consideracion of the circumstaunces /

In considering this change, apparent in the different tone and concern of the two dialogues, we should recall that More had long been a reluctant controversialist. His decision to give up disputation with his son-in-law Roper and to rely instead on prayer for his conversion to the Catholic faith—"I will no longer argue nor dispute with him, but will cleane geve him over, and gett me another while to God and praye for him"[38]—sums up the transformation from the *Dialogue Concerning Heresies* to *A Dialogue of Comfort.* Just after his resignation, as Chambers relates the story (p. 244), a large sum of money was collected by the clergy to reward More for his labors in defence of the Church. More refused, saying that he "would rather have cast their money into the Thames"; he wished people "neither to read these heretics' books nor mine, but occupy their minds better" with "such English books as most may nourish and increase devotion." Here too we see More, in the period between the two dialogues, preferring devotion over controversy.

The change in attitude toward controversy and the direction in which it would finally carry his dialogue are the fulfillment of the model whose life he translated more than twenty years before. Of Pico he wrote:

He was verie quicke, wise, and subtile in dispicions, and had great felicitee therein, while he had that high stomak. But now a great while he had bid such co*n*flictes fare wel, and euery daie more & more hated them. . . .

Though he could argue brilliantly, Pico had come to feel that

38. Nicholas Harpsfield, *The Life and Death of Sir Thomas Moore,* ed. E. V. Hitchcock, E.E.T.S., Original Series, no. 186 (London, 1932), p. 87. See also the important letter to Nicholas Wilson in which More surveys the change that has taken place in his attitude toward controversy. *The Correspondence of Sir Thomas More,* ed. Elizabeth F. Rogers (Princeton, 1947), no. 206. Cited hereafter as "Rogers."

those dispicions did great hurt, that were holden openly to thostentacion of lernyng, and to winne the fauour of the common people, & the commendacion of folies.

Thus did he set more at last by "devotion" than "conning."[39]

III

In writing *A Dialogue of Comfort* More comes to occupy a paradoxical position. His speeches under Cromwell's examination show how firm were his renunciation of disputation and his commitment to a devotional life. "And now," says the prisoner to Master Secretary, "I haue in good fayth dyscharged my mynde of all such maters, and neyther wyll dyspute Kyng*is* tytles nor Popys, but the Kyng*is* trew faythfull subiect I am and wylbe, and dayly I pray for hym. . . ." After further interrogation, with the prospect of his release,

I shortly . . . answered . . . that I wolde neuer medle in the worlde agayne, to haue the worlde gyuen me . . . but that my hole study shulde be, vppon the passyon of Chryst and myne owne passage owt of thys w⟨orlde⟩.[40]

And yet, when one thinks of it, these ready, simple speeches of renunciation recall the eloquent formulas, indeed the *pavis* or shield, with which Antony defends himself and out of which More forged *A Dialogue of Comfort.* It often seems that the prison dialogue serves as practice in responding under interrogation. The paradox of his position is that while wanting to give up contention he must continue to fight.

So great is the strain on the conventional format of objection and answer that the characters themselves seem to express More's reluctance. "I do you very much wrong to give you occasion to labour your selfe so much in mater of some study," Vincent apologizes, "with long talkyng at ones / I will therfor at this tyme move you but one thyng / & seke some other tyme for

39. *The life of John Picus Erle of Mirandula* in *EW,* sigs. a_3B–C and a_4C.

40. Rogers, p. 552; cited by Chambers, p. 309. More sustained four interrogations in the Tower: on 30 April, 7 May, 3 June, and 14 June 1535, in addition to the conversation with Richard Rich on 12 June.

the remenaunt at your more ease" (64/7–11). Vincent's reluctance to object, like Antony's reluctance to dispute, becomes the standard performance as More recasts the roles of the *Dialogue Concerning Heresies.* Still, the grim questions are asked, answers given. I have called More's position a "paradox" and suggested that it transformed his conception of dialogue. Nevertheless, in every season the author remains one man; the informing consciousness of *A Dialogue of Comfort* responds, in ways I hope to show, to the deepest concerns of the *Dialogue Concerning Heresies.*

As a prisoner More knew that death was near.[41] Correspondingly the emphasis in the prologue to *Comfort* falls on Antony's mortality. He is "now lykely to depart hens are long," says Vincent, and "what a mysse of much comfort we shall have, when ye be gone. . . ." The comfort which the dialogue seeks is not for Antony, lying in the natural disease of his old age, but for his surviving kindred in danger of persecution for the faith. On this subject he has firsthand knowledge, having been twice a prisoner of the Turks just as More is now a prisoner. The dialogue addresses the confllict created by a condemnation to die for the faith. Many complexities inhere in this central conflict. For example, to suffer persecution and die for a belief requires the continual, active vigilance of the will. More's dialogue, his letters, his spoken utterances, and even the annotations in his prayer book reveal this vigilance.

The *Dialogue Concerning Heresies* had quickened More's perception of the rooted tenacity of heretical minds. Attacking them mercilessly, he declared the faithful Christian's duty to suffer no less tenaciously for his belief.

. . . we be bounden to abyde all sorow & shamfull dethe & all martyrdome vpon payne of perpetuall damnacyon for the professyon of our fayth. . . . The ease of his yoke standeth not in bodyly ease / nor y[e]

41. From the Tower he wrote to his daughter Margaret on the 2d or 3d of May, 1535: "And I am dying alredy, and haue syns I came here, bene dyuers tymes in the case that I thought to dye ⟨within⟩ one houre, and I thank our Lorde I was neuer sory for yt, ⟨but rather⟩ sory whan I saw the pang past" (Rogers, p. 553).

lyghtnes of his burdeyne standeth not in the slackenes of any bodyly payne . . . but it standeth in ye swetnes of hope / wherby we fele in our payne a plesaunt taste of heuen. (*CW* 6, 106/10–23)

More's abhorrence of Lutheran apostasy can be measured here by the intensity of his own commitment to the Catholic faith. But in 1534, the Act of Supremacy, like a cruel peripeteia, thrust More himself into the *role* of heretic, making him one who, in the eyes of the king and Parliament, persisted in the willful adherence to unlawful belief. In England the orthodoxy of the earlier dialogue suddenly became "heresy." In treating persecution instead of heresy in *A Dialogue of Comfort* More sets his drama on an international stage.

Another conflict with which *A Dialogue of Comfort* comes to terms is the one created by imprisonment, and here too More benefits from a sensitivity to the heretical mind. Early in the dialogue, he is concerned with *desperation*—the conflict of one who has "no will to be curid" and whose reason has fallen into a "dedly dulnes . . . thynkyng almost on nothyng" (14/12–20). More's adoption of a therapeutic conversation links him directly with Boethius, who also fought to rationalize his dispiriting fate.

. . . this man was wont to telle the diverse cawses of nature þat weeren . . . hydde / / Allas now lith he emted of lyht of his thowht / / and his nekke is pressed with hevy cheynes / and berith his cheere enclyned a down / for the grete weyhte and is constreynyd to looken on the fool erthe[42]

Boethius gives the impression that Dame Philosophy is virtually the hallucination of the solitary prisoner. More's elaborate fiction doubtless served to provide him too with reasonable company in his abjection. Imprisonment naturally occasions contemplation of the loss of goods and freedom, and for both Boethius and More contemplation takes a dialectical form. But in addition, regardless of its occasion, solitary contemplation seems to be attended by a peculiar inner conflict.

42. Geoffrey Chaucer, trans., *Boece* [*De Consolatione philosophiae*], ed. F. J. Furnivall, Chaucer Society, First Series, no. 75, Book I, 2d meter (London, 1886), p. 4.

Philosophy immediately recognizes this conflict in Boethius, explaining that

he is fallen in to a litarge / / which that is a comune sykenesse to hertes þat ben desseyvyd / / he hath a litel foryeten hym self / / but certes he shall lyhtly remenbren hym self[43]

In a Christian context this "lethargy" would be called accidie. I believe that More may have this passage from Boethius in mind when he writes of those who

fall into a careles dedly dulnes, regardyng nothyng / thynkyng almost on nothyng, no more than yf they ley on a letarge / with which yt may so fall, that wit and remembraunce will were [i.e., wear] awaye, & fall even faire from them / And this cumfortles kynd of hevynes in trybulacion, ys the hieghest kynd of the dedly synn of slowth / (14/18–23)

Accidie is the peculiar conflict with which the cloistered contemplative must contend, as we are told by Cassianus, to whom More frequently refers in *A Dialogue of Comfort:*

one's mind is in an irrational confusion, like the earth befogged in a mist, one is slothful and vacant in every spiritual activity, and no remedy, it seems, can be found for this state of siege than a visit from some brother, or the solace of sleep.[44]

The monk in his cell, like the prisoner in his, fancies that a "remedy" to his accidie lies in a visit from some brother. That fantasy, deceptive as it is, suggests one possible psychological origin of imaginary dialogue. But the good monk—or any man voluntarily secluded—must fight off the desire for worldly occupations which drives him from spiritual progress.[45] Herein lies

43. Book I, 2d prose, p. 4.

44. "Of Accidie," in *De Coenobiorum Institutis,* X, 2, trans. Helen Waddell, *The Desert Fathers* (1936; repr. London and Glasgow, 1965), p. 173. Presumably More first encountered both Cassian's writings and the conflict of accidie during his four years in the London Charterhouse.

45. Cassian writes that the mind of one affected by accidie "loses itself" in the business of others "and is thus little by little ensnared by dangerous occupations, so that, just as if it were bound up in the coils of a serpent, it can never disentangle itself again" (*De Coen.,* X, 6, trans. Edgar C. S. Gibson, *Select Library of Nicene and Post-Nicene Fathers. . . ,* 2d ser., vol. 11 [1894; repr. Grand Rapids,

the conflict or, to use More's word, the temptation. It hovers in the background throughout *A Dialogue of Comfort.* Against accidie, as against other temptations, such as fear, More opposes the great monastic psalm. For, as Cassianus says at the very outset of his book on accidie:

> It is akin to dejection . . . , disturbing the monk especially about midday, like a fever mounting at a regular time, and bringing its highest tide of inflammation at definite accustomed hours to the sick soul. And so some of the Fathers declare it to be the demon of noontide which is spoken of in the xcth Psalm.[46]

In projecting imaginary conversations More's dialogue provides comfort against the conflict of accidie. At moments they are concerned specifically with temptation. The disease of the habitual solitary, however, which the device of dialogue might relieve to a degree, only stings in comparison with the painful fear of despair. Traditionally, despair is to be feared as a cardinal sin—the sin against the Holy Ghost, the Comforter. It is this conflict which Cassian calls the "most injurious passion."[47] Of the working of such a conflict in More's mind we cannot speak with certainty; nevertheless, the recurrence of this subject in the Tower dialogue indicates his preoccupation with the danger which it threatened to anyone spiritually embattled. Antony recognizes from the first that there can be no cure for "that person desperat, that desierith not his own cumfort" (14/13–14). That person's fate is like the dead end of heresy. Yet the dialogue cries out from the verge of that plight, from the conflict which Antony represents metaphorically as being on the point of drowning. All the stories of the fear of despair which are told in

---

1964], p. 268). More prays in the Tower "To be content to be solitary. Not to long for worldly company. Lytle and litle utterly to cast of the world. And ridde my mynde of all the busynesse thereof. . . . To abstaine from vaine confabulacions" (*Thomas More's Prayer Book. . . ,* transcribed and translated by Louis L. Martz and Richard S. Sylvester [New Haven and London, 1969], pp. 205f.).

46. Trans. Waddell, p. 172.

47. Trans. Gibson, *De Coen.,* IX, 13.

the dialogue can be focused in the primary category of temptation from the ninetieth psalm: "*Non timebis a timore nocturno,* thow shalt not be aferd of the fere of the night" (107/3–4). This fear can create the conflict whose only solution seems to be suicide. But, as More knows, "the nightes feare . . . casteth in our imaginacion mych more fere than cause" (110/27–30). In contending with this conflict dialogue can be instrumental.[48] Let us be clear about the conception underlying the role of dialogue in rooting out the fear of despair. We shall withstand "the depe darknes of the myd night," says Antony, by a "good hope in god" and the "light of fayth" whereby our "spirituall understandyng" shall be increased and thus dispel the night's fear. So too Cassian says that "by spiritual meditation we may keep our mind constantly occupied with hope of the future and contemplation of the promised blessedness" and thus "expel this most injurious passion from our hearts. . . ."[49] For More, then, dialogue itself is rational activity in which the mind, kept constantly occupied in spiritual meditation and contemplation, moves against despair.

More's attempt to reach the core of human tribulation refines the dialogue as an instrument of analysis. In contrast, the doctrinal disputation of the *Dialogue Concerning Heresies* seems restricted and confined. The resolution of conflict can be appreciated in the greater flexibility of the interlocutors in *A Dialogue of Comfort.* In place of the Messenger's dogmatic and aggressive tone, the nephew's becomes forbearing and tentative. The Councillor's learning and authority are overshadowed by Antony's capacity for tolerance and forgiveness. What

48. In "Suicide, Martyrdom, and Thomas More," *Renaissance Quarterly,* 19 (1972), 147n., Paul D. Green invites us to compare More's consolation of the man from Winchester with Erasmus's "Saiynges of Diogenes the Cynike," Book I, Section 8: " . . . to the hart beyng in heavines and utter discomfort: the best Phisician is good and wholsome communicacion. . . ." *The Apophthegmes of Erasmus,* trans. Nicolas Udall (1564): ed. and ann. Robert Roberts (Boston, 1877), p. 80. See also Erasmus, *Adagia* 2099, in *Opera omnia,* ed. J. Clericus, 10 vols. (Leiden, 1703–6), II, 744D–745C.

49. *De Coen.*, IX, 13.

Marc'hadour calls the "tone of quiet intimacy throughout" *A Dialogue of Comfort*[50] is the result of mutually reinforcing attitudes—a disenchantment with disputation and an increasing spirituality—whose evolution becomes prominent in this work. In returning to the trial of faith in *A Dialogue of Comfort* More confronts the problem of his *Dialogue Concerning Heresies* on its most dangerously intimate level.

IV

In the conjunction of these attitudes More's last dialogue follows St. Antony. Athanasius records St. Antony's criticism of the philosophers to their faces.

> '[S]ince, of course, you pin your faith on demonstrative proofs and this is an art in which you are masters, and you want us also not to worship God without demonstrative arguments—do you first tell me this. How does precise knowledge of things come about, especially knowledge about God? Is it by verbal proof or by an act of faith? And which comes first, an active faith or verbal proof?'
>
> When they replied that the act of faith takes precedence and that this constitutes accurate knowledge, Antony said: 'Well said! Faith arises from the disposition of the soul, while dialectic comes from the skill of those who devise it. Accordingly, those who are equipped with an active faith have no need of verbal argument, and probably find it even superfluous. For what we apprehend by faith, that you attempt to construct by arguments; and often you cannot even express what we perceive. The conclusion is that an active faith is better and stronger than your sophistic arguments.'[51]

St. Antony's position, which rings so clearly here, has a remote purity in contrast with More's Antony, who struggles in a more contaminated intellectual milieu. More recognized a complex interpenetration of reason and faith. But the precedence of faith

50. Marc'hadour, *The Bible,* Part 4, 129. See also his "Thomas More's Spirituality," in *St. Thomas More: Action and Contemplation,* ed. Richard S. Sylvester (New Haven and London, 1972), pp. 123–59, and the essays by Professors Martz and Schoeck in *Thought,* 52 (1977).

51. *The Life of Saint Antony,* trans. Robert T. Meyer (Westminster, Maryland, 1950), pp. 83f.

in the Antonine position, like other blunt distinctions of the Fathers, never lost its appeal for him. " 'We [Christians], however, do not prove, as our teacher said, *in persuasive words of Greek wisdom:* but it is by faith which tangibly precedes any constructive reasoning of arguments.' "[52] The reasoning of disputation cannot provide the assurance of things hoped for, the conviction of things not seen; a dialogue of comfort requires the persuasions of faith.

In the fourteenth century Petrarch warned of the limitations of the discipline of dialectic. His remark is suggestive, I think, of the evolution in a writer's mind which could produce changes in the dialogue form.

> All of us must cover a long and difficult road in a short set time in bad weather, almost as it were on a rainy winter day. Occupation with dialectic may cover a part of this road; it ought never to be the goal. It may be on the morning schedule but never on that of the evening.[53]

So it was with Pico, and with More. A growing spiritual preoccupation did not preclude the use of dialectic, but in More's case it led to a cultivation of the part of faith in dialectical reasoning. On the other hand, reason can be directed toward spiritual ends. By the third book of *A Dialogue of Comfort* More's disputation has been transmuted, as Martz suggests, into a spiritual meditation, showing that one "may move with the help of reason into a realm that includes and yet transcends reason. . . ."[54] In what ways has the dialogue form shared in this transmutation?

"[T]o the man that laketh wit & fayth," Antony asserts, "no comfort can serue what so euer counsayle be gevyn" (87/4–5). Comfort requires an intelligence to interpret the substance of counsel, and it requires faith. To the man who possesses both

52. Ibid., p. 85. "Our teacher" is St. Paul (1 Cor. 2:4).

53. Letter to Tommaso Caloria (ca. 1335), trans. Hans Nachod, in *The Renaissance Philosophy of Man,* ed. Ernst Cassirer, Paul Oskar Kristeller, and John H. Randall, Jr. (Chicago, 1948), pp. 137f.

54. *CW 12,* lxxvii.

wit and faith, Antony later adds, comfort "standeth in two thynges / counsayle and prayour" (151/16–17). The conceptual "road" from the outset of the *Dialogue Concerning Heresies* to the end of *A Dialogue of Comfort* might be said to follow this direction: dialectical reasoning moves through counsel and faith to prayer. Controversy moves through the wisdom of the Fathers and Catholic dogma to meditation whose purpose is the endurance of pain.

How, precisely, can faith help reason? Taken as a whole, as Sylvester has observed, the Tower works "define for us, forcefully and poignantly, the process of mind in and through which his admirable serenity ('merriness,' he called it) was attained."[55] In that "process of mind" faith plays the crucial part. Psalm 90 first attracts More's interest by its metaphor for the troubled mind: the fear of the night.[56] Our fear comes when "we be so blynd in the darke night of tribulacion," in "the depe darknes of the myd night," that we need to see "most speciall by the yee [eye] of oure fayth. . . ." Thus, More argues, faith corrects perception to a true vision of our own condition. The process of mind is a gradual *"spirituall understandyng"* which the dialogue takes rational steps to effect.

St. Antony taught his fellow monks that writing down a dialogue of sinful thoughts could help them overcome temptation.

> 'Just as we would not give ourselves over to lust within sight of each other, so if we were *to write down our thoughts as if telling them to each other,* we shall so much the more guard ourselves against foul thoughts for shame of being known. Now, then, let the written account stand for the eyes of our fellow ascetics, so that blushing at writing the same as if we were actually seen, we may never ponder evil. Molding ourselves in this way, we shall be able *to bring our body into subjection,* to please the Lord and to trample under foot the machinations of the Enemy.'[57]

55. Richard S. Sylvester, ed., *St. Thomas More: Action and Contemplation,* p. 11.
56. Book II, Ch. 12.
57. Athanasius, *The Life of Saint Antony,* trans. Meyer, p. 68 (emphasis added).

More's Antony assures his nephew (150/25–28),

> where as that ⸢thought⸣ (were in neuer so horrible & neuer so abomynable) ys yet vnto them that neuer like it but euer still abhorre yt & stryve still there agaynst, mater of conscience & merit, & not any synne at all /

Even more than the *Dialogue Concerning Heresies, A Dialogue of Comfort* may be seen as a written record of "abominable thoughts." The latter provides not only matter of conflict, as we have seen, but also "matter of merit"; for in writing of the fears of persecution and their attendant temptations, More is striving to bring the body into subjection, to please the Lord and to trample under foot the machinations of the Enemy. Vincent declares his intent to write down the comfortable counsel of Antony, but Thomas More committed both sides of the dialogue to writing.[58]

The process of More's mind habitually used a conscious technique of playing roles.[59] Late in *A Dialogue of Comfort* he provides us with an insight into the spiritual purpose of this dramatic technique. Antony asks Vincent to play a role in order to elucidate a point.[60] Vincent hardly has the heart to play the role of the rich, worldly man who would forsake his faith for his goods, but he perseveres in the scene for several pages. This technique is central in the *Dialogue Concerning Heresies,* where the Messenger is asked to speak as if he were a Lutheran.[61] At last Antony

58. Interestingly, Cicero mentions the curative power of writing dialogue at the end of the *Tusculans.* "For my part I think too that I shall write . . . out [the discussion of the last five days,]" he says. "In doing this I cannot readily say how much I shall benefit others; at any rate in my cruel sorrows and the various troubles which beset me from all sides no other consolation could have been found."

59. See Richard S. Sylvester, "*A Part of His Own:* Thomas More's Literary Personality in His Early Works," *Moreana,* 15–16 (1967), 29–42.

60. *CW 12,* 229–37. "And I pray you Cosyn take you his [lordship's] person vppon you / & in this case answere for hym" (229/2–3).

61. Rainer Pineas, in "Thomas More's Use of the Dialogue Form as a Weapon of Religious Controversy," *Studies in the Renaissance,* 7 (1960), 193, points out that, similarly, in Augustine's dialogue *Contra academicos* "the opposing side is

drives the actor into a corner, an *elenchus:* "can I not ymagyne / nor list in this mater to play their part no lenger. . . ." Vincent prays for "the grace to play the contrary parte. . . ." Virtue itself, More implies, is a *part* which we are given the grace to play. Portions of his dialogues comprise scripts to con.

The preparatory meditation of More's dialogue concerns, in a phrase that identifies Antony as a Christian humanist, *such things as pertain toward the conducting of reasonable men to salvation* (296/8–9). This process is shown to be increasingly spiritual as the dialogue moves toward its conclusion. Specifically, Antony asserts that neither reason nor prayer shall save us without God's grace.[62] "Preparation" comes at last to be defined as "labour by prayour." Again and again in the final chapters Antony's reasoning flows into prayer. Such is the process by which the many currents of the dialogue are brought under More's control.

The process in which faith helps reason is tied to the dialogue form in the most intricate fashion. In Book III, Chapter 17, Vincent gives voice to the fear of bodily pain—"the feare that forceth myne hart to tremble" (245/14–15). This fear and trembling recalls verses 4 and 5 of Psalm 54, which in his prayer book (p. 95) More marked *"in tribulatione,"* showing the special function they served in his devotions. The allusion in Vincent's speech thus sets the dialogue in the context of the psalm which begins *"Exaudi deus orationem meam,"* "Give ear to *my prayer,* O God." It is evident that the topic under debate in the dialogue is bound at the deepest level to More's spiritual exercise. To take

---

represented not by the actual opponents themselves, but by some of Augustine's pupils who are made to argue against the Catholic faith, while other pupils defend the orthodox views."

62. *CW 12,* 296/9–10: "I thinke without help of grace, mennys reasonyng shall do litle more/" In the *Treatise upon the Passion* More speaks of "natural reason, holpen forth wyth suche grace as God keepeth fro no man" (ed. Garry E. Haupt, *CW 13,* 43/14–15). Cited hereafter as "*CW 13.*" From our worldly appetites, he says near the conclusion of *Comfort,* we may "with helpe of prayour throw the grace of god, draw nere to the secret inward pleasure of the spirite" (*CW 12,* 306/8–10). See also *CW 12,* 316/19–27.

an example from the side of reason, Antony carries out a rigorous proof that all the world is a prison. The proof is important to him—for if we live in a prison, who would not happily be freed from it?—and so he marshals the most powerful arguments he can. He models his prison metaphor after Plato's great metaphor of the cave.[63] Similarly Antony's theory of knowledge—that affections are imprinted in men's minds in two manners—is strengthened by its reference to the great metaphor of the charioteer and two horses in the *Phaedrus.*[64] In both instances a problem of faith is clarified though the use of a metaphor from the master of dialectical reasoning. There are many other examples of the mutual reinforcement of faith and reason.

He whose reason and faith together reveal it is "but gloriouse to dye . . . in the sight of god" may properly be called the hero of *A Dialogue of Comfort:* he is the "faythfull wise man" (288/21–289/2). The Morean hero is in fact characterized by his opposite, the heretic, a composite figure of wretched inconsistency who glares from the pages of the *Dialogue Concerning Heresies* and the other polemical works.

Yet the man in whom reason and faith harmonize may still be in conflict with God's grace. More will not let go of this conflict. It is his bond with all other men, and it is a conflict which could only be resolved in the final actions of his life. The common

63. "And surely like as we wene our selfe out of prison now / so yf there were some folke born & brought vpp in a prison / that neuer cam on the wall / nor lokyd out at the dore / nor neuer herd of other world abrode / but saw some for their shrewed turnes done among them selfe, lokkid vpp in some strayter rome, & herd them onely callid prisoners that were so servid / & them selfe euer callid free folks at large / the like opynion wold they haue there of them selfe ⌈than,⌉ that we haue here of our selfe now / And whan we take our selfe for other than prisoners now / as verely be we now deceyvid, as those prisoners shuld there be than" (275/13–22). Cf. *Republic,* VII, 514 *et seq.*

64. "And therfor will we Cosyn assay to consider, what thinges there are for which we haue cause in reason to mayster that affeccion ferefull & sensuall & though we can not clene avoyd it & put it away: yet in such wise to brydle yt at the lest / that yt run not out so farre like an hed strong horse, that spite of our teeth yt cary vs out vnto the devill" (282/20–25). Cf. *Phaedrus,* 246B. Manley has also noted this, *CW 12,* 433.

enemy is our will. In the *Dialogue Concerning Heresies* More had cast the problem in historical terms: "the secrete operacyon of god. . .[is] workynge with mannes good wyll / to the perfeccyon of faythe in his soule" (143/8–10). Then he was concerned with the *profectus* or gradual revelation of scriptural truth. Now, in tandem with the progressive union of reason and faith, Antony stresses the imperative that a man *conform his will* to God's grace.[65] This imperative is obeyed by the process of mind which the dialogue defines. For conforming of human will to divine grace meant the cultivation of "a relationship, an attitude toward God."[66] It meant the cultivation of a spiritual dialectic. Thus Antony ends a chapter on bodily pain by saying (250/3–8):

> . . .all the good wordes in the world. . .[cannot] profit the man with the sownd entryng at his eare / but yf the spirite of god therwith inwardly worke in his soule / but that is his goodnes euer redy to do / except the let be thorough the vntowardnes of our own froward will /

More sought that dialectical relationship through prayer. After sentence had been passed on him, he would pray (*CW 13*, 231/21–23):

65. For the reader's convenience let me illustrate this continuity. Antony desires (68/18) to see a man's "will confirmyd [i.e., conformed] to godes pleasure," and again (71/4–5) to see "the obedient confirmyng of the mans will vnto god. . . ." "[T]he good man," he repeats (73/21–22), ". . . conformeth his will to godes will. . . ." Later (251/9–10) he prays for "the grace to set my hole hart vppon hym"; we should all desire to "conform our will vnto his" (316/22). The phrase is given an ironic twist by Margaret Roper when she remarks to her father in prison that many men " 'thinke that you be vpon the peryll of your soule, bounden to chaunge and reform your conscience, and confirme your owne as I said to other mens' " (Rogers, p. 524).

66. David Knowles, in *The English Mystical Tradition* (1961; repr. London, 1964), p. 95, characterizes the late medieval conception of grace as "simply a right relationship of man towards God consequent upon God's acceptation of man's love." Manley's discussion of charity is based on Aquinas's definition of it as the friendship between man and God. Manley concludes: "The realization of charity in Book III . . . emerges from a rational process, from the very structure and organization of the work itself—the movement of the mind through rational forms, categories, and distinctions, attempting to control fear and direct one's desires toward God" (*CW 12*, cv).

Lord giue me pacience in tribulacion, and grace in euerything to conforme my wil to thine: y[t] I may truely say: *Fiat voluntas tua, sicut in celo et in terra.*

But the process had already begun in the dialogues.

There are intimations that *A Dialogue of Comfort* aims beyond a conversation of the mind with itself. When Antony imagines the effect upon him "yf I get (as I may yf I will) the grace to set my hole hart vppon hym" (251/9–10), he is giving voice to the radical dialectic which More seeks. The search for this reciprocity modifies the very form of dialogue; it marks a departure not only from the earlier sections of *A Dialogue of Comfort* and the *Dialogue Concerning Heresies* but from classical dialogue, which had served in many ways as a model for both. Book III is, as Martz has shown, "a treatise on the necessity of meditation: meditation on Hell and Heaven, but most powerfully, most dramatically, meditation on the Passion of Christ, and especially on the Agony in the Garden. . . ."[67] For More meditation means, in part, as Antony tells Vincent, "communing and counseling" upon pain (199/15). Meditation involves their communing with each other but also with Christ regarding His Passion. Marc'hadour has also written of the necessity of meditation, offering an explanation for the centrality in it of the Passion:

More does not argue, he meditates. Like Erasmus he identifies with the Saviour. He is now himself dodging death, and the Master's agony provides ample justification for the disciple's recoiling from the final blow, as long as honour is safe. . . . More than one reason. . .prompted Christ to undergo an agony which, being God, he could have spared himself: his dismay bore witness to the truth of his manhood; his physical and mental ordeal, his trembling would across the ages comfort the less intrepid members of his Mystical Body. More himself is drawing comfort from his Master's fear.[68]

The dialogue offers many reasons why the meditation centers

67. "Thomas More: The Tower Works," in *Action and Contemplation,* ed. Sylvester, p. 69. In what follows, Christ's agony in the Garden is included in the term "Passion."

68. Marc'hadour, *The Bible,* Part 5, 39.

on the Passion. Antony is drawn to the Passion because of the efficacy of Christ's prayers at that time."[O]f all his holy prayours the chiefe semeth me those that he made in his grete agony & payne of his bitter passion" (67/1–3). We too should pray these prayers, he says, in the time of our tribulation. In temptation, he counsels, let one have special remembrance of Christ's Passion. He counsels in fact what the dialogue at last performs: meditation on the supreme example of faithful death. This culminates the process by which More inured himself to tribulation. Thus prayer upon the Passion ends in a perfect spiritual dialectic: "at the deth also of euery man that so dieth for the fayth, god with his hevenly companye beholdith his hole passion & verely loketh on" (289/7–9).

The process is not only Christian but also in a striking sense Socratic. As Erasmus explains, Socrates said

> that at length the soul gladly departs from the body if, through the love of wisdom, it has already thought earnestly about death and has also, long before the event, accustomed itself, so to speak, to part company with the body by despising material forms and loving and contemplating the spiritual.[69]

Erasmus adds immediately that "this is the only Cross to which Christ has called us. . . ." Like More, Erasmus conceives of the dialectical relationship with Christ in His Passion as the supreme prayer and thus the supreme comfort. The *Enchiridion* directly informs *A Dialogue of Comfort* when Erasmus asserts (pp. 171f.) that "against every kind of adversity or temptation the Cross of Christ is by far the [remedy] most potent. It is," he continues,

> at once an example to the erring, a comfort to the hard-pressed, and armor for those who fight . . ., for there is no temptation or adversity whatever that does not have its own peculiar cure in the Cross.

This is the rationale for meditation on the Passion in the Tower dialogue, and it is recapitulated in one of More's last prayers:

69. *The Enchiridion of Erasmus,* ed. and trans. Raymond Himelick (Bloomington, 1963), p. 103. Erasmus is referring to the *Phaedo,* 59A, 64A *et seq.*, and 80E–81.

> Good lorde geue me the grace in all my feare and agonye to haue recourse to that great feare and wonderfull agonye, that thou my sweete sauior hadst at the mount of Oliuete before thy moste bitter passion, and in the meditacion therof, to conceue ghostly coumfort and consolacion profitable for my soule.[70]

"[G]od ys & must be your comfort & not I," Antony tells Vincent in the first prologue. *Their* dialogue of comfort, Antony's words suggest, is only an imitation of the dialogue between the Christian and the Savior. In that spiritual dialogue a channel is opened between "my feare and agonye" and "that great feare and wonderfull agonye" of Christ's Passion. More's creation is a conception of the communion between man and Christ as intellectually active, laboring dialogue. "[T]hough you wold fayne fle from the paynfull dethe," says Antony (245/23–28),

> . . . yet may the meditacion of his gret grevous agony move you / & get & give you the grace, that you shall submit & conforme your will therin vnto his / as he did his vnto his father / and shall thervppon be . . . comfortid. . . .

Comfort against the tribulation of the body is made accessible through meditation on the Body of Christ. "Quite apart from controversial purposes," observes Marc'hadour, "More's intense devotion to the mystical Body of Christ is undoubtedly the most striking feature of his own spiritual portrait, and the central piece of his doctrinal construction."[71] It is, one might add, the center of *A Dialogue of Comfort.* Thus More's last dialogue strikes his strongest blow against heresy.[72] Just as the Body of

70. *CW 13,* 229/20–24. See the final chapter of the dialogue.

71. "St. Thomas More," *Month,* New Series, 29 (1963), 74.

72. Richard Marius also believes that an "incarnational theology" forms "the well-spring of More's being." Summarizing Marius's unpublished comments, Sylvester writes: "Unlike his polemical opponents—Tyndale especially—More could never reject the material world as merely physical. He believed, fundamentally, in the unity of body and soul. He saw man as a complex entity in whom, ultimately, body and soul must work together" (*St. Thomas More: Action and Contemplation,* p. 13). See also Marius, *CW 8,* pt. iii, 1290.

Christ occupies the central place in the sacrament of communion, so More conceives of our chief comfort as dialogue with the person of Christ. Prayer and meditation, he writes in the *Treatise on the Blessed Body,* are ultimately experienced as personal dialogue: "Let vs by deuout prayer talke to him, by deuout meditacion talke with him. Let us say with the prophete: *Audiam quid loquatur in me dominus,* I will heare what our lord will speake within me."[73]

In finding supreme value in the transcendent dialectical rapport attainable in prayer, *A Dialogue of Comfort* conveys a distinctive image of God. "More's balanced piety, like the Liturgy," writes Marc'hadour, "always addresses God with a mixture of affection and awe. So in the long prayer at the end of his *Pico,* the first line is, 'O holy God of dreadful majesty,' and the last, 'As a very tender loving father.' "[74] It is on this image that the dialogue ultimately focuses: "the very substaunce essentiall of all the celestiall Ioy, standith in blessid beholdying of the gloriouse godhed face to face. . . ." This spiritual exercise succeeds, where reason itself failed, in transcending reason, "for this state of this world, the Ioyes of hevyn are by mans mowth vnspekeable / to mans eares not audible / to mens hartes vncogitable" (308/20–309/6). The meditation ends in an apocalyptic vision of God triumphing over Turks and devils.

The evolution of More's dialogue form might be summarized as a movement from oration to orison. The second book of

73. *CW 13,* 201/22–26; quoted by Martz, "Thomas More: The Tower Works," p. 73. More actually composes a speech by Christ to the sufferer in meditation (*De Tristitia,* trans. Mary Basset, *CW 14,* pt. ii, 1190; cited by Martz, p. 76, and Chambers, p. 301). Martz's essay also contains a provocative treatment of "inward speaking" in the *Treatise on the Blessed Body.* We must reluctantly pass over the challenging question of the relation of dialogue to the Eucharist. The Catholic liturgy itself is a dialogue full of drama. C. G. Jung gives a psychoanalytic account of "mental communion" in "Transformation Symbolism in the Mass," in *The Mysteries* (New York, 1955), repr. in *Psyche and Symbol,* ed. Violet S. de Laszlo (New York, 1958) pp. 148–224.

74. "St. Thomas More," pp. 83f. "This is the very phrase he uses as a *Vale* when writing to his children from the Tower." See Rogers, nos. 202 and 216.

Utopia has been viewed rhetorically as "an extended *declamatio,*" and More seems to have written the first book to provide a dialogue setting for that oration.[75] The oratorical, conversational method, adopted also in the *Dialogue Concerning Heresies,* is supplanted in *A Dialogue of Comfort* by a meditational method. But within *A Dialogue of Comfort* the latter method does not prevail until the final book. There one observes the increasing tendency of chapters to end either in actual prayers or in acknowledgment of the efficacy of prayer in providing spiritual and rhetorical resolution. This formal development was possible only for an experienced polemicist. Where dialectic once was used to combat the devil's temptations by dispelling delusion, gradually the dialogue comes to rely upon prayer. Oratorical dialogue gives place to prayer dialogue, which is not so much a transformation as a fulfillment of the double meaning of *orare.* As a Christian humanist, More conceives of the spiritual goal as the most fundamental problem in rhetoric.

I was dumb, and was humbled, and kept silence from good things: and my sorrow was renewed. My heart grew hot within me: and in my meditation a fire shall flame out. I spoke with my tongue: O Lord, make me know my end.[76]

More shares with the psalmist the desire to set in a work of art the fire of prayer.

75. R. J. Schoeck, " 'A Nursery of Correct and Useful Institutions': On Reading More's *Utopia* as Dialogue," *Moreana,* 22 (1969), 26. On the chronology of composition see *CW* 4, xv–xxiii.

76. Psalm 38 (Douai translation).

Epilogue

A few words of summary are now in order. The humanists believed that in the deepest reaches of the self or soul they were what they read. In one of the prefatory letters to the *Utopia* Thomas More complains that he is so busy with his duties as lawyer and father that "I have no time for myself, that is, for literature." And Erasmus, using the metaphor of literature as food, says we must become what we learn. This study began by describing dialogue as a "medial art" to emphasize the idea that it mirrors the Renaissance humanists' role as mediators between the ideas of antiquity and their own sensory world. This point of view allowed us to focus classical theory and biographical information on each text and on the central topic: the emergence of the humanist dialogue as a mode for probing the conflicting ideas and indistinct feelings of self-consciousness. The chapters on the classical models which the humanists imitated attempt to enable us to experience the extent to which the humanists absorbed what they had read into their conscious selves, and thus to understand how they were transformed by ancient learning.

The discussion of the mimetic theory of literature in the first two chapters provided a context for evaluating the aesthetic aspects of dialogue. Chapter 1 related the confusion in Renaissance theory regarding the nature of dialogue as a literary form to the fact that Aristotle's *Poetics* did not set forth a clear classification of Plato's dialogues within the scheme of mimetic theory (drama as an imitation of action) because the "narrative" element, the exposition of ideas, predominates in dialogue over the dramatic. In Tasso's brief *Discorso dell' arte del dialogo* we found a concept which partially reconciles drama and dialectic—dialogue is the "imitation of reasoning" (*imitazione di ragionamento*). Because the Platonic dialogue is primarily an imitation of mental states, the mimesis of external reality (setting, action, characters) in the Aristotelian scheme properly plays a secondary or "intermittent" role. Yet, as the second chapter has demonstrated, the Ciceronian form of dialogue emphasized concreteness of historical characterization in the speakers, rather than the "abstract" function of characterization in Plato. Because the philosophical topic is viewed through the distinctive perspectives of "real" characters, there is no final synthesis of truth, as in Platonic dialogue; furthermore, with the interest in rhetoric characteristic of Roman culture, style of discourse is recognized ultimately as a reflection of personality.

The third chapter proposed another fundamental distinction in the tradition available to the humanists—that between eristic dialogue, the method of question and answer used for scholastic debate or religious controversy (More's *Dialogue Concerning Heresies*), and peirastic dialogue, which is experimental, tentative, and speculative. The chapter then traced the development of dialogue in the Renaissance, as the peirastic mode won favor with the humanists as more rhetorically effective and aesthetically satisfying than the scholastic form. At the midpoint of the book this chapter concluded with a summary of the concerns and themes of humanistic education and moral philosophy which were reflected in the dialogues of Ficino, Bembo, and Erasmus. The broad perspective of this chapter outlined the culture of humanism as a movement, while the cameo sketches of the trio of continental humanists as unique personalities anticipated the sustained analysis of dialogues which reveal the literary personalities of the English humanists Elyot, Ascham, and More. The last paragraph of Chapter 3 indicated the direction of evolution in the dialogues analyzed in the second half of the book.

Chapters 4, 5, and 6 endeavored to illuminate the interpretation of specific dialogues by reference to the critical terminology and aspects of the tradition discussed in the first three chapters. We noted, for example, the correlation between Elyot's idea of "consultation" and Socratic dialectic, his occasional use of eristic dialogue in *Of the Knowledge Which Maketh a Wise Man,* and the fact that Elyot's "imitation" of Plato was a means of grasping the master's spiritual wisdom and, in Tasso's phrase, "joining action to reasoning" in a representational form; in the chapter on Ascham, we observed the use of the *Phaedrus* as a frame for *Toxophilus* and the function of the celebrated passage on the wind in that dialogue as an emblem for "uncertainty"—the world's imperfection which the Ciceronian tradition of dialogue seeks to mitigate through the practical wisdom acquired through "experience." The chapter on the *Dialogue Concerning Heresies* and *A Dialogue of Comfort* demonstrated More's versatility in the use of both the Platonic and Ciceronian modes of setting and characterization, and in the use of eristic and peirastic forms of dialectic appropriate to the differing purposes of doctrinal debate and spiritual meditation. The central thesis of the entire study, that the Tudor dialogue evolved into a mode for the imitation of the interior world of thought and emotion, is illustrated finally by the transformational relationship between the *Dialogue Concerning Heresies* and *A Dialogue of Comfort:* both control "abominable thoughts"—heresy by means of dialectic and reason, fear and temptation by means of meditation and faith.

The humanists' recourse to dialogue signals certain deeply held conceptions of the nature of civilization and man's reason. We often see them playing with the fictional element in a primarily expository, didactic form. To us it seems that in dialogue they could dispute ideas without making a commitment to them, without being held responsible. We are struck by the tentativeness of some dialogues in which the fiction serves as a mask. On the whole, however, it would be wrong to read humanist dialogues as documents of detachment or skepticism. Rather, dialogue was adopted because it represented the mental process of resistance, judgment, and rejection or assent which characterizes conscious life; thence it might create the discursive experience which enabled writers to absorb what they had read and thought into their conscious selves and in some degree convey this to others.

Unlike complete fiction, such dialogue is not fully detached from the mental processes of its author. We do not think of it as having a life of its own; it seldom attains the transcendence of art. Insofar as dialogue is a transforming experience it remains like all human experience incomplete. It belongs to the life of civilization, which is itself a dialogue of hope and imperfection.

BIBLIOGRAPHY

Citations from Aulus Gellius, Cato, Cicero, Diogenes Laertius, and Seneca refer to the editions in the Loeb Classical Library.

Ælfric Grammaticus. *Ælfric's Colloquy.* Ed. G. N. Garmonsway, London, 1939.

Altercatio Hadriani Augusti et Epicteti philosophi. Ed. Lloyd William Daly and Walther Suchier. Illinois Studies in Language and Literature, vol. 24, nos. 1–2. Urbana, 1939.

Ambrose, Alice. "Philosophy, Language, and Illusion," in *Psychoanalysis and Philosophy.* Ed. Charles Hanly and Morris Lazerowitz. New York: 1970, pp. 14–34.

Andrieu, Jean. *Le Dialogue antique: structure et présentation.* Paris, 1954.

Anstey, Henry, ed. *Munimenta Academica Oxeniensis. Rerum Britannicarum Medii Aevi Scriptores,* vol. 50 in 2 pts. London, 1868.

Aristotle. *The Works of Aristotle.* Ed. W. D. Ross. Oxford: *De Anima,* trans. J. A. Smith, vol. 3 (1931); *De Sophisticis Elenchis,* trans. W. A. Pickard-Cambridge, vol. 1 (1928); *Ethica Nicomachea,* trans. W. D. Ross, vol. 9 (1915–25); *Rhetorica,* trans. W. R. Roberts, vol. 11 (1924); *Topica,* trans. W. A. Pickard-Cambridge, vol. 1 (1928).

———. *On the Art of Fiction: An English Translation of the Poetics.* Trans. L. J. Potts. 2d impression, with corrections and additions. 1953; repr. Cambridge, England, 1962.

———. *Poetics.* Ed. D. W. Lucas, Oxford, 1968.

Ascham, Roger. *English Works of Roger Ascham.* Ed. William Aldis Wright. 1904; repr. Cambridge, England, 1970.

———. *The English Works of Roger Ascham,* with a "Life of Roger Ascham" [attributed to Samuel Johnson]. Ed. James Bennet. London, 1761.

———. *The Scholemaster.* Ed. John E. B. Mayor. London, 1934.

———. *The Schoolmaster.* Ed. Lawrence V. Ryan. Ithaca, 1967.

———. *The Whole Works of Roger Ascham.* Ed. J. A. Giles. 3 vols. in 4. London, 1864–65.

"Ascham's *Toxophilus.*" *The Retrospective Review,* 4 (1821), 76–87.
Athanasius. *The Life of Saint Antony.* Trans. Robert T. Meyer. Westminster, Maryland, 1950.
Augustine, Aurelius. *Contra academicos libri III. PL,* 32, 905–58.
Bardy, Gustave. "La Littérature patristique des *Quaestiones et Responsiones* sur l'Ecriture sainte." *Revue Biblique,* 41 (1932), 210–36, 341–69, 515–37; 42 (1933), 14–30, 211–29, 328–52.
Baron, Hans. *The Crisis of the Early Italian Renaissance.* 2 vols. Princeton, 1955.
Bembo, Pietro. *Gli Asolani.* Trans. Rudolf B. Gottfried. Bloomington, 1954.
Bennett, H. S. *English Books and Readers, 1475–1557. . . .* Cambridge, England, 1952.
Bénouis, Mustapha Kemal. *Le Dialogue philosophique dans la littérature française du seizième siècle.* The Hague and Paris, 1976.
Biographie universelle (Michaud) ancienne et moderne. 2d ed. 45 vols. Paris and Leipzig, 1843–65.
Bömer, A[lois]. *Die lateinischen Schülergespräche der Humanisten. . . .* Berlin, 1897.
Booth, Wayne C. *The Rhetoric of Fiction.* Chicago, 1961.
Bouwsma, William J. "Renaissance and Reformation: An Essay in Their Affinities and Connections," in *Luther and the Dawn of the Modern Era.* Ed. Heiko A. Oberman. *Studies in the History of Christian Thought,* vol. 8. Leiden, 1974, pp. 127–49.
———. *The Culture of Renaissance Humanism.* American Historical Association Pamphlets, no. 401. Washington, D.C., 1973.
———. *The Interpretation of Renaissance Humanism.* 2d ed. Service Center for Teaching of History Publication no. 18. Washington, D.C., 1966.
———. "The Two Faces of Humanism: Stoicism and Augustinianism in Renaissance Thought," in *Itinerarium Italicum: The Profile of the Italian Renaissance in the Mirror of Its European Transformations.* Ed. Heiko A. Oberman and Thomas A. Brady, Jr. *Studies in Medieval and Reformation Thought,* vol. 14. Leiden, 1975, pp. 3–60.
Boyancé, P. "Le platonisme à Rome: Platon et Cicéron," in *Actes* du Congrès de l'Association Guillaume Budé à Tours et Poitiers. Paris, 1954, pp. 195–221.
Bradbury, Malcolm. "Towards A Poetics of Fiction: 1) An Approach through Structure." *Novel,* 1 (1967), 45–52.
Burckhardt, Jacob. *Die Cultur der Renaissance in Italien.* Basel, 1860. *The*

Civilization of the Renaissance. Trans. S. G. C. Middlemore. Ed. Ludwig Goldscheider. Oxford, 1944.

Burke, Kenneth. *Counterstatement.* Berkeley, 1953.

Bursill-Hall, G. L. *Speculative Grammars in the Middle Ages: the Doctrine of Partes orationis of the Modistae.* Approaches to Semiotics, 11. The Hague, 1971.

Butcher, S. H. *Aristotle's Theory of Poetry and Fine Art.* 4th ed. 1911; repr. London, 1932.

Cassianus. *De Coenobiorum Institutis.* Trans. Edgar C. S. Gibson. *Select Library of Nicene and Post-Nicene Fathers. . .*, vol. 11. 2d ser. 1894; repr. Grand Rapids, 1964.

Cassirer, Ernst. *The Platonic Renaissance in England.* Trans. James P. Pettegrove. Edinburgh, 1953.

Cassirer, Ernst, Paul Oskar Kristeller, and John Herman Randall, Jr., eds. *The Renaissance Philosophy of Man.* Chicago, 1948.

Castiglione, Baldassare. *Il Libro del Cortegiano.* Venice, 1582.

Caxton, William, comp. *Dialogues in French and English.* Ed. Henry Bradley. Early English Text Society, Extra Series, no. 79. London, 1900.

Chambers, R. W. *Thomas More.* 1935; repr. London, 1963.

Chaucer, Geoffrey, trans. *Boece* [*De Consolatione philosophiae*]. Ed. F. J. Furnivall. Chaucer Society, First Series, no. 75. London, 1886.

Cicero, Marcus Tullius. [See headnote.] *De Oratore.* Ed. A. S. Wilkins. Oxford, 1892.

Clark, Andrew, ed. *Register of the University of Oxford.* Vol. 2 (1571–1622), pt. 1. Oxford, 1887.

Clarke, M. L. *Classical Education in Britain 1500–1900.* Cambridge, England, 1959.

Cobban, A. B. *The Medieval Universities: Their Development and Organization.* London, 1975.

Coleridge, Hartley. "Memoir of Roger Ascham," in *Northern Worthies* (1833). Repr. in John E. B. Mayor, ed. *The Scholemaster.* London, 1934.

Craik, Henry, ed. *English Prose: Selections.* 4 vols. New York and London, 1893–95.

Crawford, Bartholomew Vincent, "The Non-Dramatic Dialogue in English Prose." Ph.D. dissertation, Harvard University, 1918.

Crisp, Frank. *Medieval Gardens. . . , with Some Account of Tudor, Elizabethan and Stuart Gardens.* Ed. Catherine Childs Paterson. 2 vols. London, 1924.

Cushman, Robert E. *Therapeia: Plato's Conception of Philosophy.* Chapel Hill, 1958.

Day, John T., Jr. "Elizabethan Prose Dialogues." Ph.D. dissertation, Harvard University, 1977.

Deakins, Roger Lee. "The Tudor Dialogue as a Literary Form." Ph.D. dissertation, Harvard University, 1964.

Dees, Jerome S. "Recent Studies in Elyot." *English Literary Renaissance*, 5 (1976), 336–44.

DeMolen, Richard L. "Childhood and the Sacraments in the Sixteenth Century." *Archiv für Reformationsgeschichte*, 66 (1975), 49–71.

DNB. Dictionary of National Biography. 63 vols. London, 1885–1900.

Donatus. *Ars Minor.* Trans. W. J. Chase. University of Wisconsin Studies in the Social Sciences and History, no. 11. Madison, 1926.

Dositheus. *Hermaneumata Pseudodositheana.* Ed. Georg Goetz. *Corpus Glossariorum Latinorum*, vol. 3. Leipzig, 1892.

Egan, Willis J., S.J. *The Rule of Faith in St. Thomas More's Controversy with William Tyndale, 1528–1533.* Los Angeles, 1960.

Else, Gerald F. *Aristotle's Poetics: The Argument.* Cambridge, Mass., 1957.

Elton, G. R. *The Tudor Revolution in Government: Administrative Changes in the Reign of Henry VIII.* 1953; repr. Cambridge, England, 1962.

———. "Sir Thomas More and the Opposition to Henry VIII." *Bulletin of the Institute of Historical Research*, 41 (1968), 19–34.

Elyot, Thomas. *Of the Knowledge Which Maketh a Wise Man.* Ed. Edwin Johnston Howard. Oxford, Ohio, 1946.

———. *The Boke Named the Gouernour.* Ed. Henry Herbert Stephen Croft. 2 vols. 1883; repr. New York, 1967.

———. *The Dictionary of syr Thomas Eliot knyght.* Introd. note by R. C. Alston. 1538; facsimile repr. Menston, England, 1970.

———. *The Letters of Sir Thomas Elyot.* Ed. K. J. Wilson. *Studies in Philology*, 73, no. 5, "Texts and Studies, 1976." Chapel Hill, 1976.

Encyclopedia Britannica. . . . 11th ed. 29 vols. Cambridge, England, and New York, 1910–11.

Erasmus, Desiderius. *De pueris instituendis.* Ed. Jean-Claude Margolin. *Opera Omnia, ordo* I, tome 2. Amsterdam, 1971.

———. *Dialogus Ciceronianus.* Ed. Pierre Mesnard. *Opera Omnia, ordo* I, tome 2. Amsterdam, 1971.

———. *Opera omnia.* Ed. J. Clericus. 10 vols. Leiden, 1703–6; repr. Hildesheim, 1961–62.

———. *Opus epistolarum.* Ed. P. S. Allen and H. M. Allen. 12 vols. Oxford, 1906–58.

———. *The Apophthegmes of Erasmus.* Trans. Nicholas Udall. Ed. and ann. Robert Roberts. Boston, 1877.

———. *The Colloquies of Erasmus.* Ed. and trans. Craig R. Thompson. Chicago and London, 1965.

———. *The Education of a Christian Prince.* Trans. Lester K. Born. 1936; repr. New York, 1968.

———. *The Enchiridion of Erasmus.* Ed. and trans. Raymond Himelick. Bloomington, 1963.

———. *The Praise of Folly.* Ed. and trans. Clarence H. Miller. New Haven and London, 1979.

Fenlon, Dermot. "The New Learning, the New Religion and the Law." *The Historical Journal,* 17 (1974), 185–95.

Ferguson, Wallace K. *The Renaissance in Historical Thought: Five Centuries of Interpretation.* Cambridge, Mass., 1948.

———. *Renaissance Studies.* University of Western Ontario Studies in the Humanities, no. 2. London, Ontario, 1963.

Ficino, Marsilio. *Commentaire sur le Banquet de Platon.* Ed. and trans. Raymond Marcel. Paris, 1956.

———. *Marsilio Ficino's Commentary on Plato's "Symposium."* Ed. and trans. Sears Reynolds Jayne. University of Missouri Studies, vol. 19, no. 1. Columbia, 1944.

Garmonsway, G. N. "The Development of the Colloquy," in *The Anglo-Saxons.* Ed. Peter Clemoes. London, 1959, pp. 248–61.

Gibson, Strickland. "The Order of Disputations." *Bodleian Quarterly Record,* 6 (1929–31), 107–12.

Glorieux, Palemon. *La Faculté des Arts et ses Maîtres au XIIIe Siècle.* Etudes de Philosophie médiévale, 59. Paris, 1971.

———. "L'enseignement au moyen âge: Technique et méthodes en usage à la Faculté de Théologie de Paris, au XIIIe siècle." *Archives d'histoire doctrinale et littéraire du Moyen Age,* 35 (1968, publ. 1969), 65–186.

Gomperz, Theodor. *Greek Thinkers: A History of Ancient Philosophy.* Trans. G. G. Berry. 4 vols. London, 1901–12.

Grabmann, Martin. *Die Geschichte der scholastischen Methode.* 2 vols. 1909–11; repr. Graz, 1957.

Green, Paul D. "Suicide, Martyrdom, and Thomas More." *Renaissance Quarterly,* 19, "Studies in the Renaissance" (1972), 135–55.

Greene, Thomas M. "Roger Ascham: The Perfect End of Shooting." *ELH,* 36 (1969), 609–25.

Grimal, Pierre. "Caractères généraux du dialogue romain: de Lucilius à Cicéron." *L'Information littéraire,* 7 (1955), 192–98.

Guéroult, M. "La Méditation de l'âme dans le 'Phédon.'" *Revue de Métaphysique et de Morale,* 33 (1926), 469–91.

Guez de Balzac, Jean-Louis. *Les Entretiens.* Ed. B. Beugnot. Paris, 1972.

Harpsfield, Nicholas. *The Life and Death of Sir Thomas Moore.* Ed. E. V. Hitchcock. Early English Text Society, Original Series, no. 186. London, 1932.

Hatch, Maurice A. "The Ascham Letters: An Annotated Translation of the Latin Correspondence Contained in the Giles Edition of Ascham's Works." Ph.D. dissertation, Cornell University, 1948. Kentucky University Microcards, Series A, no. 19 (PR 2201), sponsored by SAMLA.

Hernadi, Paul. *Beyond Genre.* Ithaca, 1972.

Hettler, Alfred. *Roger Ascham: sein Stil und seine Beziehung zur Antike.* Elberfeld, 1915.

Hirzel, Rudolf. *Der Dialog, ein literarhistorischer Versuch.* 2 vols. 1895; repr. Hildesheim, 1963.

Huizinga, Johan. *Erasmus.* Trans. F. Hopman. London, 1952.

Jardine, Lisa. *Francis Bacon: Discourse and the Art of Discovery.* Cambridge, England, 1974.

John of the Cross. *Ascent of Mount Carmel.* Ed. and trans. E. Allison Peers. London, 1935.

Jung, C. G. "Transformation Symbolism in the Mass," in *The Mysteries.* Bollingen Series 30. New York, 1955. Repr. in *Psyche and Symbol.* Ed. Violet S. de Laszlo. New York, 1958, pp. 148–224.

Kierkegaard, Søren. *The Concept of Irony, with Constant Reference to Socrates.* Trans. Lee M. Capel. London, 1966.

Kloepfer, R. "Dynamic Structures in Narrative Literature: The Dialogic Principle." *Poetics Today,* 1 (1980), 115–34.

Knowles, David. *The English Mystical Tradition.* 1961; repr. London, 1964.

Kristeller, Paul Oskar. "Florentine Platonism and Its Relations with Humanism and Scholasticism." *Church History,* 8 (1939), 201–11.

———. *Medieval Aspects of Renaissance Learning.* Ed. and trans. Edward P. Mahoney. Duke Monographs in Medieval and Renaissance Studies, no. 1. Durham, North Carolina, 1974.

———. *Renaissance Thought: The Classic, Scholastic, and Humanist Strains.* New York, 1961.

———. "Studies on Renaissance Humanism during the Last Twenty Years." *Renaissance Quarterly,* 9, "Studies in the Renaissance" (1962), 7–30.

———. *The Philosophy of Marsilio Ficino.* Trans. Virginia Conant. New York, 1943.

Kroeber, A. L. *Style and Civilization.* Ithaca, 1957.

Krutch, Joseph Wood. *Five Masters: A Study in the Mutations of the Novel.* New York, 1930.

Kubler, George. *The Shape of Time: Remarks on the History of Things.* London and New Haven, 1962.

Laborderie, Jean. *Le dialogue platonicien de la maturité.* Paris, 1978.

Laurand, Louis. *Etudes sur le style des discours de Cicéron.* 4th ed. Amsterdam, 1965.

Leff, Gordon. *Paris and Oxford Universities in the Thirteenth and Fourteenth Centuries: An Institutional and Intellectual History.* New York, 1968.

Lehmberg, Stanford E. *Sir Thomas Elyot, Tudor Humanist.* Austin, 1960.

Lewis, C. S. *English Literature in the Sixteenth Century excluding Drama.* 1954; repr. Oxford, 1965.

Logan, George M. "Substance and Form in Renaissance Humanism." *The Journal of Medieval and Renaissance Studies,* 7 (1977), 1–34.

Machiavelli, Niccolò. *The Chief Works and Others.* Trans. Allan Gilbert. 3 vols. Durham, North Carolina, 1965.

Major, John M. *Sir Thomas Elyot and Renaissance Humanism.* Lincoln, Nebraska, 1964.

Marc'hadour, Germain. "St. Thomas More." *Month,* New Series, 29 (1963), 69–84.

———. *The Bible in the Works of St. Thomas More.* 5 parts. Nieuwkoop, 1969–72.

Margolin, Jean-Claude. "La Critique humaniste de la Dialectique médiévale," in *La Dialectique.* Actes du XIVe Congrès des Sociétés de Philosophie de Langue française. Paris, 1969, pp. 29–33.

Marsh, David. *Quattrocento Dialogue: Classical Tradition and Humanist Innovation.* Cambridge, Mass., 1980.

Martz, Louis L. "The Design of More's *Dialogue of Comfort.*" *Moreana,* 15 (1967), 331–46.

———. "Thomas More: The Sacramental Life." *Thought,* 52 (1977), 300–318.

Massebieau, L. *Les Colloques scolaires du seizième siècle et leurs auteurs (1480–1570).* Paris, 1878.

McKeon, Richard. "Literary Criticism and the Concept of Imitation in Antiquity," in *Critics and Criticism, Ancient and Modern.* Ed. R. S. Crane, Chicago, 1952, pp. 147–75.

———. "Rhetoric in the Middle Ages." *Speculum,* 17 (1942), 1–32.

Melun, Robert de. *Œuvres de Robert de Melun.* Ed. Raymond M. Martin and R. M. Gallet. *Spicilegium Sacrum Lovaniense,* fasc. 13 etc. Louvain, 1932.

Menner, Robert J., ed. *The Poetical Dialogues of Solomon and Saturn.* 1941; repr. New York, 1973.

Merrill, Elizabeth. *The Dialogue in English Literature.* Yale Studies in English, vol. 42. 1911; repr. New Haven, 1969.

Michel, Alain. *Rhétorique et philosophie chez Cicéron: essai sur les fondements philosophiques de l'art de persuader.* Paris, 1960.

Miles, Leland. "Persecution and the *Dialogue of Comfort:* A Fresh Look at the Charges against Thomas More." *Journal of British Studies,* 5 (1965), 19–30.

———. "The Literary Artistry of Thomas More." *Studies in English Literature,* 6 (1966), 7–33.

Moors, Kent F. "Plato's Use of Dialogue." *Classical World,* 72 (1978), 77–93.

More, Paul Elmer. *Aristocracy and Justice.* New York, 1915.

More, Thomas. *The Complete Works of St. Thomas More:* vol. 2, *The History of King Richard III,* ed. R. S. Sylvester; vol. 4, *Utopia,* ed. Edward Surtz, S.J., and J. H. Hexter; vol. 5, *Responsio ad Lutherum,* ed. John Headley and trans. Sister Scholastica Mandeville; vol. 6, *A Dialogue Concerning Heresies,* ed. Thomas M. C. Lawler, Germain Marc'hadour, and Richard C. Marius; vol. 8, *The Confutation of Tyndale's Answer,* ed. L. A. Schuster, R. Marius, J. Lusardi, and R. J. Schoeck; vol. 12, *A Dialogue of Comfort against Tribulation,* ed. Louis L. Martz and Frank Manley; vol. 13, *Treatise on the Passion,* etc., ed. Garry Haupt; vol. 14, *De Tristitia Christi,* ed. Clarence Miller. New Haven and London, 1963–.

———. *The Correspondence of Sir Thomas More.* Ed. Elizabeth F. Rogers. Princeton, 1947.

———. *The Dialogue Concerning Tyndale by Sir Thomas More. . . .* Ed. W. E. Campbell and A. W. Reed. London, 1927.

———. *The workes . . . in the Englysh tonge.* Ed. William Rastell. *STC* 18076. London, 1557. Facsimile in 2 vols. Introd. by K. J. Wilson. London, 1978.

———. *Thomas More's Prayer Book.* Ed. Louis L. Martz and R. S. Sylvester. Elizabethan Club Series 4. New Haven and London, 1969.

Mullinger, J. B. *The University of Cambridge.* 3 vols. Cambridge, 1873–1911.

Nelson, William, ed. *A Fifteenth Century School Book.* Oxford, 1956.

Niemann, Gottfried. *Die Dialogliteratur der Reformationszeit nach ihrer Entstehung und Entwicklung.* Leipzig, 1905.

Noyes, Gertrude E. "A Study of Roger Ascham's Literary Citations with Particular Reference to His Knowledge of the Classics." Ph. D. dissertation, Yale University, 1937.

Oakesmith, John. *The Religion of Plutarch. . . .* London, 1902.

Ong, Walter J. *Ramus, Method, and the Decay of Dialogue.* Cambridge, Mass., 1958.

The Oxford English Dictionary. 13 vols. Oxford, 1961.

Pace, Richard. *De Fructu qui ex Doctrina Percipitur (The Benefit of a Liberal Education).* Ed. and trans. Frank Manley and Richard S. Sylvester. Renaissance Text Series, 2. New York, 1967.

Pinborg, Jan. *Die Entwicklung der Sprachtheorie im Mittelalter.* Münster and Copenhagen, 1967.

Pineas, Rainer. "More versus Tyndale: A Study of Controversial Technique." *Modern Language Quarterly,* 24 (1963), 144–50.

———. "Thomas More's Use of Humor as a Weapon of Religious Controversy." *Studies in Philology,* 58 (1961), 97–114.

———. "Thomas More's Use of the Dialogue Form as a Weapon of Religious Controversy." *Studies in the Renaissance,* 7 (1960), 193–206.

Pinckert, Robert Carl. "Sir Thomas Elyot's *The Image of Governance* (1541): A Critical Edition." Ph.D. dissertation, Columbia University, 1964.

PL. Patrologiae Cursus Completus: Series Latina. Ed. J. P. Migne. 221 vols. Paris, 1844–1903. Cited as *PL* by volume and column.

Plato. *Plato's Theory of Knowledge: The Theaetetus and the Sophist of Plato.* Ed. and trans. Francis Macdonald Cornford. London, 1935.

———. *The Collected Dialogues of Plato including the Letters.* Ed. Edith Hamilton and Huntington Cairns. Bollingen Series 71. Princeton, 1961.

———. *The Dialogues of Plato.* Ed. and trans. Benjamin Jowett. 3d rev. ed. Oxford, 1892.

———. *Works of Plato.* Ed. Irwin Edman. Modern Library. New York, 1928.

Prévost, André. *Thomas More et la crise de la pensée européenne.* Tours and Paris, 1969.

Rashdall, Hastings. *The Universities of Europe in the Middle Ages* (1895). Ed. F. M. Powicke and A. B. Emden. 3 vols. Oxford, 1936.

Rice, Eugene F., Jr. *The Renaissance Idea of Wisdom.* Harvard Historical Monographs, no. 37. Cambridge, Mass., 1958.

Robins, Robert Henry. *Ancient and Medieval Grammatical Theory in Europe. . . .* London, 1951.

Roper, William. *The Lyfe of Sir Thomas Moore, knighte.* Ed. E. V. Hitchcock. Early English Text Society, Original Series, no. 197. London, 1935.

Rose, H. J. *A Handbook of Greek Literature.* 3d rev. ed. 1956; repr. New York, 1960.

Ruch, Michel. *Le Préambule dans les œuvres philosophiques de Cicéron: essai sur la genèse et l'art du dialogue.* Publications de la Faculté de l'Université de Strasbourg, Fascicule 136. Paris and Strasbourg, 1958.

Ryan, Lawrence V. *Roger Ascham.* Stanford and London, 1963.

Ryle, Gilbert. *Plato's Progress.* Cambridge, England, 1966.

Sandys, John Edwin. *A History of Classical Scholarship.* 3 vols. Cambridge, England, 1908–21.

Schoeck, R. J. " 'A Nursery of Correct and Useful Institutions': On Reading More's *Utopia* as Dialogue." *Moreana,* 22 (1969), 19–32.

———. "On the Spiritual Life of St. Thomas More." *Thought,* 52 (1977), 324–27.

———. "Thomas More's 'Dialogue of Comfort' and the Problem of the Real Grand Turk." *English Miscellany,* 20 (1969), 23–37.

Scholes, Robert, and Robert Kellogg. *The Nature of Narrative.* New York, 1966.

Seebohm, Frederic. *The Oxford Reformers. . . .* London, 1867.

Sidney, Philip. *The Prose Works of Sir Philip Sidney.* Ed. Albert Feuillerat. 4 vols. Cambridge, England, 1962.

Sigonius, Carolus. *De dialogo liber* (Venice, 1561). *Opera omnia.* Ed. P. Argelati. 6 vols. Milan, 1732–37, VI, 431–88.

Stanbridge, John, and Robert Whittinton. *The Vulgaria of John Stanbridge and The Vulgaria of Robert Whittinton.* Ed. Beatrice White. Early English Text Society, Original Series, no. 187. London, 1932.

STC. A Short-Title Catalogue of Books Printed in England, Scotland and Ireland, 1475–1640. Comp. A. W. Pollard and G. R. Redgrave. London, 1926.

STC 2. Rev. W. A. Jackson, F. S. Ferguson, and Katharine F. Pantzer, vol. 2: I–Z. London, 1976.

Stenzel, Julius. *Plato's Method of Dialectic.* Trans. D. J. Allan. Oxford, 1940.

Stevenson, W. H., ed. *Early Scholastic Colloquies.* Introd. by W. M. Lindsay. *Anecdota Oxoniensia,* Mediaeval and Modern Series, pt. xv. Oxford, 1929.

Stewart, John Alexander. *Plato's Doctrine of Ideas.* 1909; repr. New York, 1964.

Sylvester, Richard S. "*A Part of His Own:* Thomas More's Literary Personality in His Early Works," *Moreana,* 15–16, Festschrift for E. F. Rogers (1967), 29–42.

———, ed. *St. Thomas More: Action and Contemplation.* Proceedings of the Symposium Held at St. John's University, October 9–10, 1970. New Haven and London, 1972.

———. Rev. of *Sir Thomas Elyot, Tudor Humanist,* by Stanford E. Lehmberg. *Renaissance News,* 14 (1961), 178–81.

Tannenbaum, Samuel A. and Dorothy R. *Roger Ascham: A Concise Bibliography.* Elizabethan Bibliographies, no. 37. New York, 1946.

Tasso, Torquato. *Discorso dell' arte del dialogo* (Venice, 1586). *Torquato Tasso: Prose.* Ed. Ettore Mazzali. *La Letteratura italiana: Storia e Testi,* vol. 22. Milan and Naples, 1959, 331–46.

Tateo, Francesco. *Tradizione e realità nell' umanesimo italiano.* Bari, 1967.

———. *Umanesimo etico di Giovanni Pontano.* Lecce, 1972.

Thorndike, Lynn, ed. and trans. *University Records and Life in the Middle Ages.* New York, 1944.

Thurot, Charles. *Notices et extraits de divers manuscrits latins pour servir à l'histoire des doctrines grammaticales au moyen âge. Notices et extraits des manuscrits de la Bibliothèque Impériale,* vol. 22, pt. 2. Paris, 1868.

Trimpi, Wesley. "The Ancient Hypothesis of Fiction: An Essay on the Origins of Literary Theory." *Traditio,* 27 (1971), 1–78.

Trinkaus, Charles. "Humanism, Religion, Society: Concepts and Motivations of Some Recent Studies." *Renaissance Quarterly,* 29, "Studies in the Renaissance" (1976), 676–713.

———, and Heiko A. Oberman, eds. *The Pursuit of Holiness in Late Medieval and Renaissance Religion.* Studies in Medieval and Renaissance Thought, vol. 10. Leiden, 1974.

Trollope, Anthony. *The Life of Cicero.* 2 vols. 1880; repr. London, 1882.

Trousdale, Marion. "Recurrence and Renaissance: Rhetorical Imitation in Ascham and Sturm." *English Literary Renaissance,* 6 (1976), 156–79.

Tyndale, William. *The Whole Workes of W. Tyndall, Iohn Frith, and Doct. Barnes. STC* 24436. London, 1573.

Vincent of Lérins. *Commonitory.* Trans. C. A. Heurtley. *Select Library of Nicene and Post-Nicene Fathers. . . ,* vol. 11. 2d ser. 1894; repr. Grand Rapids, 1964.

Vives, Juan Luis. *Tudor School-boy Life: The Dialogue of Juan Luis Vives*

[*Linguae Latinae Exercitatio*, 1539]. Trans. Foster Watson. London, 1908.

Vos, Alvin. "The Formation of Roger Ascham's Prose Style." *Studies in Philology*, 61 (1974), 344–70.

———. "The Humanism of *Toxophilus:* A New Source." *English Literary Renaissance*, 6 (1976), 187–203.

Waddell, Helen, trans. *The Desert Fathers.* 1936; repr. London and Glasgow, 1965.

Watson, Foster. *The English Grammar Schools to 1660: Their Curriculum and Practice.* Cambridge, England, 1908.

Weinberg, Bernard. *A History of Literary Criticism in the Italian Renaissance.* 2 vols. Chicago, 1961.

Weisheipl, James A., O.P. "Curriculum of the Faculty of Arts at Oxford in the Early Fourteenth Century." *Mediaeval Studies*, 26 (1964), 143–85.

Wilson, K. J. "The Continuity of Post-Classical Dialogue," *Cithara*, 21 (1981), 23–44.

Woodward, William Harrison. *Studies in Education during the Renaissance, 1400–1600.* Cambridge, England, 1924.

Wyatt, Thomas. *Collected Poems.* Ed. Kenneth Muir. London, 1949.

Zeller, Eduard. *Outlines of the History of Greek Philosophy.* Trans. L. R. Palmer. 13th rev. ed. London, 1931.

INDEX